Journey to Vaja
Reconstructing the World of a Hungarian-Jewish Family

Part autobiography, part family chronicle, and part immigrant saga,
Journey to Vaja tells the story of the Weinbergers over the course
of two centuries. From settlement in a Hungarian village in the late
eighteenth century to the German occupation of Hungary in the
spring of 1944, Elaine Kalman Naves places her family's triumphs
and tribulations against the backdrop of Hungarian history.

Northeastern Hungary was full of places like the village of Vaja,
where Jews had farmed for generations. Naves's ancestors had tilled
Hungarian soil since the eighteenth century. They had married into
similar farming families and maintained a lifestyle at once agricultural, orthodox, and Hungariophile. The Nyírség, a sandy, slightly
undulating region wedged between the Great Hungarian Plain and
the foothills of the Carpathians, was the centre of their world. But
all this changed irrevocably with the Holocaust; Naves's generation
is the first in two centuries whose roots are severed from the soil
that once nurtured them.

Naves's quest for her past began with her father, one of the few
members of a vast extended family to survive the Nazi death camps.
His stories and memories of ancestors were a well-spring from which
he drew strength, and they became an obsession for Naves as she
was growing up and when she had children of her own. *Journey
to Vaja* is her attempt to record the lives of these ancestors and
reclaim their lives as part of her and her children's birthright. It in-
corporates myths and stories with family letters and detailed archi-
val research to provide an extraordinary look at the landscape of
memory and a testament to the redemptive power of love and family.

ELAINE KALMAN NAVES is a writer and journalist living in Montreal.
She is a literary columnist for the *Montreal Gazette* and has written
a radio documentary entitled "Journey to Vaja" for the CBC series
Ideas.

McGill-Queen's Studies in Ethnic History
Donald Harman Akenson, Editor

Journey to Vaja

Reconstructing the World of a
Hungarian-Jewish Family

ELAINE KALMAN NAVES

McGill-Queen's University Press
Montreal & Kingston • London • Buffalo

Legal deposit fourth quarter 1996
Bibliothèque nationale du Québec

Printed in Canada on acid-free paper

McGill-Queen's University Press is grateful
to the Canada Council for support of its publishing
program.

Portions of this book, some in different form, have
appeared in *Prairie Fire*, the *Jerusalem Post*, the
Montreal Gazette, *Viewpoints*, and the *Canadian Jewish
News*.

Canadian Cataloguing in Publication Program

Naves, Elaine Kalman
  Journey to Vaja : reconstructing the world of a
  Hungarian-Jewish family

  (McGill-Queen's studies in ethnic history)
  Includes bibliographical references.
  ISBN 0-7735-1511-9 (bound)
  ISBN 0-7735-1534-8 (pbk.)
  1. Naves, Elaine Kalman – Family.
  2. Weinbergers family. 3. Holocaust, Jewish (1939–
  1945) – Personal narratives. 4. Holocaust, Jewish (1939–
  1945) – Hungary. 4. Hungary – History. I. Title.
  II. Series.

DS135.H93W45 1996   943.9'0099   C96-900559-8

In memory of my father,

for my mother,

and for Dr Philip Beck

Where I was before I came here, that place is real. It's never going away. Even if the whole farm – every tree and grass blade of it dies. The picture is still there – if you go and stand in the place where it was, it will happen again; it will be there waiting for you.

Toni Morrison, *Beloved*

Contents

Acknowledgments

This book began in conversations with my father, and many other family members have shared in the joy and struggle of its creation. My sister Judith Kalman participated in some of the interviews, helped with early transcriptions, and acted as an invaluable sounding board and critic throughout. My father's cousins – Susan Rochlitz Szőke of Toronto, the late Jenő Weinberger of Boston, and Ágnes Békés Walkó and the late Sámuel Derzsi of Budapest – searched their memories for me at often painful cost. I am also grateful to them – and to Magda Székács Erdős – for their gifts of many wonderful photographs. My husband, Gary Naves, prepared the genealogies, maps, and floor plan of the Rákóczi Estate House with loving attention to detail.

László Vincze and Zsiga Morvay of Budapest and Márton Grosz of Toronto provided much useful information about the farmsteads of the Nyírség and village life during World War I. Peter Hidas generously opened his Montreal library of Hungarian sources. The late Professor Sándor Scheiber of Budapest pointed me in the right direction at an early stage of research; the late David Rome of Montreal gave me encouragement at a crucial moment. Zsuzsa Walkó and Dr Katalin Berend acted as volunteer long-distance research assistants, tirelessly tracking down obscure references in Hungary.

I am indebted to Bryan Demchinsky for his two readings of the manuscript, detailed comments, and advice relating to the book's structure. Maureen Garvie was an ideal copy editor: both hawk-eyed and sensitive. The people at McGill-Queen's were a pleasure to work with. I thank Don Akenson and Philip Cercone for their enthusiasm for *Vaja*, and Joan McGilvray and Susanne McAdam for their sound counsel and great sense of fun.

To my husband, Gary, I am profoundly grateful for first suggesting that I write this book and then for nagging, cajoling, and supporting me in uncountable ways through a very long haul. And I thank my daughters Jessica and Rebecca for re-anchoring me in the present by their sanity and good grace.

Elaine Kalman Naves
Montreal, March 1996

Author's Note

Even though the people of whom I write in this book have assumed life in my imagination, this is not a work of fiction. Certain scenes are dramatized, and at times dialogue has been reconstructed based on what others have told me. But every effort has been made to verify facts, and all dates and place names are real. So are the names of the cast, although in some cases these have been anglicized for the ease of the reader.

The sizes of estates are given in the Hungarian measure, *hold*. A *hold* is .57 hectares or 1.42 acres.

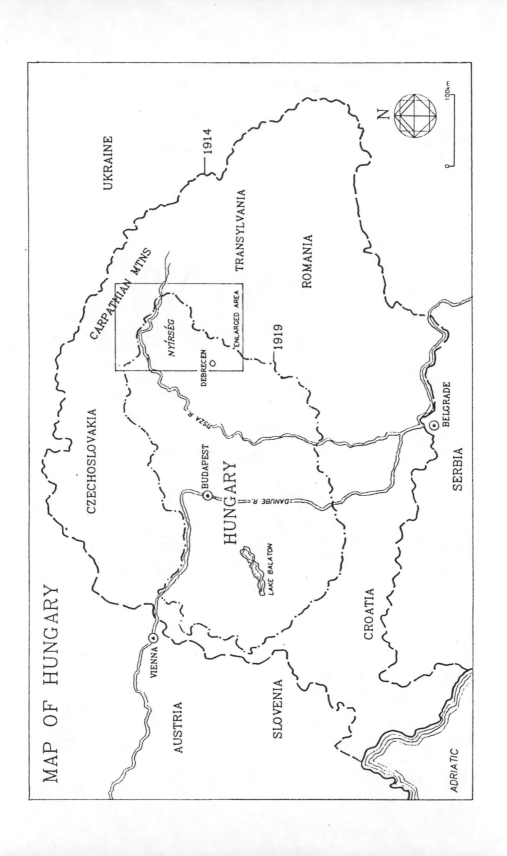

MAP OF HUNGARY

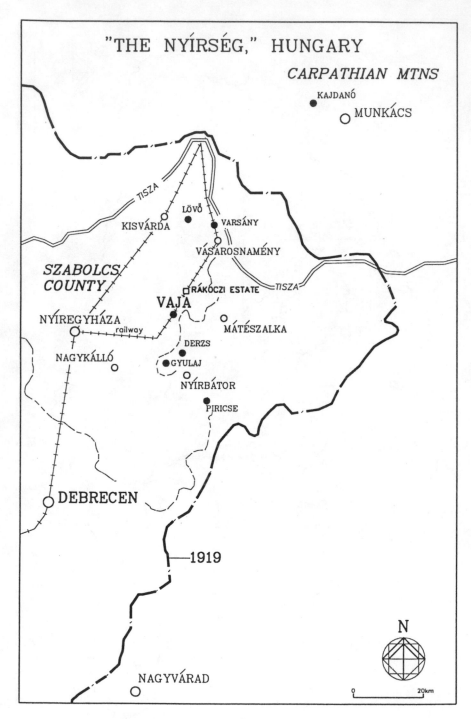

"THE NYÍRSÉG," HUNGARY

CARPATHIAN MTNS

KAJDANÓ

○ MUNKÁCS

TISZA

LÖVŐ

KISVÁRDA

VARSÁNY

VÁSÁROSNAMÉNY

TISZA

SZABOLCS COUNTY

□ RÁKÓCZI ESTATE

VAJA

NYÍREGYHÁZA

railway

MÁTÉSZALKA

DERZS

NAGYKÁLLÓ

● GYULAJ

NYÍRBÁTOR

PIRICSE

DEBRECEN

1919

N

NAGYVÁRAD

0   20km

xvi

SIMPLIFIED SCHWARCZ (SZÉKÁCS) FAMILY TREE

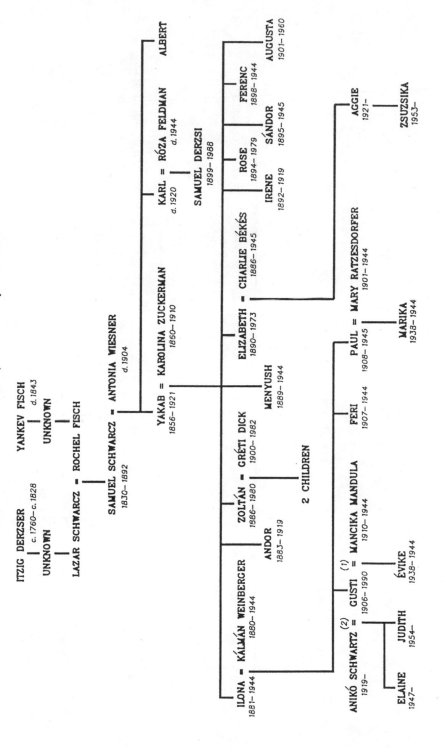

SIMPLIFIED WEINBERGER FAMILY TREE

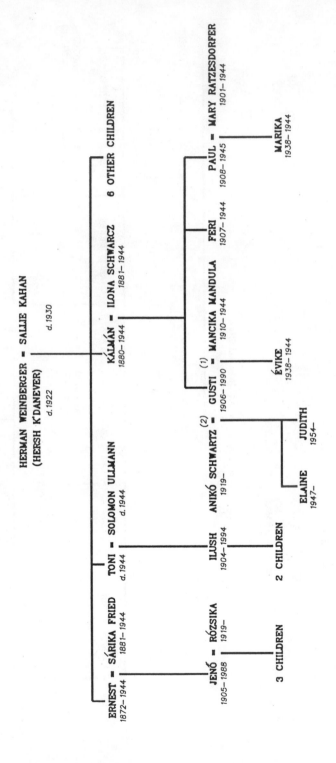

HERMAN WEINBERGER = SALLIE KAHAN
(HERSH K'DANEVER)
d. 1922   d. 1930

ERNEST = SÁRIKA FRIED
1872–1944   1881–1944

TONI = SOLOMON ULLMANN
d. 1944   d. 1944

KÁLMÁN = ILONA SCHWARCZ
1880–1944   1881–1944

6 OTHER CHILDREN

JENÓ = RÓZSIKA
1905–1988   1919–

3 CHILDREN

ILUSH = ANIKÓ SCHWARTZ (2)
1904–1994   1919–

2 CHILDREN

GUSTI = MANCIKA MANDULA (1)
1906–1990   1910–1944

ÉVIKE
1938–1944

ELAINE   JUDITH
1947–   1954–

FERI
1907–1944

PAUL = MARY RATZESDORFER
1908–1945   1901–1944

MARIKA
1938–1944

Yakab at the Villa Nada on the Adriatic, with his daughters Rose, left, and Irene, in 1911.

Prologue: "No Wide Estates"

> My father bequeathed me no wide estates;
> No keys and ledgers were my heritage.
>
> A.M. Klein, "Heritage"

In the beginning there was me and my father.

I can see us now as we were in the Budapest of the early 1950s: a rotund, middle-aged man and a small, brown-haired girl pacing hand in hand in front of our apartment house, oblivious to the suburban surroundings, to the see-saws and swings of the playground, to the yellow trams grinding along Queen Elizabeth Street.

Out of a seemingly bottomless reservoir, my father was telling me a story.

The story had a preface: "I feel sorry for you because your world starts only with me and Mummy."

Children loathe pity, but they love stories. I loved my father's stories, and I loved the special closeness between us on Sundays. During the week he was away in the countryside, inspecting the state network of collective farms. Sundays were story-days when he told of places and people I didn't know: places we didn't visit, people I couldn't know.

A natural storyteller with the gift of total recall, he included in his repertoire two broad subjects: stories from the Bible and stories about Vaja. In my child's mind these stories jelled into a complex amalgam of the biblical and the apocryphal. Fables of Hungarian-Jewish farmers fused with accounts of the Garden of Eden and the sacrifice of Isaac. My confusion reflected a central truth in my father's thinking. For him Vaja represented both the beginning of the world and a lost Garden of Eden.

Two hundred and fifty kilometres northeast of Budapest, the village of Vaja is a dot on the map of Hungary. It takes its name from that of a noble family, the Vays, a detail I did not at all grasp when I was six. For me the name Vaja was rooted in the Hungarian word *vaj*, "butter." Vaja conjured up golden, buttery images in my head: of round slabs of bread smeared thickly with pale yellow, of fields of ripening wheat on a hillside. The Vaja of my imagination was a smooth, lipid, bountiful place.

Fifty years earlier my father had been born there on the Rákóczi Estate, a property leased from the Counts Vay. Three years before my birth he had set foot in Vaja for the last time. Within space of those three years he had lost every important human tie it is possible to lose. In those years he had also found new happiness, a new wife, and planted a new life.

He drew the energy required for this second life out of the well-spring of a Vaja recalled. It was a well that replenished itself with each bucket lowered into its depths. My father took strength from dipping into its waters, and he offered the jug to the rest of the family. My mother didn't care for the taste; my sister swallowed small gulps. But I took to the tastings naturally, as if by osmosis.

The Vaja stories recounted in the street were reinforced by Vaja memorabilia and photographs in our apartment. The dining room held salvaged treasures from the Rákóczi Estate: a Persian carpet used as a table throw, a set of demi-tasse cups in the china cabinet, a pair of silver candlesticks that had belonged to my grandmother.

Our family had three photograph albums, one belonging to my mother of her dead family, one to my father of his, and a joint one of the family they had created together. My mother was superstitious about mixing the new pictures with the old. I was allowed, even encouraged to leaf through my parents' albums of the dead, but I must not contaminate the pictures of the living by mixing them in. My mother carefully tucked loose photos back in their slots in the appropriate album.

But I didn't have to search in albums for the faces in my father's stories. The walls of the Budapest apartment were adorned by photographs from his past. His first wife, Mancika, looked down from one wall, head propped on a slender wrist in a pose reminiscent of the one in which he had first glimpsed her long ago. Their wedding picture occupied another wall. Évike, the half-sister I never knew, took gawky, uncompromising stances in several spots on the wall, locking her slightly bowed legs just the way my father and I tended to do when we stopped during our walks.

4

I don't remember ever asking what had happened to the people in the photographs. I always *knew* that they had died during the war, that they had died because they were Jewish. Sometime in the course of my childhood I must also have found out how they had died, but I don't remember that either.

I do remember thinking often about my father's brother, Uncle Feri. He and my father were exceptionally close, hardly more than a year apart and raised virtually as twins. Somewhere, somehow I had picked up the notion that, unlike the rest of the family, the precise circumstances of Uncle Feri's death were unknown. I imagined him to be alive somewhere, perhaps in Israel, suffering from amnesia, unable to return to us. Someday he would remember, someday he would come back. First to Vaja – as my father had done after his liberation – and then to us.

I could recognize the members of my mother's family equally well from her photographs, but I knew little about them. Unlike my father, my mother refrained in those days from telling me about her family. She did not approve of my father peopling my head with ghosts. It was hard enough to be married to a man whose emotional life was so deeply rooted in the soil of Vaja without having one's child haunted as well. After all, my mother had to live with me on weekdays as well as Sundays. And I was not an easy child, hurling the cry, "I wish Aunt Mancika were my mother instead of you," at her during my tantrums.

My mother's distrust of our returns to the past was amply justified for, along with a legacy of second-hand memories, my father bequeathed to me a nostalgia for a time and place that were not my own. Wherever we lived, a part of me remained a foreigner. Budapest, London, Montreal – a part of me searched for the "true" place I came from. Deep down I believed Vaja to be that place.

We left Hungary in 1957 and arrived in Canada two years later. The photographs were put away; my father's stories surfaced less often. When they did, I felt acutely uncomfortable, appalled at the terrible watershed separating my birth from the world predating it. Yet the past still exercised a powerful fascination for me. I studied history at university and subsequently worked as a professional historian. I specialized in Canadian history, a fresh page of the past, free, it seemed to me, of the terrible baggage of the part of the world I came from. When I travelled to Europe in those days, like my father, I did not journey to Vaja.

And yet I travelled to the Vaja of my imagination at all the critical junctures of my life. The people who had lived there informed my most intimate decisions more powerfully than my living parents did. What would my pious grandmother and grandfather think of my marriage to a gentile? How must I bring up my children so that my beloved, never-known grandparents could take pride in them?

When my first daughter was born, I began once again to listen for the siren call of the family's past. I had heard my father's stories many times, yet if pressed I could hardly have recounted a punchline. For one thing, he spoke a textured Hungarian far richer than the one I retained from my childhood. For another, the locales and historical backgrounds of his tales were foreign to me. If I wanted to pass on his legacy to my children, I would have to understand it a lot better myself.

When I invited my father to speak into a tape recorder, he wasn't stilted for long. Soon he launched into his old storytelling mode and – with my toddler daughter fiddling with the mike and cooing background noise – we spent a summer taping. I had no intention of writing a book; in fact, to brush up my Hungarian, I transcribed all the original tapes in that language instead of translating them directly into English as I would subsequently do.

Over that summer twenty years ago, I was introduced to my father's family as an adult. They were no longer characters from a fairy tale for me. Despite his penchant for idealization, I could make out warts on many faces. Yet as soon as I conjured up my uncles Feri and Paul, my grandmother and grandfather, they dissipated in smoke before my eyes. I had wanted to know about their lives, not their deaths. But a process of free association invariably led my father, without warning and from one instant to the next, to flit from pastoral scenes on the estate to Auschwitz, from a wedding feast in Vaja to the clearing of Buchenwald.

Was this the tradition I wanted to pass on to my children? I would not address this question for many years. At the end of the summer, I put the brown spiral notebooks that held the transcripts in the bottom drawer of my desk. When my father hinted at resuming what he called "the sessions," I made feeble excuses.

In 1981 a magazine article in Hungarian arrived for my parents from Tel Aviv. Forwarded by a labour-battalion comrade of my father who lived there, it was an anonymously written history of the Jews of Munkács, a town that now belongs to Ukraine but was formerly part of the Austro-Hungarian Empire. The author described in intimate and authoritative detail a paternal branch of my father's relatives, the Weinbergers of Kajdanó and Munkács, as one of the prominent families of the region.

I was thirty-three years old when this article arrived, not a child of six. By now I understood very well that Uncle Feri, my father's brother, had perished somewhere, anonymously, in one of any number of death camps. Yet – my heart thudding with excitement as I read this first of many accounts of my family I would read by strangers – my initial thought was: *my uncle is alive, he has written this.*

My uncle was dead. A few years later I would trace his death conclusively. But that article represented a turning point in my affair with the past.

The family had a history. Its past was not some kind of hallucination in which my father and I colluded. Someone else, a *stranger*, had written about them. I had ancestors who lived and died in normal ways before the world went mad.

The family had a history and I was a historian.

Some basic research taught me that northeastern Hungary was full of places like Vaja. Jews had farmed there for generations, at first leasing small plots, eventually owning latifundia. Since the eighteenth century my ancestors had been tillers of Hungarian soil. They had married into similar farming families and perpetuated a lifestyle at once agricultural, orthodox, and Hungariophile. The boundaries of their world stretched from Ukraine to Berlin, from the Adriatic to

Transylvania, but its heart was the Nyírség, a sandy, slightly undulating region wedged between the Great Hungarian Plain and the
foothills of the Carpathians. My generation is the first in two centuries whose roots are severed from its soil.

I resumed my tape-recording of my father, no longer as a fount
of family lore but as a source of data about the farmsteads and
their ways. I enlisted others to help me. I advertised for information.
Word spread about my project. People sent me extraordinary documents: a hundred-year-old autograph album from Israel, a wartime
diary, an unpublished manuscript.

And then my father mentioned that he had some papers of his
own to show me. He took out a yellowing packet and thrust it in
my hands.

Unknown to me, for nearly forty years through every move from
country to country, from apartment to house, with dogged attachment he had taken along a sheaf of letters written to him during
World War II by his wife, his parents, his brothers, his child. He
had no sense of their historical value. They were personal mementoes
he expected would be discarded after his death. He no longer even
looked at them, merely holding onto them by reflex.

During the war, my father, like other Hungarian-Jewish men of
military age, was assigned to a series of labour battalions. These
letters, sporadically preserved in the early war years, were intact from
the time of his last leave in February 1944. On March 19, 1944,
the German army occupied Hungary.

Until then, the position of Hungarian Jews was, relative to that
of the rest of Nazi-dominated Europe, a sheltered one. Now Hungarian Jews were targeted for immediate execution. Aware of the
mortal danger of his family, my father kept all the letters written
to him from then on. In May, the daily accounts stopped.

For as long as I could remember I had been searching for the
people who had written these letters. Now I held their very essences
in my hands. In tiny, pearl-like characters, my grandmother wrote,
"My faith in God to which I cling more convulsively than ever sus-
tains me through every trial." On dainty, flowered stationery reminiscent of the kind I purchased for my daughters, my half-sister
painstakingly inscribed in block capitals the loss of her first tooth.

8

I read their everyday concerns. I saw them each day stepping closer to destruction. I was trying to maintain a scholarly objectivity, but I became obsessed with these letters, spending every available moment on translating them, speaking of little else. I fell ill and spent six months on the floor, immobilized by back pain and a kind of psychic paralysis.

When I recovered, my father suffered a stroke. His speech became badly impaired; great chunks of his remarkable memory were washed away. I considered dropping the project forever.

But I couldn't drop it. I couldn't forsake them. They had left too much of themselves behind.

My father had been right all those years ago: I did need to know the world that came before him and my mother. I needed my birthright, a right not merely to living parents, but to parents who exist in a continuous chain of generations with a past that reaches beyond a single cataclysmic event.

And so I traced the remnants of this family first in North America. And travelled to Budapest for more interviews and research.

And then I journeyed to Vaja.

Going Back

Queuing up for a British Airways flight to Budapest in London's Heathrow Airport, I became aware of the sound of Hungarian being spoken in progressively shriller and more panicky accents by someone near the head of the line. The flight had been announced in English only, and an old woman laden with string bags was drowning puzzled-looking English flight attendants in a flood of colloquial Hungarian. Taking pity on both parties, I tapped the old woman on the shoulder and assured her in rusty Hungarian that yes, indeed, this was the flight to Budapest; I, too, was headed there.

On the plane we switched our assigned seats so that we could sit together, although by this time such was the lady's effusive delight at finding a fellow Hungarian-speaker that I regretted my gesture of help. My companion invoked blessings on my head and regaled me with the history of her children and grandchildren in London. When my polite responses dried up, she asked me why I was going to Hungary.

This was mid-June of 1986, almost exactly three years after I had last been to Budapest. Then, I had spent virtually all my time in the capital researching in libraries and interviewing family members, and just barely managing a day trip to the part of the country my family came from. This time I intended to spend more time in the Nyírség, the sandy northeast of the country that originally took its name from the birch tree. I planned to start with the town of Nagykálló, the Nyírség's oldest and most famous Jewish centre.

None of this was a secret, yet I found myself reluctant to discuss it with my seat-mate. It is common for Hungarian Jews, even ex-patriates like myself, even today, fifty years after the Holocaust, to be slightly paranoid about our Jewish origins with Hungarians we don't know. Frequently, Jews who work together in mutual respect in Budapest will wonder about the origins of each other's names or about the shape of a particular nose – yet will never ask the forthright question, "So are you Jewish too?" The history of assimilation is long; anti-Semitism – covert or open – lurks around the corner. Many feel grateful to leave common backgrounds unexplored.

On the other hand, my choices were apparently to listen to more anecdotes about the old woman's family or to tell her something about myself. In any case, I wanted no part of hiding my Jewishness. I began to explain that I was heading for the Nyírség to exhume my Jewish family's past – feeling annoyingly aware of a nervous quickening of my heartbeat. The octogenarian babbling her gratitude next to me had the appraising eyes of a shrewd peasant. Was she more likely to cut or patronize me for my answer?

I was startled by her response. The broad Slavic face with its marked cheekbones and generous mouth broke into an enormous smile. She grasped my hand in a gesture of introduction. "My name is Mrs Benjámin. I am also from the Nyírség."

Benjámin, I thought, now really surprised – could she possibly be Jewish? We were now well-launched in the game of "guess the Jew." I had revealed myself; in her encouraging body language and use of her name, she was telling me either that she was no anti-Semite or that she herself was Jewish. The typical response would have been to equivocate further. It's not playing the game by its subtle and intricate rules to ask bluntly, "Is the lady Jewish?" It is far too direct – and insulting, too, if the lady is not. I broke the rules and asked.

"Of course I'm Jewish." Mrs Benjámin nodded. "Born and bred Jewish in Nagykálló."

Nagykálló. My destination.

Groping in my hand luggage for my tape recorder, I reflected that this was one of those moments that my father, in the days when he was still well, would have called being fingered by God.

Since the late Middle Ages, the town of Nagykálló has been a centre of Jewish life. It eventually became the seat of Szabolcs County and, until the Holocaust, one of the great Jewish meccas of Eastern Europe. Legends still abound about its most famous citizen, Rabbi Itzhak Eisik Taub, better known as the Tzaddik of Kálló or the "Kallever." Since his death in 1821 his grave has drawn throngs of pilgrims to Nagykálló's two historic Jewish cemeteries annually on the seventh of Adar – "Zayen Oder" in the old toothsome Yiddish pronunciation of the region.

The Kallever had been the first chief rabbi of Szabolcs County and the importer of Hasidism to Hungary from *yeshivot* in Poland and Moravia. Born in Hungary, he was deeply attached to the local populace. In the legends spun about him, it was said that he sat about with shepherds at campfires, rubbed elbows with fishermen and innkeepers in taverns, and made dawn-time appearances dressed in braided folk costume in the vineyards around the town. Tradition has it that he ministered equally to the gentile population as to the Jewish, that he incorporated local tunes into Jewish liturgy, and was the composer of a famous Magyar melody. So imbued was he with the folk culture of his native land that each year at Passover he recited the *Haggadah* in Hungarian instead of the customary Hebrew.

Mrs Benjámin, my seat-mate on the plane to Budapest, had grown up near the older of Nagykálló's two historic Jewish cemeteries, the one that was closed in 1821 when the Tzaddik was buried there. Her first childhood memories were of preparations for the Jewish hordes who descended upon the town each year on the seventh of Adar. A holiday atmosphere prevailed then, with the bustle of cleaning, shopping, and baking for the arrival of both friend and stranger. Mrs Benjámin remembered polishing the petroleum lamps in the living groom till they gleamed; she recalled her mother serving macaroons and schnapps to her guests before bedtime.

They swarmed to Nagykálló in every species of vehicle, by train, carriage, or barrow-cart. The fame of the Kallever was so great that other great European holy men sought burial near him. Latter-day disciples of a Budapest rabbi and a Cracower *rebbe* streamed to Nagykálló as much to pay their respects to their own leaders as to the original holy man. They came to worship, they came to beg favours.

As a little girl, the future Mrs Benjámin peered through the slats of the wooden palisade that surrounded the cemetery. The crush of dark-coated men was too thick to make out the boxed wooden structure that housed the Tzaddik's grave. There was a slot in the side of the mausoleum into which pilgrims popped the slips of paper, the *kvitlis*, on which they had scrawled their pleas and plaints, praying for the Tzaddik's intercession in their lives. "I looked on in wonder and a frightened awe," she told me. "I knew that they were dropping in the *kvitlis* they had brought with them."

Gazing into the eyes of this garrulous old woman, I wondered if by some unbelievable chance they may have caught a glimpse of an old man and an adolescent boy in March of 1920 – my great-grandfather and my father.

My great-grandfather Yakab Schwarcz had pilgrimaged to Nagykálló on many previous occasions. It was a town of importance in the story of his life. His great-grandfather and namesake had played a significant role in the Jewish annals of the town. Yakab himself had attended its famous *yeshiva*. In 1920 Yakab took with him on the pilgrimage his oldest grandson, my father, Gusti. Yakab had reasons to thank the Tzaddik for favours granted in the past. Over the years he had penned many *kvitlis* begging for the Tzaddik's help in the healing of the boy now crushed to Yakab's side by the mob around the mausoleum. And now the boy was well.

This time Yakab was pleading on his own behalf. Had the old lady on the plane perhaps spied my great-grandfather Yakab dropping his last *kvitli* in the special slot? By March 1920 Yakab was very ill with diabetes. But he was a believer in miracles – he would have said with good cause. He also believed in blessings. A few months later, he would compose an extraordinary will in which he catalogued the many blessings God had showered upon him personally. But there was another blessing that had been meant not only for him but for his ancestors and descendants as well. The legend has come down through the ages in many versions; this is the one that I have heard:

Once a prosperous sheep farmer – our ancestor – was driving his sheep to be shorn in a village neighbouring Nagykálló. Caught by nightfall, he put up at a simple inn where, lying on his pallet of straw, he was disturbed by the groans of someone in pain. The sheep farmer went to investigate and found a rabbinical student in a state of semi-delirium. Despite the young man's protests that he needed no help, the farmer insisted on nursing him through the night, bringing him soothing tea and adjusting his straw ticking.

When the young man groaned that in his weakened state he would make a terrible impression on his future congregants in Nagykálló where he had been invited to serve as rabbi, the farmer offered to drive him there in his wool cart the following morning. Hearing these reassuring words, the rabbi-elect sank into a healing sleep.

The farmer was good as his word and dropped his passenger in Nagykálló's market square the next day. As he bade him good-bye, our ancestor was astonished to see the young man raise his arms in a gesture of benediction.

"*Yevorechecho* ...." the future Tzaddik intoned. "For your act of goodness, accept this blessing. It will accompany not only you but your descendants as well. Your family, like our forefather Abraham's, will be wealthy and numerous. Your name will live long and the veneration of your offspring will preserve it for hundreds of years."

Amidst the yellowing grass that grows outside the Tzaddik's mausoleum today are humps of ancient graves dating back to the Middle Ages. On the other side of the village my long-ago forbear, Yankev Fisch, great-grandfather of my great-grandfather Yakab, rests in the larger graveyard that was opened up after the Tzaddik died. Although they are separated in death, the two men's lives were intimately linked, and in the many myths about the great rabbi, Yankev features as a loyal sidekick.

Situated along a busy trade route between Bohemia and Transylvania, Nagykálló was a centre of commerce visited by Jewish merchants as early as the fifteenth century. Reckoned the oldest of the Nyírség's Jewish settlements, its beginnings are difficult to pinpoint. Three dispersions destroyed the community's written records, but the old graves bear witness to a long-standing Jewish presence. Despite the dispersals, stubborn and persistent remnants of the community crept back each time to the thick walls and crenellated ramparts of the fortress of the Kállays, the family of aristocrats who offered them protection from Magyar highwaymen and Turkish janissaries.

In the late eighteenth century the Emperor Joseph II, a disciple of Voltaire and of the Enlightenment, made a heroic effort to sweep away the shackles of medievalism on his dominions. His efforts to modernize extended even to his Jewish subjects to whom he granted the right of freedom of movement, settlement in most towns, the practice of agriculture, industry, the trades, and fine arts. Most of these and other grand reforms were disregarded by local authorities who preferred medievalism to entry into the modern age and who emphatically preferred the Jews to remain in unassimilated enclaves.

Nagykálló, however, was different. Decades before the toleration edicts of Joseph II, eleven Jews had received permission to settle permanently in the town. One of them was probably the father of Yankev Fisch, a long-lived gentleman who, according to apocrypha, was a landholder in Nagykálló and had been married to a *first* wife for eighty-eight years.

The vast majority of modern Hungarian Jews are descendants of immigrants from Poland who arrived in Hungary in the nineteenth century. But – well into even the nineteenth century – Jews of Nagykálló prided themselves on being "indigenous," distinguishing themselves from the large influx of eastern Jews then submerging earlier Jewish settlement. These native Jews disdainfully sequestered themselves from the hundreds of Polish and Galician immigrants attracted by Joseph II's reforms.

The Nagykálló natives were precursors of a later widespread tendency among Hungarian Jews to feelings of separateness from the mainstream of Jewish history. During the forging of Magyar nationalism, they cast their lot wholeheartedly with that of the emerging Magyar nation – only one of the many ethnic groups in the polyglot Austro-Hungarian Empire which included Slovaks, Ukrainians, Slovenes, and many other nationalities. Even the orthodox among Hungarian Jews described themselves with self-conscious pride as *Magyars* of the Israelite faith.

While the majority of Hungarian towns were enacting local legislation shutting Jews out of settlement and the right to own real estate, Nagykálló's Jews were noted for their prosperity and lived in such amity with their Christian neighbours that at the beginning of the nineteenth century they were allowed to own all the houses in the market square. Linguistically too they were unusually well integrated, in a country where the official language until 1844 was Latin and a motley mix of languages was spoken of which vernacular Magyar was only one. Though the Tzaddik of Kálló spoke flawless Magyar, in his petition of 1792 requesting a raise in salary from his congregants, he wrote in Yiddish. But the president of the congregation, my ancestor Yankev Fisch, granted him the request in a memo written in Hungarian.

In the two centuries that have elapsed since those days, Nagykálló has languished. Overtaken in size and importance by Nyíregyháza, ten kilometres away, today Nagykálló is a sleepy, overgrown village shrunk to suburban status beside its industrialized neighbour. Hollyhocks grow by its roadsides; sheep graze on its outskirts as they did centuries ago. Inexplicably stuck in the middle of one of its sere fields, an unnatural outcropping juts from the flatness of the Nyírség plain. This curiously sterile promontory is the "Hill of Misery," constructed long ago by serfs at the whim of an early Kállay whose stunted imagination devised this mode of relieving the monotony of the terrain.

For decades after World War II, Nagykálló died out as a mecca for pilgrims. In the 1980s, however, there was a flurry of renewed interest in the village by Hungarian Jews feeling the stirrings of the democracy movement and by expatriate Jews exploring their roots. Nowhere on the scale of the throngs of the past, pilgrims nonetheless began to arrive from Israel, from America, and even from Budapest. Nyíregyháza taxi drivers chauffeuring western visitors to the village knew to steer me to the man they called the "old farmer Jew," who kept the keys and guarded the two Jewish cemeteries at opposite ends of the village. The farmer was the head of one of the last Jewish families who still lived there. Pathetically pleased to show off the recently refurbished graveyards, he pointed to the finely scalloped stone fence and the renovated mausoleum. Once made of wood, the building enclosing the Tzaddik's tomb was now of lemon-coloured stucco crowned by a tin roof. Inside, the chill smell of death and burnt wax emanated from the iron casket on which sat a tray of used *yahrzeit* candles.

In a corner, a plastic bag held scraps of paper. "What are they?" I asked.

"*Kvitlis*," the old man said. "Do you want to leave one too, for the sainted rabbi?" he added, smiling encouragement. Caught off guard, I said no so brusquely that the old man's watery blue eyes registered dismay.

What could I have possibly asked the Tzaddik, had I believed in his powers to intercede? Should I have appealed to him to turn back the clock to when Mrs Benjámin helped her mother bake macaroons for the seventh of Adar? To when the carriage deposited my great-grandfather Yakab and my father, come to plead for Yakab's life in 1920?

Where would I have been in that old-world bustle of men in caftans and dark business suits like Yakab's? My birth, after all, was predicated on the destruction that swept through this region a quarter century after my father and great-grandfather pilgrimaged here together. But for the old cemeteries, a great storm had wiped away the traces of a lifestyle that had taken centuries to evolve. Gone today are the farmers and drivers and tavern-keepers and matchmakers and shopkeepers. Gone the bailiffs, the warehouse and distillery owners and operators, the lumber merchants, the potato, cabbage, and grain wholesalers. Gone the seamstresses and milliners, the teachers, the children.

I didn't leave a *kvitli* for the Tzaddik. I slipped some money to the farmer Jew and drove to another village, looking for my great-grandfather Yakab.

Yakab's Journey

Yakab Schwarcz was a methodical man. His will, a remarkable document written in 1920, a year before his death, ran to seventeen legal size pages of type. Each of his eight surviving children received a copy, with notes added in Hungarian and Hebrew in Yakab's beautiful hand. One copy, annotated by Yakab in purple ink, eventually was salvaged by my father, saved by him through what travails and strange endeavours I can only begin to imagine.

My father loved Yakab dearly. His first memories were tied to the old man, still in his prime in the first decade of the twentieth century when Gusti was just beginning to take cognizance of the world around him. He recalled how as little boys he and his brothers would wait expectantly by the train tracks that cut through their farm; how their mother would march them there knowing her father would be travelling that morning. What a thrill it was to see Yakab framed one moment in the window of the speeding train, then to be scrambling in the grass for the candies he had flung at them before disappearing from sight.

My father also venerated his grandfather, a man of ambition, achievement and overarching piety. His will – my father's one tangible legacy from Yakab after everything save a few photographs and a beloved Psalter had been destroyed – was an artifact from which Gusti would regularly quote from memory. Once he sat me down and read me the document from beginning to end. When he came to the passage where Yakab had written, "I made night into day and worked every minute, so that I could earn my family's bread the honest way while financial pressures perpetually pressed upon my skull," he covered his face and began to weep.

Gusti had inherited not only a testament and a prayer book from his grandfather. Yakab was emotional as well as methodical, as likely to have a tantrum as to break down in tears. In the will he begged his children's forgiveness for his "nervous outbursts"; he also had cause to note that, in writing it, he had succumbed to sobs several times. My father's tearful displays of feeling were also unpredictable and heartfelt – and always unsettling to witness.

"He had such a hard life! *Such* a hard life," Gusti sobbed.

"*Apu*," I started to remonstrate, as one would with a child, "he didn't. Not really. Not compared with you."

This heresy sobered my father completely. He removed his glasses and began briskly to dry them on a handkerchief. "How can you compare me to him?" he exclaimed in genuine puzzlement. "My life was a picnic compared to his!"

He meant this breathtaking assertion in all sincerity. My father, who had lost nearly everyone in the Holocaust, who had had to re-build his life so many times in so many ways and places, did not view his life through the same prism as I did. To me the idea that his life was a picnic in comparison to anyone's, but especially in comparison with his wealthy grandfather's, was laughable. Yakab, who now lay beneath an ornate gravestone in the family plot, buried according to precise instructions that took him more than a page of type to specify? Yakab, who had had the good fortune to live and die without the need to challenge the eternal verities of faith and observance, whose belief in miracles had been substantiated many times over before the world went mad?

But then my father, self-deprecating and modest, habitually made light of his wartime physical sufferings, waving them off as trifling compared to what my mother had endured. The depressions that beset him every fall around the time of the high holydays and every spring when the 19th of March evoked the time of the family's an-nihilation were for him an albatross to be borne as his due. "Survivor guilt," we would now call it, although he was oblivious of the concept. His neurotic dread of Canadian snowstorms, his exaggerated pro-tectiveness of my mother's health, his inability to sleep until my sister and I were in our beds as teenagers – all this he considered part of the normal baggage of a normal life.

My father, a corner of whose heart was a permanent graveyard, nonetheless managed to conduct his life in an entirely matter-of-fact way. At the time that he read me Yakab's will, I challenged his interpretation of his grandfather's life. But now I wonder if his view of Yakab was not more realistic than mine. For if I allow myself for a moment not to be blind-sided by the Holocaust, Yakab's life appears more complex, more textured and, yes, harder than I had first assumed.

Great-grandfather Yakab was born in the Nyírség village of Derzs in 1856, "two weeks before Purim, of the exact date I am not certain," he wrote in his will. He was the fourth generation of his family to be born in the ancestral home. The adjective "ancestral" should not mislead one into thinking it a grand or luxurious house. Its walls were mud, its floors packed earth, its roof thatch – lowly materials in cheap and abundant supply in the Hungarian countryside. The peep-hole-sized front windows looked out on a low-eaved wooden porch typical of Nyírség architecture. Designed to keep out the merciless summer sun, it also doomed the two front rooms to perennial murkiness. One of these rooms was used as a prayer house by the village's Jewish males. Another in the back served a similar function for women. Yakab's eight siblings and his parents crammed into the rest of the quarters: a kitchen, a vestibule, and two all-purpose chambers for eating, sleeping, and living.

From such beginnings Yakab Schwarcz became one of the most prominent Jews in Szabolcs County, one of its most progressive farmers and indubitably its most giving man. Having meticulously itemized donations totalling 160,000 Crowns, an amount that represented virtually all of his cash assets, he wrote in his will to his children in 1920, "you all know that in my lifetime it was always my greatest pleasure if I could give to the poor."

In the category of the poor, Yakab clearly did not include said children, although in 1920 – following the Great War, following Hungary's Bolshevik Revolution, following the Romanian occupation of the country – even the most affluent of the eight surviving children stood in a tenuous financial position. But Yakab, like all his philanthropic ancestors, regarded acts of charity as an investment that would yield a profit and dividends: "Let us trust in our good Lord, who does not remain in anyone's debt, that for my contribution He will abundantly repay you, as well."

He was the self-made son of a self-made man. The epitaph on his gravestone, a quote from Genesis, reads, "Then Jacob went on his journey." Yakab travelled far and wide both within the Austro-Hungarian monarchy and in east-central Europe – to rabbinical courts in Galicia, to agricultural fairs in Berlin and Dresden, to spas in Carlsbad and Abazia – but the nucleus of his world remained his native county.

A middle child, raised in the main when his father was still a struggling land tenant in Derzs, he attended *yeshivah* in nearby Nagykálló, whereas his younger siblings were educated at posh schools in Vienna during the family's more affluent days. He married up – choosing a wife from a similarly devout but considerably more wealthy and cultured Szabolcs Jewish family. Like his parents before him, he and his wife, Karolina, also struggled. Since his earliest dawning of understanding, Yakab had known that his father, Samuel Schwarcz, would honour the Jewish custom of favouring the eldest son to whom he would eventually bequeath half his estate. To his three youngest boys Samuel would leave the rich leasehold that became the foundation of his wealth after Yakab's marriage. Samuel's only daughter received a dowry. But the three remaining sons had to scramble for their fortunes. Explaining away the small estate he was leaving for his own children, Yakab noted in his will, "From my late dear parents and my late dear Father-in-law I received a scant inheritance indeed."

And the hardships were not only financial. Two children died in childhood, and he was widowed relatively young. "It is to this day ten years that I am an unfortunate widower," he wrote in Carlsbad where he had gone to take a cure for his diabetes in 1920. "Here I must put down my pen, for I have begun to weep terribly! I was fifty-four years old when your poor, good, sweet mother who rests with God left me here!"

We may smile at his extravagant use of exclamation points and unabashed sentimentality, but he had been devoted to Karolina. During the decade after her death, blow upon blow rained down on his head. He came close to bankruptcy. The Great War tested his faith and shattered his complacency. As for 1919, that was his *annus horribilis*: Hungary's Bolshevik Revolution forced him to flee his home and, while in exile, he lost his oldest son, the family's darling, and a cherished daughter, the child who most resembled Karolina.

No, Yakab's journey had not been particularly easy. Yet it had been travelled with gusto. Even in Carlsbad, a grey-haired gentleman with a neatly sculpted spade of a beard, he mustered surprising energy, considering his weakened state. He typed with intense concentration, determined to convey a complicated message to the generations ahead.

Nor did he neglect the generations past. He had a delicate task to delegate to his sons: they must, after his death, pilgrimage to the family cemetery in Derzs where all his ancestors were buried, and formally apologize to his dead parents for his defection. For, after much thought and soul searching, he had chosen to lie next to Karolina in Nyírlövő in her family's graveyard, rather than among the Schwarczes of Derzs.

But he was still proud of his Schwarcz lineage, proud of the tradition of philanthropy he had inherited, proud most of all of the long-standing Schwarcz association with the Hungarian soil.

After all, he wrote in the will, he claimed descent not only from his namesake and great-grandfather, the illustrious Yankev Fisch of Nagykálló, but also of his great-great-grandfather "honest Itzig the Jew," also known as Itzig Derzser, the first of the Schwarczes of our line in Hungary, albeit he was not yet called Schwarcz. It was Itzig who, legend has it, had first bought land in Derzs, Itzig who was "famed in faraway lands for his matchless acts of charity."

A Wandering Jew Strikes Root

The house in Derzs where Yakab had been born in 1856 stood at the intersection of two county highways much frequented by travellers. "Honest Itzig" had built it there because he had known a thing or two about travel by the time he reached Derzs, a village with a history dating back to 1329 when it became the fief of a nobleman named Dersi. The Jews of the village, however, were generally of the Johnny-come-lately variety. Itzig was in the vanguard, probably one of fifteen Jewish settlers enumerated in the hamlet in 1784-85, forerunners of one of the great population movements of Europe.

Beginning with the dislocations caused by the nightmarish Khmelnytsky (Chmielnicki) pogroms of 1648-49 in Ukraine and further stimulated by the successive Partitions of Poland, waves of Yiddish-speaking, primarily Hasidic Jews washed over the northeastern counties of greater Hungary – a region today divided between the Czech Republic, Slovakia, Romania, and the former Soviet Union. By the early decades of the nineteenth century they were pressing into the more southerly Hungarian counties of Szabolcs and Szatmár between which the Nyírség is spread.[1]

The Polish and Galician newcomers were not popular with either the Hungarian authorities or their earlier-arrived co-religionists. Local administrations passed measures preventing their settlement, and Jews who had struck root earlier – even recently arrived Polish Jews – tried to obstruct them from staying. In 1770 in the village of Mád a case was brought against a Polish Jew who had failed to pay the rent on his tavern. All the witnesses against him were Jews, the majority like himself from Poland. They blackened him in the eyes of the court and succeeded in securing his expulsion from the village. The hapless man's reputation preceded him even in the next place, where he was described as "a Jewish newcomer from Poland who has no possessions, he is a mere wanderer, which is why he was chased out of Mád where he has caused a great rumpus and opposition among the Jews."[2]

Itzig probably arrived in the Nyírség in the early 1780s. He must indeed have been weary of travel to have stuck there, for Derzs's land flowed neither with milk nor honey. Over millennia, northerly winds had battered and raked this southern section, eroding its soil and piling its characteristic sand into rolling dunes. Between the sand-hills lay treacherous basins of marsh and reed. Yet there was desolate beauty in these backwater ponds, which bred waterfowl and fish of every variety. And the white-trunked birch was beautiful too, the famous birch that had given its name, *nyírfa*, to the region and to many villages in the form of the prefix "Nyír."

Itzig took the name "Derzser" – of Derzs – a surname he would not be allowed to pass on to his progeny. During the reign of the enlightened Habsburg despot Joseph II (1780–90), as part of several measures of Germanization and centralization, the emperor decreed that his Jewish subjects must choose permanent German family names. Unlike the existing informal nomenclature based on places of origin, patronymics and physical descriptions, these German sur-names were to remain constant within a particular family. Special naming commissions of the central government toured the country-side, foisting names upon a sullen population. Itzig's descendants settled for "Schwarcz."

Though he did not bequeath them his name, Itzig left an enduring legacy. The memory of his wanderings fostered in him an undying sympathy for the footsore migrants who passed in front of his white-washed cottage. And so, as Yakab would write later of his great-great-grandfather, Itzig became "famed in faraway lands for his matchless acts of charity." In his front yard, Itzig placed a trestle table under the shade of the hardy-rooted acacias that were even then starting to supplant the birch as the Nyírség's emblematic tree. On the table Itzig's wife set simple refreshments from their own board. The poor would knock at the front door to receive their fill of milk, bread, or potatoes. For a time the travellers rested there, then hoisted their bundles onto their backs once more. There was no question of payment: a word of thanks sufficed.

My great-great-grandfather Samuel, Yakab's father, ritualized his respect for Itzig by honouring the old table in a singular way. By then the Schwarcz family had grown in social standing, affluence, and numbers, and had left Derzs for greener pastures. Samuel had the original table enlarged to accommodate the forty or fifty family members who now congregated around it on occasions of joy and sorrow. He chose a different kind of wood for the new leaves in order to emphasize the original dimensions of the table and to call attention to its pious past. And a new tradition related to the table grew up. Each time a venerated family member died, a leg was hewn off the old table and placed in the coffin along with the corpse, a reminder at the time of judgment of the individual's acts of goodness. So did the Schwarczes strive to remind the Almighty of their efforts in this world on His behalf.

Family legend has it that Itzig came to own a small plot of land in Derzs long before such ownership was officially granted to Hungarian Jews. Be that as it may, the very existence of the legend poignantly illustrates the desire of Jewish migrants to be rooted in their new country. Landedness, in fact, was the true litmus test of Jewish fortunes in Hungary. Nearly one thousand years earlier, at the time of the national territorial conquest by Magyar tribes, Khazar-Jewish allies of the conquerors received land grants upon which they practised agriculture. In later medieval times, when Jewish power brokers enjoyed the protection and favour of Hungarian monarchs, Jewish noblemen occasionally received landed estates from the sovereign. But these isolated acts of largesse disappeared with the loss of Jewish legal status in the later Middle Ages.

Only with the reforms of Joseph II at the end of the eighteenth century was the right of Jews to engage in agriculture reasserted. Even so, the Hungarian legislature did not lift the ban on the leasing of nobles' estates by Jews until 1844. As for their ownership of land, the Diet merely hinted at it in 1840 and did not grant it fully for another twenty years. In the meantime, though, there were legal loopholes through which the prohibition could be bypassed, and by the turn of the twentieth century, more than a third of Hungary's arable land was estimated as being owned by Jews.

Landownership symbolized their true arrival as full-fledged members of Hungarian society. It was quintessential proof of permanence and security in a country where, even in the twentieth century, land was overwhelmingly the main form of property. For what could be more yearned for by the preternaturally "wandering Jew" than to be rooted in this way? And in the late eighteenth and early nineteenth centuries, Hungary was awash with wandering Jews. Even as individual Jews prospered in their new country, they were reminded of their own or their parents' uprooted past by the regiments of poor itinerants who, in an age devoid of organized social services, moved day by day from one wealthy (or at least relatively more affluent household) to the next, unsure of where their next meal was coming from. The ambition to own land was equally great for the modest Jewish land tenant or the overseer of a magnate's estate as it was for the *nouveau riche* industrialist or banker seeking social legitimacy in a society wedded to feudalistic values and symbols.

In their desire to purchase land, Jews handily found sellers among the nobility and gentry. The abolition of serfdom and of the nobility's exemption from taxation in 1848 ushered in a new order for Hungary's notoriously spendthrift aristocracy. To manage their agricultural estates successfully required a new efficiency and an eye for profit that most were either unwilling or unequipped to assume. Sooner than develop business skills, they sold off or leased their properties to ensure the supply of funds that maintained opulent country estates and town flats, expensive casino memberships, and enormous gambling debts.

My great-grandfather Samuel, Yakab's father, acquired his first plot of land shortly after Yakab's birth. The legend of how this came to be is wreathed in magic, mystery, and a tinge of humour. One crisp winter night, so the story goes, as Samuel's household slept, a carriage pulled up in front of his snow-covered, thatched dwelling in Derzs. Summoned by urgent rapping, Samuel staggered to the door. At the threshold loomed a stranger, wrapped in the garb of a well-off peasant, a coat lined with sheep's wool. The man had brought an invitation from Samuel's landlord, Albert Gencsy, the squire of Kisléta, which could hardly be declined: "A few hours ago, madam, his wife was – Lord be praised! – safely delivered of a baby boy. My master bids your immediate presence."

Throwing britches hastily over his nightshirt, Samuel breathed a brief goodbye to his wife and patted the heads of his sleeping babies. It took only moments for him to complete his toilette and for the coachman to reverse the horse in the direction of Kisléta. Anxious thoughts assailed Samuel over the course of the journey. What had he done wrong? What had the birth of his landlord's son to do with him? The fifteen kilometres seemed as long as all the trips he had ever taken in his life. At dawn they finally pulled up under the arched eaves of the squire's manor and were met in the hallway by the beaming master himself.

"Welcome, Sam," the squire greeted him with bluff heartiness. "You must be hungry after your journey." And at the sudden worried look that clouded the young man's face, Gencsy clapped him jovially across the shoulder.

"Don't think I don't know better than to give you ham and sausages," the squire joked with heavy humour, leading the way to the dungeon-like kitchen in the basement. There, as a mark of his consideration, a Jewish woman from the village was bustling about preparing refreshments in her own kosher pots. More and more mystified, Samuel sat down in the dining room to partake of this breakfast. Only after the woman had served him and left the room did his host get to the point.

"I've asked you to come here today because I want my son's first kiss to be bestowed by a Jew. Yes, indeed – you yourself will be the first to kiss the newborn. I'm convinced, you see, that this will bring him luck in life."

Samuel stared back in perplexity. If he questioned his host as to how a Jew's kiss could possibly bring luck to a squalling newborn, neither the question nor Gencsy's answer has been passed down the generations. He must have felt foolish as he bent over the cradle and tickled the infant's cheek with his beard. His puzzlement deepened when Gencsy announced his intention of naming the child "Samuel." (Later he would be less mystified when he learned that he shared the name with the Gencsy ancestor who had built the manor house.)

Not until the two men had returned to the dining room from the nursery and lit up their pipes did Samuel begin to relax. Apparently the midnight summons was a harmless caprice of his landlord. But yet another surprise awaited him.

"What say, Sam," puffed Gencsy companionably, "what say I sell you my estate in Derzs? You know, the one you've been leasing?"

"But I can't afford it!" Samuel exclaimed.

"Who said anything about money?" the squire retorted. "You'll pay for it when you can. We'll draw up a contract right away. And we don't have to bother with an advance."

And that's how, according to legend, my great-great-grandfather Samuel Schwarcz became a landowner. It would be years before he paid up the squire. His subsequent prosperity would be built not upon its thin *holds* but upon a future fat leasehold in a neighbouring village. But the symbolism and social status conferred by the original purchase strengthened both his faith in himself and his conviction that the Power on high was with him.

Samuel's fortunes improved sufficiently for him to begin to lease a prosperous property in the village of Gyulaj where he moved in the mid-1870s. When renovated by Yakab's younger brother, Karl, a quarter of a century later, it became the comfortable new establishment to which the enormous extended family would troop to mark the great and sombre *yahrzeit* observances of their parents.

Great-grandfather Yakab's younger siblings grew up in Gyulaj and profited from the family's latter-day affluence. Yakab himself was twenty when the move occurred and he lived there for only three years. Nevertheless, he commemorated the village with a small donation in his will because, as he wrote in Carlsbad, "from here I was a happy bridegroom."

Finding the Exemplary Wife

In 1879 when nineteen-year-old Karolina Zuckerman married twenty-three-year-old Yakab Schwarcz, her brothers were attending university in Budapest and Vienna and her older sisters had wed landowners and professionals. Yakab Schwarcz had neither a university education nor a profession nor riches. He was a fortuneless middle son on the make, handsome, ingratiating, and clearly impressed by the artistic pretensions of the Zuckermans of Nyírlövő, who diversely dabbled in architecture, literature, and fine horticulture. Yakab brimmed with plans – to find a good leasehold, to experiment with new farming methods, to make his mark. Allying himself with the Zuckermans could only help him.

He surely admitted as much in his will when in the hierarchy of his gratitude to God he gave thanks for being able to "marry into such a distinguished family as was my late Father-in-law's" before noting his appreciation "that I had such a matchlessly good, high-minded and exemplarily religious wife."

Within the extended family, the very model for happy marriage was set by the union of Mina Moskovits and Gustav Zuckerman, Karolina's parents. Doubtless, setting and caste had something to do with their status in the family, for the Zuckermans of Lövő – cultured and, more importantly, rich – represented the cream of Nyírség Jewish society. Every bit as religious and philanthropic as the Schwarczes, they were several notches higher in social standing. At the time of Yakab's marriage, the Zuckerman mansion that would become the family's showpiece was still in its planning stages. Near the end of the century the new stone manor with its three arched French doors fronting on lush gardens would be photographed and written up in the Szabolcs County *Monográfia*, a snobbish tome devoted to the area's history and the stately homes of its aristocratic or gentrified families.

The designer of this particular mansion was a sleepy-looking giant with brown eyes and black beard, my great-great-grandfather Gustav Zuckerman, my own father's namesake. He had begun his career as the manager of a monastery distillery. A quiet, reserved man, he had a prodigious capacity for work and, in a business that lent itself to flagrant abuses, a reputation for strict honesty. His employers grew fond of him, and he eventually bought the Lövő estate with its 1,000 *holds* from the Jesuit order.

The landscaping of the Lövő grounds and garden was a shared joy for Gustav and his wife, Mina. A lively sparrow of a woman, she had been Gustav's foster sister, adopted by his parents as company for their only child, and groomed to become his wife. In front of the house the two ardent gardeners planted flower beds in long ribbons of colour down to the row of chestnut trees that curtained the house from the dusty road. Behind palms and rubber trees in the back stretched an orchard and vegetable gardens. A profusion of heliotropes, narcissi, daturas, and geraniums flourished in several greenhouses, ready to be brought into the house in winter. Throughout the years of their long marriage Gustav paid homage to Mina's love of growing things by bringing her a long-stemmed flower each morning, from the garden or a greenhouse, depending on the season.

The fundamental male bias at the core of Judaism is reflected even in the way a chronicle such as this one has preserved and passed along stories almost solely of a family's patriarchs. But once in a while, from the store of accumulated anecdotes a particular woman practically leaps into life. So it is with Mina.

The Zuckermans kept a room set aside in the Lövő mansion exclusively for the comfort of poor, itinerant Jews. Once, a nameless beggar protested as the lady of the house herself made up his bed for the night. "Frau Zuckerman ought not to trouble herself with such a task for one such as I," the beggar demurred in Yiddish.

"It's not *your* bed that I'm making," replied my great-great grandmother, "not yours at all, but *mine*."

When my father told me this story, its moral was meant to underscore Mina's pious and humble nature. But instead I see in the vignette a woman who knew equally her station in life and the wandering Jew's. It wasn't humility that prompted her to change his linen, but a canny perception of her reward in the hereafter.

An anomalous photograph commemorates the engagement of Karolina and Yakab. Although both were scions of orthodox families, nothing in the picture denotes their Jewishness. Yakab's wavy chestnut hair remains uncovered and, save for fashionable sideburns, he is as yet clean-shaven. Karolina stands intent and unsmiling beside her seated fiancé, a proprietorial hand on his wrist. Endless childbearing would within the decade transform her into a stout matron with the demeanour of a healthy peasant. Even in this youthful picture, her heart-shaped face with its wide cheekbones and blunt chin falls short of conventional prettiness. But the deep-set eyes, the coils of high-piled hair, the hourglass figure make her a comely bride.

She was the right wife for Yakab, even-tempered like her father. Her serenity would centre her highly strung husband as long as she lived. He was of a sudden and ignitable temperament, in worship in particular transported by great yearnings and enthusiasms, but the rages for which he apologized in his will only plagued him in the decade of his widowerhood.

A slight smile plays about Yakab's sensuous mouth in the engagement photograph, as if his bride's fingers both soothed and aroused his pulse. Out of Karolina's fecund body he would have the many children promised his line by the Tzaddik of Kálló. I imagine him blushing at such thoughts before the wedding, and shifting to the logistics of the event with which he was much preoccupied in those days.

The wedding plans neatly reconciled Yakab's social pretensions with his religious zeal. "For the Isr. poor of NYÍRBAKTA – 300 Crowns," his will directed, "for here in front of the Count's castle took place my wedding on June 3, 1879, the ceremony being performed by the famed former honourable Chief Rabbi of Újfehértó, Reb Herzke."

In 1879 Yakab was crisscrossing Szabolcs County in search of the contacts necessary to secure a solid leasehold of his own. His enquiries and interviews took him beyond the northern spheres of his future in-laws' influence and his father's southern connections. In the central Szabolcs villages midway between Lövő and Gyulaj, the young man canvassed prospective landlords for a likely property he might afford.

The lesson of Gustav Zuckerman's success had not been lost on Yakab. Distilling alcohol was one of the most profitable enterprises in the region. Potatoes for the making of mash were readily available, and the by-products of distilling made valuable fodder for livestock. As for the prime product, alcohol was the one commodity with a guaranteed market even in a poor agrarian society. As the Hungarian economy expanded in the latter part of the nineteenth century, distilling proved to be one of its great success stories. So Yakab was prospecting for a leasehold already furnished with a distillery and a licence to distil. The Rákóczi Estate which he would lease a year later was so equipped, and a mere stone's throw from the Nyírbakta property of Count Dégenfeld, one of the local luminaries upon whom Yakab called with a letter of introduction in 1879.

Impressed by the personable young man who solicited him as a future tenant, the count offered his grounds as a fitting site for the approaching wedding. A love of ostentation was one of Yakab's weaknesses, and he accepted the offer with alacrity. But as if to balance his social and pecuniary aspirations, he called upon an old mentor of his boyhood to officiate at the ceremony. A local wonder rabbi, Reb Herzke Halévy enjoyed national renown for mysticism. In the midst of his studies he might raise his head and call for firefighters to be dispatched to a distant village. Such was his repute that the firemen, gentiles all, obeyed his instructions without question. And indeed they were said to arrive barely in time to save a village from flames.

In the fullness of time, Yakab would inherit a number of prized religious objects from the man who officiated at his wedding. The coffin in which he would one day be lowered into the soil of Lövő was fashioned from the holy man's study table. One of the lesser talismans has remained in the family to this day. In 1944 when my father, Yakab's oldest grandson, parted for the final time from his mother, Yakab's daughter Ilona, she gave Gusti a tattered fragment of much folded-paper bearing mystical notations in Reb Herzke's hand. This amulet would guard, and be guarded by, my father in 1944-45 when every Jew in Hungary daily faced the threat of extinction. In 1947 and again in 1954, the yellowed scrap accompanied my mother to the Budapest hospitals where she brought me and my sister into the world. And, nearly a century after Yakab's wedding, it devolved upon me – shrugging cynically, yet surprisingly gratified to have it beneath my pillow when in turn I gave birth to my daughters in a Canadian city far removed from the world of Reb Herzke, Yakab, and Karolina.

As was usual at the time, Yakab and Karolina moved in with her parents at the beginning of their marriage; their first child, my grandmother Ilona, was born in Lövő in 1881. By the spring of 1882 the young couple were ready to set up house on their own and moved to the village of Vaja from where Yakab would farm the Rákóczi Estate for the next eight years.

It was a pretty village, its greater and lesser landmarks alternating with two hundred whitewashed cottages studding a sprawling Main Street. On the spring morning of the Schwarczes' arrival, Karolina had to shield the baby in her arms against the sand and grit of the thoroughfare when the carriage finally came to a halt. Other than the rabbinical blessing of long ago, there was no intimation that one day Yakab's business would turn big profits. The house by which the carriage stopped consisted of a mere two rooms and a primitive kitchen, just like most of the rest. Leased from a Jew named Grunstein, it was considerably meaner than the original ancestral home in Derzs.

During the eight years they lived in the Vaja house, Karolina gave birth to their sons Andor, Zoltán, and Menyush, and to two other babies who died infancy. These were the years of which Yakab would write that he "made night into day and worked constantly so that I could earn my family's bread the honest way ... [while] financial pressures perpetually pressed upon my skull." Business setbacks forced him to give up the farm in 1890 and move to the nearby town of Kisvárda where, in a similar modest establishment, daughters Elizabeth and Irene were born. "There is not a more industrious, active, and ambitious man than I in the world," he wrote in Carlsbad. "From my dear late parents and my dear late in-laws I received a very insignificant inheritance; in relation to my business I disposed over but trifling capital, and, without citing anything else – even when there was peace – I was always obliged to buy twelve pairs of shoes at a time for my dear family."

Twelve pairs of shoes, for, when he returned to Vaja in 1895 – this time taking up residence on the estate itself – four more children were born within six years to the by-then middle-aged couple. Whether burning the midnight oil over his accounts or locked in conjugal embrace, great-grandfather Yakab did indeed "turn night into day."

Despite the five-year sojourn in Kisvárda, Yakab's fortunes were wedded to Vaja, a village that in 1882 still bore more resemblance to the feudal world than to the modern. It took its name from that of the aristocratic Vay family whose historic castle dominated the face of the village in much the same way that the Vays dominated its life.

The ornate portals of the Vay park opened on to the mid-point of Main Street at the heart of the village. Within the iron gates stood two castles. The sixteenth-century Big Castle occupied the site of an earlier medieval fortress, of which a sturdy reminder still survived in the form of the northern tower, a square, sun-bleached edifice complete with rooftop battlements, grilled windows, and arrow slits. In the Middle Ages the old fortress had been an extensive affair, and where the shapely nineteenth-century stone church now stands near the gates on Main Street was the site of its former chapel. With time, the ramparts of the fortress crumbled, and both church and castle underwent structural and ideological changes. Like the Vay family, the church turned Calvinist during the Reformation. It was rebuilt in 1821 outside the castle gates, flanked by the houses of the richer peasantry on Main Street.

The rest of the Big Castle represented Renaissance elegance: three-storey walls of cream-coloured stone, high windows outlined by stone lintels. Facing it stood the more modern eighteenth-century Little Castle, a scaled-down, two-storey building with mock gothic windows. When Count Adam Vay visited Vaja – for generally he lived in his grander residences in nearby Nyírberkesz and distant Budapest – he preferred the comforts of the Little Castle to the cold formality of the historic one. The Big Castle was nevertheless maintained like a jewel box in which were displayed the ornaments of the Vay family.

Old swords, firearms, and great maces were displayed in the ground-floor hall. Carpeted stairs ascended two flights to the magnificent, mahogany-furnished Rákóczi chamber where a huge fresco on the ceiling depicted the fourteenth-century Battle of Nicopolis in which Count Titus Vay had saved the life of the King of Hungary from the hands of the infidel. In gratitude for this and other services, the King had granted the Vays their coat of arms and the power of life and death over their serfs.

The feudal system had been abolished in Hungary since 1848, but, even without the exercise of the right of life and death, many feudal realities remained intact on the Vay estates. The count owned over 2,000 *holds* in Vaja divided unequally between two properties, the larger Rákóczi and the lesser Kuruc estates. The majority of Vaja's 1,600 villagers depended on working these lands for their livelihood, either as day labourers or share-croppers. To supplement their sparse incomes, they vied with each other to earn a little extra money tending the count's race horses or raking the paths of the Vay grounds, so neatly swept that every footprint showed in the sandy gravel.

Stretching for sixteen *holds* behind the two castles, the great park was maintained as carefully as the interiors. The areas closest to the buildings were landscaped to provide a setting for the crypts and headstones of ancient Vays scattered about, while the back regions were allowed to run picturesquely wild for hunting. Great oaks and chestnuts blended with slender birches and sweeping acacias, as the cooing of pigeons joined the screech of game birds. And here in these wilder sections of parkland were buried the meritorious greyhounds of past Counts Vay, the resting place of one favourite marked by its own carved gravestone.

Ironically, the most famous member of the Vay family, the one whose life story had bequeathed the names of Rákóczi and Kuruc to the two estates, would not rest here beside his forebears and descendants until a quarter century after the arrival of Yakab and Karolina to Vaja. For, despite the historic prominence of the Vays, the official rehabilitation of Adam Vay the Kuruc – who had died in exile in 1719 – did not take place until 1906, the year that his body was brought back to Hungary, the first of Prince Ferenc Rákóczi's followers to be granted posthumous pardon by a Habsburg monarch.

36

This earlier Adam Vay, whose career spanned the late seventeenth and early eighteenth centuries, was intimate friend and chief marshal to the prince, leader of an ill-fated nation-wide rebellion against Austrian rule known as the Rákóczi Uprising. The eight-year insurrection temporarily united members of the Hungarian aristocracy and an army of serfs against the tyranny and religious bigotry of the Austrian dynasty. Like so many others in Hungarian history, the uprising was doomed. Rákóczi and his chief lieutenants fled first to Poland, then to Turkey. Faithful Adam Vay died in exile in Danzig and was not allowed to return home for nearly two centuries after the Treaty of Szatmár had ended hostilities.

The memory of the charismatic and talented Rákóczi left a permanent romantic legacy in Hungarian music, poetry, and folktale. (Berlioz's famous march takes its title from the prince's name.) Locally the legacy endured even in communist times, the award-winning collective farm of the region acquiring Rákóczi's name and the Vay castle restored as a museum in his honour.

In 1882, as Main Street wound past the Calvinist church and the gates of the castle, there was little to break the regularity of the reed-thatched cottages with gay displays of potted geraniums in their tiny front windows. Even the odd shop or tavern was similarly housed, since only prosperous peasants and village notables could afford to build out of the unglazed brick representing village affluence. The rest of Vaja's 200 houses resembled Grunstein's humble dwelling. Beneath the cheerful whitewash, mud plaster held together walls woven of twigs and branches. Sixteen hundred villagers in 200 houses spelled out a simple equation: an average of eight people inhabited each small dwelling.

Towards the outskirts of Main Street stood a slightly larger tin-topped building. This was the village hall where administrative matters were settled and announcements proclaimed as they had been since time immemorial, the village headman with a drum strapped to his side pounding out a solemn rhythm and bellowing forth the messages of local and national authorities. Behind the hall, its patch of garden sprouting a few hollyhocks and poppies, stretched an empty field of yellowing stubble, the buffer between the zone of the living and that of the dead.

Beyond this field, almost outside the limits of the village, lay Vaja's cemetery. In ironic counterpoint to the stone monument of the count's greyhound in the castle grounds, the villagers' graves were marked by simple wooden crosses bearing names painted in white. Local surnames such as Olah, Tisza, and Dobos repeated themselves over generations of wooden markers arising amidst rock roses and portulacas. The graveyard's very simplicity gave it a touching, arresting charm.

A knoll sinisterly named Hanging Hill, where the historic right of life and death of the Vays had been exercised in earlier times, rose behind the cemetery. It seemed an anomalous name at the time of Yakab Schwarcz's arrival.

Facing the village hall across the dusty Main Street stood a similarly unprepossessing building, distinguished slightly from the others, nonetheless, by its architectural style. Built of stucco with a sloping tiled roof, its street-facing arched windows gave it an exotic look. Vaja's Jewish synagogue was one of the earliest to be built in the Nyírség after the reforms of Joseph II brought Jewish settlers to the area. Inside it was murky and musty and slightly mysterious to one used to worshipping in the homier atmosphere of farm prayerhouses. Another difference was the accommodation of women in a proper if tiny gallery upstairs.

Jews had first settled in Vaja in the 1770s. A century later Vaja numbered some 120 Jewish inhabitants. Modest shopkeepers, tavernkeepers, and tradesmen made their small livings here. After Yakab began to produce his record harvests, a few potato and grain merchants rose in prosperity above the ranks of the rest. In the main, though, the Vaja congregation remained small and impoverished, composed of poor craftsmen and labourers – drivers, tinkers, blacksmiths – serving the agricultural trade of the region.

A bitter schism divided Hungarian Jewry in 1869, two years after the Emancipation Proclamation had granted them full civil and political rights. The gentile parliamentarians who ushered in a golden era during which Hungarian Jewry flourished as never before believed implicitly (and stated explicitly) that Jews must earn their freedom. To show gratitude for their new rights, they must take on the traditions and ideology of the Magyars. And, in fact, fuelled by the energies released during Emancipation, the majority of Hungarian Jews were beginning to find the customs of the synagogue strange and outmoded. Increasingly they chafed against the tyranny of prayer ceaselessly dictated by daily life – the prescribed blessings at hand-washing, eating and drinking, departure and arrival from home. At a congress convened by the same government that had shortly before granted Emancipation, the rigidly observant minority separated itself from the liberal congregations of the majority to form "orthodox" communities. Those who accepted the theories of the congress called themselves "neolog" and gradually abandoned the dietary laws, introduced organ music in their synagogues, and increasingly used Hungarian as the language of worship. The orthodox regarded the neologs as close to apostates; the neologs despised the orthodox as the transmitters of medieval superstitions.

Despite the virtually unanimous espousal of orthodoxy by Nyírség congregations, even among the orthodox there was no true uniformity of orientation. For even most orthodox Hungarian Jews accepted the premise upon which Emancipation had been granted: that Jews were a religious group and not a people. Scions of long-standing Magyar-Jewish families such as Yakab might well travel to famous Hasidic courts in Galicia to worship with and consult noted wonder rabbis, but they still took pride in their own distinctly secular garb and culture. In orthodox villages such as Vaja, it was altogether rare to see a Jew in the Hasidic gaberdine. Only the rabbi wore sidelocks and a long, shiny black coat, and even he was shod in heavy black knee boots like any peasant, not the white stockings of the Hasidim. Christian villagers greeted him with a respectful tip of the hat and the same "Good day, your reverence" due the Protestant minister.

Yet trouble was brewing for Hungarian Jewry in 1882, the year that Yakab journeyed to Vaja – and, figuratively speaking, it was brewing in Yakab's backyard, in a Szabolcs-County village forty kilometres from and not dissimilar to Vaja. In the 1880s the Tiszaeszlár ritual murder case became an international *cause célèbre* foreshadowing the Dreyfus affair in its notoriety. In April 1882, Esther Solymosi, a gentile servant girl mistreated by her (Christian) employers, disappeared from Tiszaeszlár coincidentally with a flurry of activity in the village synagogue. On *Shabbes Hagadol*, the Sabbath before Passover, a well-attended audition was held in the synagogue for the post of a new cantor. After Esther failed to return home, one of the cantorial candidates was accused of killing her, assisted by other local Jews in the synagogue, allegedly in order to bake her blood into Passover *matzoh*.

When the sensational case came to trial, it was characterized by torture, vandalism, and exhumation. Anti-Semitism became a political and social fad: an anti-Semitic party was formed to save the nation from the "Jewish menace." Mass meetings were held demanding the abrogation of the law of Jewish Emancipation. Eventually these resolutions were debated in the Hungarian Parliament where both government and opposition members denounced the anti-Semitic delegates as reactionaries and demagogues, and the resolutions were quashed.

Locally, however, the fate not only of the Tiszaeszlár accused but of all the Jews of the countryside depended on the decision reached by the court in Nyíregyháza. Crucial to the eventual acquittal of the accused was the retaining of a nationally respected defence attorney, Károly Eötvös, a distinguished legal expert with impeccable social and personal credentials. In the acceptance of the case by the aristocratic Eötvös, Yakab Schwarcz of Vaja also played a bit part. Disguised in peasant costume and driving a cart under cover of darkness, Yakab's father, Samuel, accompanied in turn by each of his sons, called on Jewish homes in the neighbouring villages to help raise funds for Eötvös's fee.

The Tiszaeszlár accused were eventually exonerated, but suspicions about the Jews of that village continued to linger. Its synagogue sacked, the Tiszaeszlár community fell apart.

Esther Solymosi never turned up.

The Rákóczi Estate

Primitive anti-Semitism was only one symptom of the Nyírség's backwardness in the last quarter of the nineteenth century. In fact, great-grandfather Yakab's campaign of modernization was launched in one of the least promising areas of the country. While western Hungary was beginning to experiment with crop rotation and intensive agriculture, the northeast remained mired in traditional patterns that had not advanced appreciably since the Middle Ages. Count Adam Vay's property was no exception.

The Rákóczi Estate had the rough shape of a circle with the distillery at its centre. Radiating from it were the outbuildings and servants' quarters, and then, like spokes of a great wheel, the thirty-odd fields of some thirty *holds* each into which the property had been divided. Each field was subdivided into three equal parts as it had been since time immemorial. Spring grains were planted in the first, autumn grains in the second, while the third was left fallow. Some of the fields were worked by farm hands on a contractual basis defined as the *convention*, by which they were paid a combination of cash and kind. The majority were share-cropped, large teams of workers under an overseer parcelled up the land amongst themselves, each man receiving a strip in each of the field's three subdivisions, the plots generally at inconvenient remove from one another. Payment to the share-cropper consisted of one-third of the fruits of the harvest. Generally, a peasant combined contractual labour with share-cropping, hiring himself out as part of a team to thresh and harvest for the count and share-cropping parts of one or more fields.

The constant subdivision of land guaranteed a modicum of fairness in that no peasant worked exclusively poor or rich lands, but it was an enormously inefficient system, wasteful of time and energy. Large chunks of land left fallow, desultory fertilization, the absence of the

owner, the venality of his overseers, and widespread thievery by workers helped account for Yakab's later comparative success. For even
if the system remained the same in its large outlines, its rational-
ization generated profits for the new entrepreneur leasing the estate.

And the new entrepreneur was dedicated to producing a profit.
During his business travels Yakab was once inspired by the example
of an energetic peasant woman on her way to market in Dresden.
On her head she balanced a basket of tomatoes. Knitting needles
clicked briskly between her fingers as she marched. "Imagine," Yakab
enthused on his return home, "*three* concurrent activities – walking,
carrying *and* knitting! A model for us all."

By contrast, Yakab was bemused by Count Adam's lackadaisical
attitude to the functioning of his many estates. When great-
grandfather had called upon the count with a problem in one of
the early years of his tenancy, Count Adam had waved him in the
direction of his bailiff, a distant impoverished relative who also nevertheless had a title. "Please see Count Abraham about that matter,
Mr Schwarcz. You should know I don't care to meddle unnecessarily
in my own affairs."

From the beginning, Yakab treated the count's property as his
own. Anything that needed replacing he not only replaced but improved upon, with the view that one day he would buy the estate
and the improvements would revert to him. When he won a lucrative
licence from the Treasury permitting him to cultivate 150 *holds* of
tobacco, he added five huge tobacco barns and housing for twenty-
odd tobacco farmers at his own expense. He built fifty extra servants'
huts, new barns, stables, and corn lofts and enlarged the distillery.
Small wonder then that in 1895 Count Adam was delighted to welcome his tenant back from Kisvárda. No longer would he have to
bother with drunken overseers and universal theft. (Interviewer to
old peasant in contemporary Vaja: "How did those who did not own
land manage to live?" Old peasant in response: "They stole from
the big estate. I did it, too. If you got away with it, fine. If not,
the gendarmes gave you a beating.") Moreover, his property was improved, his taxes and insurance paid, and three times a year his
rent arrived at the appointed moment.

So pleased indeed was the count to have Yakab back and so willing to trust him with his possessions that he now magnanimously offered him the Little Castle for his personal use. The era of the mean village hut was over. Within the enterprising, now middle-aged *pater familias*, bearded but still trim and spare, there yet lived the vain young man who had been married in the landscaped grounds of a count. Yakab could not bring himself to refuse the offer, yet something held him back from accepting it, and he postponed an answer until he had consulted his wife.

Karolina's sense of decorum – and practicality – carried the day. Not for her the wild parkland in which she foresaw that she would constantly be chasing an uncontrolled and ever-growing brood. Nor did she relish proximity to the Vay crypts, the maces and swords, the fresco of Nicopolis. Out of the count's presence, Yakab's own common sense also returned. Better to live in the thick of the estate where he needed to be to boss, to supervise, to control his peasants, instead of away in a castle like the indolent counts.

He had two centrally located bailiff's houses to choose from. Built late in the eighteenth century in the traditional manner of painted stucco over mud and plaster, the larger stood on a little hill and contained three ramshackle rooms. Yakab would make additions to it higgledy-piggledy, transforming it into a comfortably sprawling dwelling as his family continued to expand. Eventually he constructed a separate office building of stone, windowed on every side so that even from his desk he could view the farmhands at work and bellow at the slackers among them. The second existing house Yakab converted into a synagogue, for the one in the village, four kilometres from his new residence, was too far to walk to on the Sabbath.

And now began the era of the Rákóczi Estate's history that Yakab's children and grandchildren loved to recall. Concerning the sojourn in Grunstein's house they remained taciturn, but they waxed eloquent about both their father's business innovations and his improvements to the farmhouse. The telephone and the new bathroom with its running water supply in particular became the wonders of the local countryside.

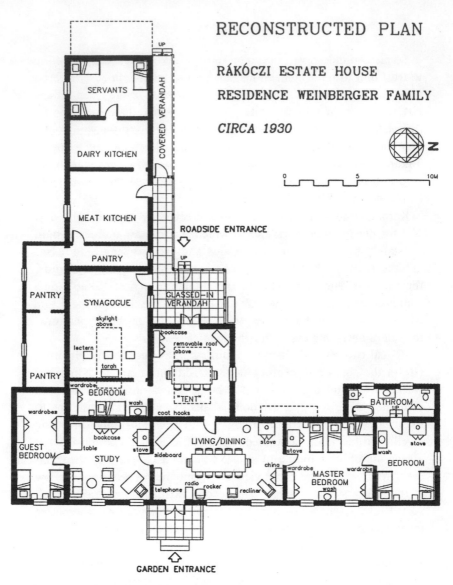

RECONSTRUCTED PLAN

RÁKÓCZI ESTATE HOUSE

RESIDENCE WEINBERGER FAMILY

CIRCA 1930

No one ever thought to take a photograph of the old family home because it was thought to be so unremarkable. This plan, drawn up by an architect, is based on descriptions from those who once lived or visited there.

Yakab's standards were those of the capital, not of country backwaters. And nineteenth-century Budapest was a model of urban development and sophistication. Its first telephone exchange began operating in 1881 with fifty subscribers. The Budapest subway system, Europe's first, opened in 1896 as part of the nation's millennial celebrations. Hungarian moving pictures under the name of "animatographs" were being shown, and at the turn of the century there were enough automobile owners to band together in a Royal Automobile Club.

In many respects a typical nineteenth-century believer in modernization and progress, Yakab tried every innovation he could lay his hands on. Steam ploughs and harvesters imported from the West, lupinus seeds from Germany, a typewriter, a gramophone all found their way in due course to the Rákóczi Estate. The steam ploughs and harvesters proved costly white elephants relegated to the machine sheds, their rusting skeletons jungle gyms for farm children. But experiments with the green fertilizer lupinus by a handful of local farmers who included Yakab eventually revolutionized agricultural yields in the Nyírség, cutting down on the amount of land left fallow and anchoring the unstable sand. Yakab's most inspired achievement was to bring the railroad literally to his garden gate. And this success sprang from his ability to bend others to his will, not by force but by persuasion.

A constant source of frustration in the marketing of his produce and the shipping of alcohol and tobacco to distant markets was the estate's distance from the nearest railway station. In the 1880s Yakab was obliged to cart his goods nearly thirty kilometres to Kisvárda. Even at the turn of the century his nearest stop was half that distance. Besides the expense and time involved, there was the inconvenience of trips in bad weather and the risk of shipments freezing en route in winter. When rumours of a projected railway line running northeast from Nyíregyháza began to circulate in the county capital, Yakab immediately started to lobby the county council to make sure Vaja was allotted a station. In 1904 the branch line to Vásárosnamény was completed and Yakab's dream realized. The Vaja station was a mere three kilometres away.

But his victory spurred him towards an even bolder project. The new steel tracks ran parallel with the fields below his house, curving northward so that three times a day he could see the cars rolling by his dining-room window. Watching them, Yakab calculated that he could kill his competition if he had his very own station.

He proceeded to lobby the directors of the railway company as persistently as he had previously solicited the county council. "The Rákoczi Estate is a very large property with an extensive amount of traffic. Freight transports, of course, but also much passenger trade. We have hundreds of business passengers."

At his own expense, with no encouragement that his investment would pay off, he built 140 metres of siding – enough to accommodate the five cars he required for an extra-large shipment of potatoes. Then he returned to canvass the company once more.

"I have built a siding on my estate because of the extent of my traffic."

"But Mr Schwarcz," the chairman of the board protested, "please ... The train can't stop at an ordinary *farm*!"

"My *estate* does a very extensive business."

"With all due respect, we don't believe it."

"Then make a test!"

Worn down by his badgering, the board agreed to a trial. "If at least one person gets on or off every day at the Rákóczi Estate in the next thirty days," sighed the beleaguered chairman, "we'll make a stop there."

Once a day for the next month, Yakab sent someone – anyone – into the village by train, a journey normally more conveniently undertaken by carriage. Thus fobbed off with proof of passenger traffic, the railway company duly gave its consent. After World War I, the station was even provided with a little station house.

In the course of the next forty years there were several occasions when the estate hung on the brink of bankruptcy. Extravagance and outside events conspired to keep Yakab showily poor, so that he never achieved his ambition of buying the count's property. At his death in 1921, his material possessions amounted to a string of farm buildings and bequests to charity, their value shortly to be wiped out by runaway postwar inflation. Yet, in the long run the Rákóczi Estate enjoyed the most sustained success of all the farms in the huge extended family, right until the fateful day in April 1944 when it was expropriated under Nazi rule. A key to its success was Yakab's vision of the railway as a necessary tool in undercutting competition.

Decades after the genesis of the original station, my father and his brothers reaped the benefits of Yakab's perspicacity. The midwinter potato orders for the Budapest market came their way purely because the great potato merchants of the capital knew that shipments would arrive on time and in perfect condition. The existence of the station had cultural and social ramifications as well. The farm, though 250 kilometres distant from Budapest, did not feel like a remote outpost of civilization in a backward county. The morning papers from Budapest arrived by the noon train. It was possible to make the return trip to Nyíregyháza in an afternoon and to daytrip with almost as much ease to the larger city of Debrecen.

And, as if in retribution for Yakab's ploy with the railway company, a steady stream of business traffic plagued the women of the house. For once they alighted from the morning train, the ranks of merchants, veterinarians, notaries, distillery inspectors, and the like had to be fed and entertained until the next train took them away. Years later when my grandmother Ilona became chatelaine of the household, she would grumble to the housemaid each morning, "Run along, will you, and see who got shaken off that train today."

Twelve Pairs of Shoes

Though he was keen to embrace progress and modernity, Yakab by no means espoused change in everything. The world, even in rural Hungary, was at a crossroads as the nineteenth century edged into the twentieth. The circumstances of Karolina's death in 1910 themselves symbolized a rejection of change. The strangulated hernia that killed her at the age of fifty had gone unattended because of her primitive fear of the scalpel. When a Budapest surgeon summoned by a desperate Yakab arrived at her bedside in Vaja, the professor could only shake his head and pronounce her too far gone for his skills.

Less starkly, Yakab's belief in progress stopped short at the education of his children. Though he himself was a man of some culture, not one of his ten children attended school beyond the age of fourteen. They grew up in an atmosphere at once permissive and unbending. Their father denied them little else, giving in to their whims, getting down on the floor to engage in horse-play with the younger ones, heaping extravagances on all of them. He showered them with material possessions, outfitting each son with a private carriage driven by a liveried, heron-plumed coachman and horses splendid enough to turn the heads of sophisticated city-dwellers in Debrecen. Tulip and hyacinth bulbs arrived by the thousand from Holland for the pleasure of his daughters. A tennis court beneath the walnut trees in the garden provided the family's youth with exercise and its older members the pleasure of spectating. Yet Yakab refused intellectual nourishment to his children beyond a rudimentary level. In their early childhood, Jewish governesses and tutors taught them at home. Later, they were packed off to board at *polgári*, a sort of higher elementary school which they completed by the age of fourteen.

Religious orthodoxy was the altar at which Yakab sacrificed his children's schooling. But his own form of orthodoxy was not aridly formal. One had only to witness him in prayer to recognize the strain of intensity that underlay his compliance with the Law. Invariably it was he who led the family in prayer when the whole clan assembled on the grand occasions of the *yahrzeits* of his parents. He had a splendid, resonant voice and an unusual, if histrionic delivery. Tears coursed down his cheeks and his body heaved with suppressed sobs, yet he still managed to give voice to a yearning melody. Wrapped in his prayer shawl, swaying back and forth as he pleaded with the deity, he was an impressive sight illuminated by the great flickering memorial candles on the eastern wall of the dining room.

Yakab's personal piety was coupled with concern that his offspring would be tainted by despised reformist notions if they were allowed to pursue higher studies. While he himself mingled expansively in society, with age gaining additional social stature and popularity, he feared his children's premature exposure to the worldly influences education would open to them. In the end, despite his efforts to shelter them, secular life did make inroads on his family's level of observance. Yet even when his children strayed, Yakab's indulgent love proved stronger than his outraged piety. He accepted without demur the name change to Székács which his oldest son deemed necessary for admission to the Seventh Hussars during World War I – and which the younger children adopted with alacrity, although surely all of them would not serve in elite regiments. He closed his eyes to the fact that in the army his sons would not observe the dietary laws. He even looked the other way when Elizabeth, his second daughter, flouted the rules of the Sabbath in numerous small ways under his nose.

Noisy, energetic, and confined to their farm-bound world, in their childhood Yakab and Katrina's offspring were an unruly bunch. They ran through governesses and private tutors; they wore their mother down. Karolina devised a primitive punishment when she was at the end of her tether. Having managed to catch the culprits, her last resort was to tie them to the legs of the mahogany table in the dining room, so that many of the nine carved legs often had prisoners lassoed to them. Even Ilona, my grandmother, who later acquired a reputation for an almost aberrant saintliness, confided to her sons that she had been an impossible child, given to hiding under beds when it came time to do her lessons. (She claimed to have chewed up the slippers of a visiting cousin on one such occasion.)

Not surprisingly, the parents took turns leaving home as often as they could. Karolina visited the spas in Carlsbad in the summer; Yakab vacationed in the slacker winter season, but was also frequently away on business. Invariably, catastrophes greeted their homecomings.

On one of his returns from holiday, for instance, Yakab was greeted by Karolina who, wringing her hands, begged him to do something immediately about his second son, Zoltán, as he had been so bad that she could no longer cope with him.

Green-eyed, brown-haired Zoltán, demonstrated in early life an amorality which Yakab, ever blind to the faults of his children, conveniently ignored. As the silver-haired Uncle Zoltán I knew in my childhood, he wore a veneer of ingratiating geniality, but his childhood pranks foreshadowed a certain unfeelingness as an adult.

Yakab commenced the obligatory lecture with an unfortunate choice of words: "Zoltán, my boy, even the geese have gaggled to me about your recent exploits." An unpenitent youngster headed for the poultry yard a few minutes later. He picked up the first goose that crossed his path, gazed into its hapless eyes and asked, "Are you the one who betrayed me to Papa?" Receiving no answer, he wrung its neck. He then caught a second, addressed it with the same question and hung it next to the first on the slats of the corn loft. A dozen geese met their end before anyone took notice.

Just after the century turned – when Yakab's square beard was shot with silver and he had assumed the stoutness of affluence, when Karolina's blunt chin rested on a solid cushion of flesh and her waist had permanently disappeared – their family was finally complete. Augusta, the last baby, was born in 1901 when Ilona, the oldest, had already reached the marriageable age of twenty. Five boys and five girls, no two were alike, either in looks or personality.

Ilona had round cheeks and light brown hair that rippled away from her smooth face. Merry, with a lilting laugh, she loved sports and was frequently photographed on the tennis court in the required costume of the day, a ground-sweeping flounced skirt and starched white blouse. Only her habit of chewing her nails to the quick hinted at the compulsiveness that would overtake her in later life.

Tall, blue-eyed, dashing Andor, the flower of the family, dreamed of little else than cutting a fashionable figure in society. He would come to exemplify the essence of the "gentry" Jew who patterned his behaviour on that of profligate Hungarian aristocrats. This prototype included the ability to consume astonishing amounts of alcohol, to lose or win a fortune at cards in late-night parties without a facial flicker, and to defend one's honour by the code of the duel. Andor did not gamble, but he satisfied the other requirements handily. He attained the pinnacle of his career when he made his way, by dint of his father's money and his own impeccable bearing, into the elite Seventh Hussars of Debrecen where he bore arms with the oldest son of Count Adam Vay, his father's landlord.

Jolly, boastful Zoltán came next in line. He was the only one of the children to have inherited his father's looks and agility in business, albeit without Yakab's scrupulousness. In his youth at the turn of the century Zoltán's chief preoccupations were showy parade horses and fine carriages; later his eyes would never stray far from the main chance.

No one did Yakab ever misjudge more than his second son. Highly sensitive to the enmity and bickering among his own brothers (two of whom had taken to the courts to battle out their differences), Yakab established a family tribunal to adjudicate possible disagreements among his children after his death. In his will he assigned the presidency of this tribunal to Zoltán, "for I am convinced that he loves each of his brothers and sisters equally and is an entirely impartial party.

"It is written," Yakab added, "that parents may rest tranquil in their graves only if there is peace among their children. Regarding this I ask you, my dear Children, to look to it that there be peace among you, because only thus can you most fittingly honour the memory of your late dear Mother and myself. Love one another, for you are one flesh and blood; and if, God forbid, one of you requires help, let the rest rush to his assistance immediately."

What anguish would Yakab have suffered had he guessed the indifference with which Zoltán would treat the one brother and three sisters to return from the hell of Auschwitz and Bergen-Belsen: Zoltán, who had managed to weather the Holocaust relatively safely in Budapest and, by the time his siblings returned, had found a lucrative tap with which to milk the postwar transition economy.

The third son was Menyush, a delightful scamp who ought to have gone on the stage, for he was born to perform. His business affairs were doomed to failure as his mind teemed with a dozen scatterbrained notions. Cross-eyed and homely, he could contort his mobile features into almost any form while his mind revolved around pranks and schemes suitable for a schoolboy. His comic virtuosity succeeded in lightening even the pall of despondency that periodically hung over his oldest sister.

"Do you remember, Ilona," he teased my grandmother as she sat in the twilit living room in thrall to one of her bouts of melancholy in the 1930s, "Do you remember that time you and I went to Budapest and there were no seats on the train?" And he began to dramatize the scene in the crowded compartment where he had promised to obtain her not only a seat but enough room to stretch out in comfort. Casually mentioning that they were on their way to the Pasteur Institute, he had dropped broad hints about rabies to their fellow travellers, who hastily decamped. Mimicking the horrified expressions of the other passengers, he continued the routine to the point of frothing at the mouth, relentlessly playing the fool till Ilona, who had not spoken for weeks, succumbed to peals of laughter.

Eighteen months apart, Elizabeth and Irene, the two girls who followed Menyush, were raised as a unit. They were sent away to boarding school together at an early age, and perhaps because of this or their complementary natures, formed the tightest bond among the siblings. Irene died young, but Elizabeth survived hard labour in Austria and starvation in Bergen-Belsen. She became the most cherished highlight of my childhood, as boundlessly indulgent in her treatment of me as her father Yakab had once been with his own grandchildren.

Short and plain except for the fine hazel eyes which could size up a situation in an instant, Elizabeth was quicksilver personified. She moved so quickly that even in great old age it was impossible to photograph her properly – she never stayed still long enough to allow the camera to focus. In contrast, Irene was a gentle, self-effacing beauty with fine blonde hair and light eyes. When their mother died, Ilona was already established in her own household, and it was upon these two "big girls," then twenty and nineteen respectively, that the mantle of responsibility for the four younger children descended. They also shared the role of housekeeper, learning to perform in the kitchen at lightning speed since Yakab, testy in his grief, brooked no breach of Karolina's standards.

As nimble-witted, intelligent, and industrious as her father, Elizabeth wanted to go to university to study medicine. Yakab forbade it, so Elizabeth, not one to bemoan her fortune, applied her considerable talents to the sphere in which she found herself. In a family of outstanding housekeepers, she became the best of all, eventually setting up a cooking school and a lingerie salon.

Irene showed a vocation for nursing, spending weeks on end in her married sister Ilona's new home in Piricse, devotedly caring for my father, who was an invalid during his childhood. She herself developed diabetes in 1917, though the treatments prescribed by a professor in Transylvania brought her symptoms under control. So well did she feel that in the fall of 1919 during a lull in the political turbulence to which Hungary had succumbed after the First World War, she and Elizabeth ventured to the capital to order dresses for the winter. They were in Bertha Neumann's exclusive salon when Irene suffered a sudden attack. Elizabeth rushed her to hospital where, within a few hours, she fell into a coma from which she never awoke.

Horrified, grief-stricken, but always resourceful, Elizabeth made the complicated arrangements to have her sister's body transported by train to Lövő, to lie beside their mother and their brother Andor, who had died earlier that year. Disrupted by the uncertain political conditions, the trains ran erratically and along detoured routes. Elizabeth obtained permission to have the coffin attached to the end of the train in a sealed car. Amidst rumours that the wagon had been broken into and the corpse stolen, the dreadful journey took two full days as the train crawled along. The bridges were barely negotiable; at Tiszahid where the train crossed the Tisza River, the guard rails had been destroyed on both sides of the bridge and the train seemed to traverse the span by levitation. Elizabeth stared out of the window at the abyss below, as terrified of the scene beneath as of the prospect of life without her closest friend and confidant.

While Ilona became the family matriarch in the years before World War II, history would thrust upon Elizabeth the burden of care for the three youngest siblings who survived the Holocaust.

The four youngest children had always borne heavily the imprint of Karolina's untimely death and their father's passing a decade later. Sándor and Ferenc were quiet, self-effacing men, a little colourless next to their flamboyant older brothers. Sándor in particular was inordinately reserved, a thin, dry man who inhabited a windowless cupboard in the service wing of the house. It was this painfully shy brother, who adored the family with a mute devotion, whom Zoltán and his wife turned away from their Budapest apartment, refusing him a night's lodging when he returned, dying, from Auschwitz.

Rose and Augusta, the two youngest girls, managed to maintain a delicate emotional equilibrium within the sheltered cocoon of the Rákóczi Estate, but broke down after they married and left home. Even before the war they had begun to succumb to bouts of mental illness. Looking after them became a constant leitmotif in Elizabeth's life when she returned to Hungary from Bergen-Belsen in 1945.

I remember vividly the quartet of Yakab's surviving children: silver-haired, flat-nosed great-uncle Zoltán, smooth as butter; my great-aunt Rose, obese and slatternly, napping in our living room exhausted by garrulity, a scarf spread over her face to shut out the world; beautiful Augusta, the youngest sister, in one of her transported states, liquid eyes burning, skin stretched taut over high cheekbones, her mouth an angry wound spouting venomous words like a stream of lava. And I remember Elizabeth.

To me it seemed as if the two emotionally afflicted aunts had survived merely to cause trouble for my father and Elizabeth. While I did not actively dislike them, I felt no real affection for them either. But Elizabeth was a constellation in my firmament who often out-shone even those two other great stars, my mother and my father, whose parental roles caused them to beam frequent rays of disap-proval in my direction.

Rounded of body, sharp of face and eye, Elizabeth in all but biological fact was my grandmother, lavishing on me the doting, indulgent love that had characterized the Vaja family. She travelled from Debrecen to Budapest for my sake though she barely had money for train fare, bought me toys she could not afford, treated my glaring faults as virtues. Later she would become a grandmother in her own right and recite for her granddaughter a litany of my exploits which began in true fairy-tale fashion with "Once upon a time, there was a little girl who was very, very pretty and very, very bad."

After my family's departure from Hungary in 1957 I did not see Elizabeth for twelve years. In the sweltering summer of 1969, my whole family, including my new husband, visited Budapest for the first time since we had left. At almost eighty, Elizabeth was as spry and sparkling-witted as ever, whipping up feasts in her cupboard-sized kitchen while indoctrinating me in the vital women's lore she felt I had missed by being absent from her side.

"You must learn to cook well, for the way to everyone's heart, not just a man's, is through their stomachs.

"Birth control is very important. Always remember, a vinegar douche *right after*, and you needn't fuss with those silly pills." (Overhearing this, my mother pulled me into a corner. "Don't listen to a word of that. She had fertility problems.")

When I parted from Elizabeth at the end of that holiday, I happened to be with my father. At twenty-one I was still nonchalant about farewells and said a blithe good-bye upstairs in the apartment, the possibility that we might not meet again not even crossing my mind.

Down below on the parched, gasoline-reeking sidewalk I kept craning my neck for a last glimpse of the tiny woman waving from the fourth-floor balcony, white handkerchief billowing in her fingers. "Don't look back," my father said, face resolutely set forward. "It's easier if you don't look back."

I felt a chill unwarranted by the close heat of the Carpathian basin. Once more I turned around and she was still there, the handkerchief now invisible. My father continued marching along soldier-like. He would meet her again many times, although I never did.

55

Kálmán Came from Kajdanó

Therefore shall a man leave his father and his mother,
and shall cleave unto his wife, and they shall be one flesh.

Genesis 2, v.24

If Elizabeth was my surrogate grandmother, I had no surrogate
grandfather. There was never anyone to step into the laced-up boots
left empty when my grandfather Kálmán perished in 1944. Though
his Székács brothers- and sisters-in-law had nicknamed him *Kálmán
Sógor* – "Brother-in-law Kálmán" – he was a brother-in-law in name
only. By marrying the oldest daughter and by his devotion to her
whole family, Kálmán almost overnight assumed the role of eldest
child.

He was too respectful a son, too tender-hearted a brother, and
too pious a Jew to admit that he preferred Ilona's family to his
own. The biblical fourth commandment to honour his father and
mother, the parents to whom he owed his being and whose hands
he unfailingly kissed upon each arrival and departure from home,
was engraved in his consciousness. Yet in time he would inherit Yakab's mantle as organically as if it had been his blood right, as
he could never have inherited the mantle of his own father.

From above the piano in my living room in Montreal, two old Jews
in square skullcaps stare down at startled visitors. Dressed in black
against black backgrounds, the two bearded, white-haired patriarchs,
framed in identical gold, draw eyes magnetically to the wall where
their portraits hold court.

They were father and son, my great-great-grandfather Benjamin
Weinberger and his son Herman, although the painting of Herman
depicts the older face. Benjamin's smooth, sallow visage with its high
brow, prominent cheekbones, and calm brown eyes radiates tranquillity. In my family we have always called him "the big grandfather"
when we have meant "the senior grandfather."

Herman, "the little grandfather," aka "the Kajdanó grandfather,"
wears a tortured, belligerent, forbidding expression. His ferocious

eyebrows virtually bristle on the canvas; his little grey eyes are disquiet, the lines of his face set in a permanent suspicious frown. It is hard to believe that Herman was the father of my pliant grandfather Kálmán.

One of Herman's other sons had these portraits painted in the 1930s from photographs. This son, a Budapest lawyer and businessman, had given them place of honour in his study. That's where I first met the little and big grandfathers in postwar Budapest, when I was taken to visit the great-uncle who had been the only one of Kálmán's eight siblings to survive. I pecked away at a typewriter beneath the portraits, writing mock letters while my father chatted with his uncle. Occasionally my eyes would lock with those of my father's grandfather Herman. Despite the angry cast of his features and the full beard, I could see that the bushy brows and the jutting nose were the same as my *Apu*'s.

At the time that the marriage brokers were negotiating the match between Ilona Schwarcz and Kálmán Weinberger, the village of Kajdanó numbered 1,000 predominantly Ukrainian inhabitants. A scant seventy-five kilometres from Vaja, Kajdanó fell in a different part of the world from the Nyírség even in those days, when only a county boundary separated Szabolcs and Bereg counties. This county boundary was nonetheless formed near the arch of one of Hungary's great rivers, the Tisza, which at its northeastern source goes through a triangular bend, carving out Szabolcs, Szatmár, and Bereg Counties, then the administrative departments of a small corner of the Austro-Hungarian monarchy. Today the Tisza's curve roughly approximates the international boundary between Hungary, Ukraine, and Romania.

Kajdanó was part of a region known as Subcarpathia, which has had an astonishingly chequered modern history. In Kálmán's youth it belonged to Hungary, then fell to Czechoslovakia after World War I, was re-annexed by Hungary in 1938, became part of the Soviet Union after the World War II, and today belongs to Ukraine. Quipsters from Munkács, the large town ten kilometres away, coined the following deadpan conversation between two individuals in Communist times:

"Tell me the story of your life."

"Me? I was born in the Austro-Hungarian Monarchy, went to school in Czechoslovakia and I now reside in the Soviet Union."

"Then you're a widely travelled person."

"Me? I've never moved away from Munkács!"

Relative to the norm of Subcarpathian penury, Kajdanó village was a prosperous little place, its source of wealth a fat black soil dramatically different from the loose sand of the Nyírség which had to be coaxed into production. Even a few *holds* of Kajdanó loam guaranteed a good living to its owners. It was, for example, not uncommon for Kajdanó natives, Jew and gentile alike, who had emigrated to America at the turn of the century, to return home in the years after the First World War to offer $1,000 for a *hold* – a relative fortune for those days in that village – to anyone foolish enough to sell off land.

Herman Weinberger, the village's largest landholder, was in no way inclined to be so foolish. His 400 *holds* stretched back from the Munkács-Ungvár highway in exemplary order: deep-ploughed dark furrows on which grew the potatoes that fed his distillery, whose slops in turn nourished the prize-winning cattle in his barns. On his land stood an alcohol refinery, a warehouse for storing liquor and yeast, and an oil mill to which neighbouring peasants and farmers brought their sunflower seeds to be pressed for a fee.

From his father Herman had learned a cardinal lesson: to be rich, you held on tenaciously to what you owned. It was a lesson he taught in turn to his own sons.

The son of a brewer of slivovitz in the mountain village of Patkanyoc, Herman's father Benjamin – "the big grandfather" – had begun his career as a distiller. From this he graduated to a *regalé* tenancy, leasing from the Crown the right to collect the excise taxes on meat and alcohol for the region. A pernicious method of tax collection frequently leased out to Jews (whose popularity it was hardly calculated to enhance), the *regalé* was sold at a fixed sum by the state, with any profits collected in excess of this price accruing to the lessee. Profits did indeed pile up for Benjamin Weinberger, and he soon purchased a liquor store in Munkács in the same building

58

as the office of alcohol and meat excises. When he had gave up tax collecting, he bought the building, kept the store, and opened a rum distillery next to it. Then, like the Nyírség families into which his grandson Kálmán would marry, he turned his attention to land.

The Kajdanó lands, ripe for plucking from a Hungarian noble fallen on hard times, provided a base for further expansion. No international boundaries stood between Benjamin and the best cattle which he found in the Galician town of Lemberg, today the Ukrainian city of L'vov but then still part of the Austro-Hungarian world. Benjamin shipped the cows back to Kajdanó, fattened them up with the by-products of distilling, and sold them at a premium on the profitable Viennese and Prague markets.

The town of Munkács was the true heart of Benjamin's business empire. Its Jewish inhabitants at the end of the nineteenth century numbered 7,000, nearly half the town's population. One of the largest orthodox communities in Hungary, it was renowned for its conservatism and pronounced inclination towards Hasidism, counterbalanced by a strong Zionist impulse. In fact, with Yiddish-speaking Jews in Hasidic garb teeming its narrow streets, a score of small prayerhouses and two great synagogues, world-famous rabbis and *yeshivot*, religious feuds, enlightenment-seeking Zionists, and Hebrew press, Munkács resembled the Polish communities celebrated in the writings of Isaac Bashevis Singer far more than the Hungarianized-orthodox Jewish circles of the Nyírség.

Despite an abundance of local talent, Herman Weinberger (in Jewish circles known as Reb Hersh K'danever, a Yiddish corruption of "Kajdanó") was a disciple of the Belzer *rebbe* for whose sake he crossed the Carpathians at least once a year into Galicia. This exertion was signal proof of his regard, for unlike his father, Benjamin, who relished travel, Reb Hersh K'danever was a homebody. Those who did not know him well (and he had few intimates) thought that he conducted his Munkács affairs without descending from his carriage purely out of arrogance. But it wasn't just that he was a stay-at-home; he found it painful to move altogether. Even in the days when his waist-length beard was a youthful chestnut, Herman was debilitated by an enormous hernia for which he refused surgery. Wrapped in a heavy plaid travelling rug, he transacted his dealings with grain merchant and bank manager alike from the seat of his carriage. Even his doctor took his pulse perched on the carriage step.

Though Herman Weinberger was a great burly bear of a man, the title of "little grandfather" which my sister and I had given him in Montreal contained a hidden kernel of insight into the heart of this secretive and irascible ancestor. All his photographs depict him in venerable old age, so we have tended to think of him as somehow having been born old. In truth, he was robbed of his childhood and youth and prematurely catapulted into adulthood.

There's a charming if apocryphal story about Herman and his wife, Sallie, playing in the sand with her new married-woman's wig soon after their wedding. That account may be loving embellishment, but it illustrates the central enigma of the Weinberger family, the marriage arranged between the thirteen-year-old only son of Benjamin Weinberger and the twelve-year-old daughter of a Transylvanian landowner and *regalé* tenant. What had possessed the calm-eyed Benjamin, head of the *regalé* tenants of his region, regularly representing them on missions to the Hungarian Parliament, a man known for his intelligence and polished manners, to inflict the responsibilities of marriage upon a pair of children? And it wasn't a marriage in name only, to be consummated at some later date. A year after the wedding, when Sallie was thirteen and Herman fourteen, they produced their first son.

Amazingly, it was one of the best marriages in the family. Herman leaned and depended all his life upon the judgment of his child-bride, Sallie Kahan, playmate and companion of his youth. She was the strongest, most humanizing connection of his long life, more important even than the father whom he hero-worshipped and the first-born son upon whom he doted. Years after she left him a widower in 1922, the old man could be seen tramping towards the back of the garden with bowed shoulders to weep inconsolably by himself.

Sallie was a tall, swarthy, heavy-featured girl, well-matched in size for her mate. Later generations would credit her with the brains of the family and him with the rigorous religious piety. She came from an educated family (one of her nephews was the noted Hungarian Zionist Dr Nison Kahan, another the American cardiologist and medical researcher Dr Soma Weiss) and was a prodigious reader. The enigma asserts itself once more: how did the daughter of an educated family come to be married off at such a cruelly tender age? And how did a girl upon whom motherhood was thrust as she entered her teens have time to read? Yet her children and grandchildren swore by this fact. My father would point to his carefully tended hands with their thick knuckles and rounded nails and say that they were his inheritance from Sallie; her broad, capable hands had been as accustomed to holding a novel or newspaper as a wooden spoon. In her absorption in the subject matter, her coarse black wig would fall to one side, giving her a rakish appearance.

It was Sallie who insisted – at times fiercely – on having their nine children properly educated. All seven boys were sent away to good *gimnáziums* in scattered parts of the country; two of the middle sons attended university. The girls were given the fashionable lessons deemed suitable for women of breeding. Sallie sent my grandfather, second son Kálmán, to the Transylvanian city of Nagyvárad (Oradea Mare), historically the home of religious tolerance and liberal democracy in Hungary. The broadening effects of this free-thinking, dissipated, westward-looking city known as Hungary's "little Paris" on a boy whose circumscribed world until then had only encompassed a feudal village and a strait-laced inward-looking town were enormous.

A cosmopolitan city of 100,000, Nagyvárad's population was one third Jewish, but paramountly neolog. Gentry-inspired bourgeois Jews, they were as proud of Nagyvárad's Freemason lodge as of its seven newspapers, its sixteen brothels, and the international reputation of its native son, the brilliant anti-establishment poet, Endre Ady. These liberal influences and literary breezes had a profound impact on young Kálmán Weinberger, even though he lived in a sheltered orthodox enclave of the slightly *louche* city. More than anything else, his Nagyvárad education would account for his future ability to blend a love of world affairs and of rationalism with the religious faith into which he had been born.

Eight years and two sisters separated my grandfather Kálmán from his older brother, Ernest; five other brothers followed. Herman loved his first three children – his first-born, his junior by only fourteen years, with a curious admixture of brotherly and fatherly affection, the two girls with bemused indulgence – in a way entirely different from the off-hand gruffness with which he treated the six boys who came after. Clearly, he loved them, too: when they grew up and moved away, he insisted on paying their fares home from the furthest reaches of the country. And if they did not bring their wives and children along as well, they earned a tongue lashing that made them smart even if they were adult, bearded men.

But those six younger boys were simply too numerous for Herman to treat as individuals. He himself had been an only son, used to his father's almost undivided attention. After Benjamin's death, Herman set great store only by his wife and eldest child. In any difference of opinion between his sons, he invariably sided with Ernest. Ernest's almost lordly appearance and stringent orthodoxy bore witness in Herman's eyes to the legitimacy of his regard for this most deserving of sons. The young man rose quickly through the ranks of Munkács's businessmen to become a member of the municipal council, president of its largest congregation, and head of its Chevra Kadisha, the burial society to which belonged the city's most socially prominent and pious Jews.

Herman and Sallie were particular about Ernest's choice of a mate. Their own early marriage had clearly steered them away from similar arrangements. Not one of their children approached the *chupah* in unseasonable youth; Ernest was all of thirty before he married the daughter of a Nyírség wool merchant and landowner in 1900. With the dowry brought him by his bride, Ernest bought a forest and set himself up in a comfortable house in Munkács. A year later, when his father-in-law died, he inherited a small but lucrative property in the Nyírség.

By one of those coincidences that knit the Jewish world together, Ernest's bride had gone to school in Kisvárda with the oldest daughter of Yakab Schwarcz, a man Herman Weinberger had heard of through mutual connections at the rabbinical court of Belz. When a marriage broker touted the name of Ilona Schwarcz to him as a possible match for his second son, Herman asked brusquely about the state of Yakab's finances. Oh, the matchmaker responded airily, Yakab Schwarcz was a wealthy man. Did not his grown sons gallivant about in fancy carriages drawn by the finest steeds in his county? Did he not have a telephone in his house, and had he not recently installed a *bathroom*?

Reb Hersh K'danever listened, his frown deepening. The horses of Kajdanó, often mere overgrown mountain ponies, were seldom evenly matched for size, let alone for beauty, yet they pulled him into Munkács as efficiently as if they had been prize thoroughbreds. What use had he, Herman Weinberger, for telephones? He heard enough babble from people face to face, let alone having to listen to their disembodied voices! And as for a *bathroom* on a farm ... Reb Hersh K'danever glowered at the matchmaker for his foolishness.

The man switched tactics. Not only was Yakab Schwarcz a man of means, he continued, he was an extraordinarily pious and giving man. He had almost single-handedly financed the construction of the *mikvah* next to the synagogue in Vaja; now that he lived at a distance from that village, on his farm he had his own *shul*. He never turned a needy man away from his door. Why, the poor were positively enjoined to give him *minyan* and were rewarded generously for their pains. Furthermore, no man held his ancestors in greater awe: he observed their *yahrzeits* with much pomp and singular generosity. A man who gave as much as Yakab Schwarcz must surely have plenty out of which to give.

Herman Weinberger nodded slowly. He had heard mention of these things, in Belz. A devout man, a generous man. Let the matchmaker bring him a photograph of the girl next time.

And so twenty-three-year-old Kálmán Weinberger met his bride, his junior by one year, under a marriage canopy in the Subcarpathian town of Ungvár on June 9, 1903. ("For the Isr. poor of Ungvár – here was the wedding of my dear daughter Ilona ... 600 Crowns," Yakab would write many years later in Carlsbad.) No wedding photograph survives, but there is a picture taken earlier, at their engagement in Nagyvárad, by one Sándor Fekete, "court photographer to his Grace, the Archduke Joseph." Ilona's wide, full-lipped mouth – my father's mouth – turns gently upward, but Kálmán does not smile. He gazes straight ahead out of heavy-lidded eyes. His shoulder grazes the puffed and pleated taffeta sleeve of the round-faced, apple-cheeked girl into whose family he is about to merge. He looks level-headed, sober, and – his eyes evading direct confrontation with the camera – stoical.

By the time the wedding took place, it was evident to Herman Wein-berger that his new *mechetonem* merely gave the appearance of wealth, but lacked financial substance. Instead of a dowry such as the one brought by Ernest's wife, Kálmán received an invitation to come live on the Rákóczi Estate until such a time as the young couple could afford to set themselves up in an independent establishment. The much-vaunted profits made by Yakab Schwarcz's progressively run business were clearly squandered on charity and show, show and charity. Herman Weinberger, who gave as much to the poor as was seemly for a man in his position, opened his coffers only when he had to. It would never have occurred to him, for instance, to pave the road of the overgrown Nyírség village of Újfehértó so that the *rebbe*, who had settled there temporarily during World War I, need not soil his shoes on the way to *mikvah*. Neither would he have cause to boast in his will as Yakab did (with an element of flamboyant pride at distinct variance with the God-fearing humility at the root of his generosity) that during the entire war he had been the largest contributor in all the region to the umbrella charity known as the Mayer Baal Ness.

On the other hand, neither would Herman have cause to excuse himself to his children, pleading the size of a family as large as Ya-kab's, for leaving them a paltry inheritance. For old Hersh K'danever left his children well provided. It would be he who would posthu-mously rescue a bankrupt Rákóczi Estate, a tenth portion of his legacy proving enough to free Kálmán and his sons from the bog of insolvency into which they would sink in 1930. That, however, stretched more than a quarter century into the future at which Ilona Schwarcz smiled with touching hope and Kálmán Weinberger gazed with hooded eyes.

Great-great grandfather
Benjamin Weinberger of
Munkács and Kajdanó, who
made his fortune as a distiller
and tax collector and invested
it in land.

Great-grandfather Herman Weinberger with one of his daughters-in-law
and two granddaughters. The image of an irascible patriarch, he was
married at thirteen to his bride, Sallie Kahan, who was twelve. A year later
Sallie gave birth to my great-uncle Ernest.

Great-uncle Ernest Weinberger, my grandfather Kálmán's oldest brother,
with his family in Munkács. Ernest was the apple of great-grandfather
Herman's eye. When relations turned sour between Ernest and Kálmán over
a business partnership, Herman automatically sided with Ernest.

My great-grandparents Yakab
Schwarcz and Karolina
Zuckerman at the time of
their engagement in 1879.
Yakab was high-strung,
temperamental, and religious.
With Karolina to steady
him, he made a fortune as a
progressive, large-scale farmer.
When she died, he lost nearly
everything.

The engagement photograph of my grandparents Ilona Schwarcz and Kálmán Weinberger. The picture was taken by Sándor Fekete, "court photographer to his Grace, the Archduke Joseph," in 1903.

Feri, Paul, and Gusti Weinberger, circa 1911. My grandmother kept the two younger boys' hair long because she longed for a daughter. My father, Gusti, is about five here, shortly before he succumbed to the near-fatal illness that blighted much of his childhood. Paul holds my grandfather's pocket watch as a bribe not to cry.

Paul, Gusti, and Feri with their beloved Schoolmaster Sas, who bore a distinct physical resemblance to Lenin.

Weinberger cousins in Munkács. Jenő, second from left standing, as pious as his forebears, managed to make it through the war without eating food that wasn't kosher. Both my father, Gusti, and my uncle Feri adored Ilush, seated far right, one of Debrecen's belles in the 1920s.

Yakab and Karolina at a spa on the Adriatic in 1909,
a year before her death at fifty.

Great-uncle Andor on the Romanian front in 1916 around the time of his engagement to the Viennese film-star Liane Haid.

Brothers Ferenc and Andor Székács, circa 1918. Ferenc was too young to serve at length in World War I, but Andor joined up at the first opportunity and was repeatedly decorated for bravery. This picture was taken not long before the chaos that erupted at the end of the war.

Honeymoon in Vaja

In preparation for the arrival of the newlyweds, Yakab tacked on a final addition to the house. A long, narrow room, its one window looking out on the garden, it would later be converted into a tight guest room into which Kálmán and Ilona and their three little boys squeezed themselves when they visited the estate from their own home. In this cramped space Ilona would pick her way between the wardrobes and dressers in the small hours of the night, up and down, up and down, her head drooping in fatigue as Paul, her tyrannical youngest, buried his face in her hair, and droned on in a sleepy litany, "I want only Mother to carry me about, only Mother to carry me about."

A solitary candle sputtered on the bedside table beneath the window, bathing the two beds on either side in a flickering amber glow. Kálmán, eiderdown over his head, dozed fitfully in one; in the other, three-year-old Feri slept undisturbed, but four-year-old Gusti's eyes were wide open as he faced the door in front of which his mother paced. It was an odd-looking door, covered in white chintz, the only one in the house padded for soundproofing. On its other side, in the study, slept his recently widowed grandfather Yakab.

The same attentiveness to the welfare of others that would subsequently incline Yakab to pave a muddy village byway for the convenience of the refuge-seeking Belzer *rebbe* had induced him in earlier days to protect the privacy of the newly married Kálmán and Ilona in their original love nest. In those days Yakab still slept at the opposite end of the house beside his Karolina. It was not the sanctity of his own middle-aged passions but the young couple's right to uninhibited lovemaking that he had thought of when he instructed the carpenter to pad the interconnecting door between the study and new bedroom, on the one side with brown leather, on the other with white quilting.

Sleeping arrangements on the Rákóczi Estate changed easily as a child left for school or a new baby was born. In the seven years since Yakab had tacked on that little room, Kálmán and Ilona had moved to a neighbouring farm; Ilona had borne three sons; Karolina had died; and Yakab had exchanged his old bedroom with its memories of his wife for the chaste and neutral study. The love murmurs of newlyweds had given way to the peevish wails of a teething toddler.

"I want Mother to carry me about," Paul sobbed, coming immediately awake on contact with the bed, as Ilona, thinking him asleep, set him down.

Kálmán's head emerged groggily from beneath the eiderdown, and Feri moaned in his sleep. Ilona sighed, picked up the baby, and began once more to pace. Then the white quilted door creaked open. A dishevelled grandfather Yakab, tufts of grey hair escaping his nightcap, eyes bloodshot, stood framed in the doorway.

"Listen here, son," thundered the apparition in the white nightshirt, pointing an accusing finger at the baby. "Grandfather doesn't want to hear another infernal word of this 'Mother, carry me.' If Grandfather hears it one more time, he will come in here with a big stick and give you a thorough paddling!"

Not for nothing had Yakab raised ten children. Paul's cry froze on his lips, and he burrowed under the covers between his brothers, never again to make a peep at night on outings to the ancestral home.

Kálmán had not known what to expect of life on the Rákóczi Estate when he had first arrived in 1903. Shy, ill at ease, he began married life by growing a neat goatee. If anything, the newly sprouted beard beneath the existing Franz-Josef moustache emphasized his callowness. Of medium height, with a boy's slightness that he retained all his life, he was dwarfed by his strapping brother-in-law, Andor, his junior by three years. Much later, sitting at Ilona's right hand at the head of the table at which he had once felt so gauche and tongue-tied, Kálmán would regale visitors with the anecdote of how through his own ineptness he had sentenced himself to a diet of giblets in his new home. Originally he had accepted the innards of the goose – a choice morsel in Vaja, a despised leftover in Kajdanó – out of shocked politeness when they had been pressed on him. He thereafter found them floating in his soup bowl as a mark of his mother-in-law's special favour.

Despite his shyness, he found his place quickly. In the approving atmosphere of the Rákóczi Estate he even seemed to grow in stature. The sensual pleasures of marriage (unaccompanied for some time by corresponding responsibilities), the kindness of his in-laws, and his popularity among Ilona's siblings all helped to make his first year in Vaja an extended honeymoon.

He had a malleable nature that thrived on acceptance and praise of which he had received scant measure at home. Always in Ernest's shadow, he now found himself singled out by Yakab, fussed over by Karolina, catered to by his bride. Yakab consulted him about the education of his sons and in response to his advice dispatched the youngest to Nagyvárad. Daily Yakab drove him out to the fields, glowing with pride as he showed him around and inquiring with genuine interest about the methods used in Kajdanó. Finding out from Ilona that the Kálmán had brought from home a considerable library of secular books, his father-in-law installed a new bookcase for his use in the "tent," the integrally constructed *sukkah* that doubled as a second dining room.

Kálmán's eyes widened at some of the practices of his new family. At Kajdanó, the norm had been to raise profits prudently, according to tried and true methods. But here no expense or effort was spared to make the estate attractive and comfortable. In late spring the tall windows of the dining room were flung open to admit the heavy fragrance of the hundreds of hyacinths grown in a huge round flowerbed below, the focal point of the garden. As Kálmán glanced out, the unseasonably warm April day changed with sudden capriciousness. Within moments a violent wind began to gust, the sky rumbled, and hailstones pelted down. Farm hands rushed to bring in the animals, the washerwoman dashed to collect bobbing white sheets from the line. But his little sister-in-law Elizabeth had eyes for nothing but her mother's beloved hyacinths. As he bolted the windows and doors, Kálmán watched her racing among the blue and purple flowers, capping each with a clay pot so that they appeared to be wearing bonnets in the storm. He smiled a little to himself. His father, Herman, might disapprove of the flowers but surely would unbend a little at the sight of Elizabeth's ingenuity.

Kálmán was in no doubt as to what Hersh K'danever would think of some of the other epic goings-on of this place. When Yakab ordered material for his womenfolk, it arrived in bolts so numerous that they had to be stored in crates. And when the seamstress came to run up the new outfits, she was installed for weeks at a time, helping the girls select colours and fabrics from a choice as varied as a good shop's.

And then there was the gramophone. Kálmán chuckled out loud trying to picture his father's reaction to that particular innovation. Although Hersh K'danever was actually two years younger than Yakab, it was impossible to imagine him taking to such a newfangled invention. If by some freak of circumstance one found its way to Kajdanó, Herman would doubtless hole it up in some cupboard, out of sight and sound, whereas Yakab proudly hauled the great box with its trumpet-shaped speaker out to the terrace on summer evenings. Arm about Karolina, ensconced on the wicker sofa, he crooned along with the sentimental ballads. "There is but one little girl in all the world," serenaded Yakab, making sheep's eyes at his buxom wife of thirty years. Then, switching to Tchaikovsky's Violin Concerto, he turned the volume up high enough for the blast to reach the village.

If Kálmán had reservations about some of his father-in-law's excesses – if he wondered to himself about rusting harvesting machines or steam ploughs bogged down in mud – he kept them to himself. His own subsequent stewardship of the Rákóczi Estate was far more thrifty than Yakab's, but his economies were implemented only after his partnership with Zoltán – who could have taught even Yakab a spendthrift trick or two – had foundered to the point of bankruptcy. Even under Kálmán's more parsimonious management, there were areas that austerity's finger never pinched. When it came to charity, he was guided by the same principles as Yakab; when it came to the education of his children, he was guided by principles Yakab had never entertained.

Kálmán was deeply moved by the religious life of the small farm community. His secular education and bone-bred Magyar culture co-habited willingly with the orthodoxy into which he had been born. The spiritual life of the Rákóczi Estate with its little synagogue-on-the-spot struck a deep, responsive chord in him. With a twinge of guilt at his disloyalty, he realized that he found even the Sabbath more beautiful here than at home in Kajdanó. Here there was no necessity of trudging to the neighouring village Friday nights and Saturday mornings over a muddy or dusty thoroughfare, or in winter snowdrifts, in the testy company of his father, whose hernia made every step painful.

Here, in fact, there was nothing to detract from the beauty of the weekly holiday. Not that the synagogue, just north of the house and next to the distillery, was in any way imposing: a plain, white-washed room equipped with thirty seats, each with its own individual lectern for the prayer book and *chumash*, its few decorative accents were the silken curtains over the Ark, and the velvet robes and silver crowns of the Torah, specially commissioned in Belz.

Only on the major festivals did the full complement of thirty wor-shippers congregate in this room. To round out the regular Sabbath *minyan* provided by his older sons and the few Jewish employees on the estate, Yakab depended on villagers from the neighbouring communities of Rohod, Vaja, Ör, and Nyírmada. Though these vil-lages had their own synagogues, there was the inducement for those prepared to walk a few kilometres of staying overnight at the manor house and sharing the Sabbath table, possibly in the company of a visiting rabbi or traveller with news from afar. The most dependable of these village pilgrims would eventually be rewarded by bequests in Yakab's will "for always readily bringing me a minyan."

Here Kálmán met Uncle Ger, an old cobbler from Rohod with a retinue of three or four young scamps rounded up on Friday af-ternoons, glad of the prospect of their only hot meal of the week, for most of Rohod's Jews were very poor. No one knew why Uncle Ger had fled to Hungary from Germany years ago, nor why he had converted from Christianity to Judaism in his adopted country. But they were unfailingly impressed by the fact that this convert had studied at the *yeshiva* of Nagykálló established by the Kallever nearly a century ago, and by Uncle Ger's reputation as a favourite of the current Nagykálló sage, Reb Mendele. Uncle Ger always acquitted himself honourably when called up to the Torah and, on the occasions when Reb Mendele was also a Sabbath guest in Vaja, he and the shoemaker strolled about arm in arm in the afternoon, the teacher visibly doting on his unlikely disciple.

Then there were Reb Chone Grűn and Reb Berish of Nyírmada, who were inseparable. Reb Chone was an inveterate practical joker; every year at Purim he arrived dressed in a general's uniform of the revolutionary army of 1848. Berish, his alter ego, was a florid-faced consumptive with whom Chone argued incessantly. One of them could no more say that something was white without the other immediately declaring it black.

And there was the swarthy villager from Ör whose complexion made Kálmán think of the Jews of the Holy Land and who was known simply as "the Water-carrier." With an ancient sway-backed nag and a rickety cart, he made his living as a driver; his job on the farm consisted of bringing water to the threshing machines for the two or three weeks in the summer when threshing took place. It was a job that normally would have fallen to one of the peasants, but they didn't seem to begrudge him it. The Water-carrier took his meals in the kitchen of the house rather than out in the fields and lived off his three-weeks' work all winter long. He too would turn up for Yakab's *minyans*.

Worship was an uplifting though simple affair in the prayerhouse. Yakab had taken to heart the dictum of the Belzer *rebbe*, that it is preferable to pray briefly with devotion than to go on mechanically at great length. In Yakab's era the tempo of services was quick and the prayers affecting. (Kálmán would later revert to the traditions of his childhood and, in older age, became a stickler for lengthy services.) Those of the worshippers who had both learning and good voices took turns leading services, with Yakab usually acting as cantor and Uncle Mordechai replacing him on the high holydays when Yakab travelled to Belz. Uncle Mordechai – who was no relation, but was addressed this way out of affection – was noted for his fine voice, sweet temper, and cleanliness of an order rare in a village Jew. His Sabbath suit positively shone with the care he lavished on it. Yakab dispatched a carriage to fetch him each Friday afternoon to his home as a special mark of favour to the elderly man.

Uncle Mordechai loved services at the little farm *shul*. "As long as I live, Mr Schwarcz," he would say, "I hope to have the privilege of worshipping here, because this is a holy congregation." Once the ritual slaughterer of Nyírmada, despite his easy disposition he had managed to become embroiled in a bitter controversy with the rabbi. No one was tactless enough to refer to it on the estate, but the rabbi had forbidden his congregation to eat meat slaughtered by Uncle Mordechai. Yakab had sided with Mordechai, claiming he had been unjustly wronged, and had taken him under his wing.

Despite his conscientious nature, Kálmán did not spend all his time in field, office, or synagogue. At meals he drew close to his bride at the dining-room table. By night, as he stroked the chestnut hair spread out on Ilona's pillow, he counted it a blessing that the women in his new family did not adhere to the strict orthodox custom of shaving off their hair on marriage as his mother and sisters had done. By day Ilona pinned the glossy tresses away in a demure bun which she did not find necessary to hide under a hat unless she were about to pray or go visiting. By night in the narrow bedroom with the quilted door, she took out the pins deliberately, then brushed the released waves until they glistened in the candlelight, while Kálmán, propped on one elbow, watched her from bed.

The honeymoon year elapsed without any sign of pregnancy. The young couple began making plans to lease a small farm in the neighbourhood. When they moved there the following year, Ilona still had not conceived. It was curious, it was worrisome. Both came from large families and had taken it for granted that their union would be blessed by many children. But it was almost three years after the wedding that my father was born in February 1906, after a harrowing birth for which the couple returned to the Rákóczi Estate.

Three days and nights Ilona struggled – not in the honeymoon-guest room but in a bedroom adjoining the bathroom at the opposite end of the house. On the fourth day, since matters had apparently reached a pass where the midwife's skills had been exhausted, Yakab sent for Uncle Saul, his physician brother-in-law in Kisvárda. The baby arrived before the doctor, delivered after all by the midwife, with the umbilicus wound treacherously around his little neck.

Karolina, jolted out of her habitual tranquillity by the tensions of the past days and transported by the newfound joys of grand-motherhood, swaddled the infant herself and gathered him up in her arms for display to the rest of the household. He was an unsightly newborn, battered after his ordeal, with a squashed nose and great ears that stuck away from his head, but Karolina, released from a great fear, found him singularly beautiful. Bearing him triumphantly to the dining room, she encountered her son Andor at the threshold.

"Just look," she exclaimed, aglow with pride, "just look at what a *lovely* baby Ilona has given us!"

Out of bold blue eyes, hot-headed Andor stared down at the swaddled bundle. The infant returned his gaze with an unfocused goggle. The future first lieutenant was not one to censor his opinions. "Why, Mother, he's the ugliest thing I ever saw," he declared. And as if there were any doubt as to his meaning, he spat in his brand-new nephew's face.

They called him Gusti and gave him the Hebrew name of Gad, in honour of Karolina's recently deceased father, Gustav Zuckerman. Ilona had no milk after the exhausting delivery, and a strapping peas-ant girl whose husband was the foreman of the oxen stables was hired as wet nurse. And now – the fertility problem apparently solved – Ilona promptly became pregnant again. Feri was born a year after Gusti, and Paul another fourteen months later. This third delivery was again complicated, the baby's large head being blamed for the problem. From the mysterious whispers of anxious adults overheard by a quiet, ruminative little boy, from later repetitions and embel-lishments of the tale of his own traumatic birth, would emerge my father's full-blown phobia of birthing. It would not only render him useless at the deliveries of his own children, but would make him, a farmer, flee the stalls of foaling mares and birthing cows in shame and terror.

The years when her children were young were the happiest of Ilona's life. She and Kálmán had their own small home but still lived near a Rákóczi Estate presided over by both her parents. In later years it would seem to her that this had been a charmed time, fresh with the promise of the many babies her heart craved and her energies required, when the differences between her and Kálmán were as yet masked by the demands and daily joys of raising their boys.

That those growing differences never turned to disaffection was the result of Kálmán's good nature and tolerance. With time and experience, he exchanged naiveté for poise while over the years she became retiring, introspective, and obsessed with religion. The man formed equally by the orthodoxy of Kajdanó and the liberalism of Nagyvárad, whose bookshelves held the great Hungarian classics, entertained interests of far greater sophistication than the woman whose education had stopped at fourteen and who seldom even picked up a newspaper. Yet early in their life together this discrepancy seemed irrelevant. Kálmán had read Marczalli's histories, Ady's verses, Mikszáth's satires, the theorists of the 1848 Revolution long before he ever set eyes on the smooth-faced girl who used to hide under her bed when she ought to have been doing her lessons. A common purpose continued to unite them as they reared their sons in the ways in which they themselves had been reared.

It was only as it became less and less likely that Ilona would have more children, when it became obvious that, barring a miracle, there would be no daughter to name after Karolina, that Ilona began to display the eccentricities that age would magnify. She arranged first Feri's, then Paul's hair in styles reminiscent of bewigged Bourbon monarchs, their curls cascading to waist level. Increasingly her piety took a form that was extreme even in a home renowned for its orthodoxy. While her brothers served as soldiers in the Great War, she observed full fasts two days a week. The strictness of her observance of the dietary laws became fanatical; she divided the kitchen into two separate rooms, one for meat and the other for dairy, each with its own oven, furnishings, and accessories.

As adolescents, her three sons teased her about her idiosyncratic notions, chuckling over her concern that the vapours of cooking meat and dairy dishes would mingle in an unkosher cloud if both were cooked at the same time in the same room. Kálmán, however, let her have her way in almost everything.

He balked only when she decided to shave her head. "I ought to have done it long ago," she reasoned. "It was wrong of me not to have cut it off in the first place." By this time the splendid chestnut locks had darkened and thinned, but Kálmán recoiled at the idea of mutilating even the sparse little chignon.

It went against the grain for him to forbid her, nor was it her style to flout him, so she did not, in the end, shave off her hair, or even take scissors to it. Fastidious in all her ways, she designed a head covering of white batiste edged with fine embroidered trim. Fitting it low over her forehead, she tied it at the back so that not a speck of her hair showed; the effect was similar to a nun's wimple. At home from then on she always wore this head piece. She detested wigs. When she travelled to town, off would come the wimple; like any proper matron, she wore a proper hat.

"Honour Thy Father
and Thy Mother"

Yakab was fifty-four, Gusti, my father, exactly half a century younger, when Karolina died in 1910. What was for one the shattering, unexpected loss of a life-partner became for the other the first identifiable childhood memory. The dying woman lay in the room where Gusti had been born, the house's traditional sickroom. It was called "the small bedroom" in relation to the others, but it was nonetheless spacious because it had been so sparsely furnished. There were two brass beds and bedside tables, a marble washstand, and a grey-green tiled stove in which a fire struggled to ward off a pervasive chill.

Karolina lay in one of the two burgundy-lacquered beds with posts topped by gold knobs. When Gusti was raised to her pillow, a medicinal odour assailed his nostrils from the array of jars and glasses on the marble-topped table. Karolina smiled wanly and reached out to press him to her bosom. "*Gadi*," she murmured, "my little Gad" – the Hungarian diminutive of the Hebrew name of her father, by which her grandson would be known within the family all his life.

Gusti's next memory was of Karolina's *shiva* and of being brought to the dining room with his brothers to lighten the spirits of the assembled mourners. The cushions had been removed from the couch and chaise-longue. The children stared solemnly down at their elders who sat on cushions on the floor in stocking feet. Yakab's eyes were streaming, and he was flanked on the floor by his children who dashed away their own tears when the little nephews entered in their sailor suits. What to make under these circumstances of their jovial grandfather whom they loved best in his persona of candy-strewer from the train window or of their jolly aunts and uncles who could now barely muster a smile?

Of the various death rituals – funerals, *shivas*, pilgrimages to family burial grounds, and to the Tzaddik's grave in Nagykálló – the commemoration of the *yahrzeits* of Yakab's parents, Samuel and Antonia Schwarcz, attained a level of truly heightened refinement. These twice-annual ceremonies when the entire family returned to the ancestral home in Gyulaj were marked by rites of unrivalled pomp, solemnity, and pious ostentation. The celebrations were hosted by Yakab's younger brother Karl, who had inherited the Gyulaj estate with Albert, a third brother.

Like the hall of a medieval castle, the Gyulaj dining room was the main living area of the house, converting to a bedroom at night for master and mistress. On one of its walls, between the beds hung a heavy copper tablet inscribed with the dates of Samuel's and his wife's *yahrzeits* reckoned many years in advance. Antonia's always fell on the winter holiday of Tu B'Shvat, Samuel's a few months later in early spring – the Hebrew date remaining constant but varying from year to year on the Gregorian calendar.

Upon Karl and his wife, Róza, fell the responsibility for huge gatherings of a precise size almost impossible to gauge. The observance of the two great Schwarcz *yahrzeits* was of importance not only to the extended Schwarcz family, not only to its invited local and distant rabbis, but also to numerous acquaintances and alms-seekers who generally crashed the event. The *yahrzeits* were the occasions of charitable disbursements of an extraordinary nature even in a family where giving was a way of life. Prior to the event, money orders were mailed to the needy; sizable additional sums were sent to charities both in Hungary and the Holy Land. Karl kept these receipts in his Torah chest, with the stipulation that when his time came they were to be placed in the grave with him. In an effort to obey the dictum that the truest form of charity is anonymous, he also sent his cook and coachman out late at night in carts laden with food and firewood to be distributed to the poor without revealing the benefactor's identity.

In the days leading up to the *yahrzeits*, carriages awaited the arrival of rabbis and notables at the Nyírbátor train station. The poor who came unbidden found their way on foot, a ten-kilometre hike from the station. By twilight on the eve of the big day, the yard, porch, and dining room were packed with guests and beggars, while the stables and coachhouses filled with the teams of family members.

The ceremonies opened before nightfall with the lighting of memorial candles. Eight metre-long candles in large flower pots filled with sand had been installed on a table on the eastern wall of the dining room. In order of seniority and with tearful solemnity, the seven surviving sons and one daughter each kindled a candle that would burn for twenty-four hours. Though the room was crammed with people, in these moments a hush reigned, broken only by an occasional strangled sob from one of the mourners.

All the women now left the room and the men began the afternoon prayer, which was immediately followed by evening services during which the brothers recited Kaddish. Though Karl was the host, it was Yakab, the most devout of the brothers, who took the floor to conduct the worship. At its conclusion, servants pulled out the extensions of Itzig Derzser's table and added more leaves to accommodate as many diners as possible. At the head sat the most venerable of the rabbis. Then came the brothers ranked by age, followed by their sons and the visitors. More than fifty men crowded the great dining room, but tables had also been set up for lesser guests in the other rooms, while the women dined next door in the smaller manor house belonging to Albert, the youngest Schwarcz brother.

A veritable feast followed. The braided loaves blessed and sliced by the rabbis each weighed some ten kilos. Wine flowed freely. Beneath the flickering light of a petroleum-fuelled chandelier, gesticulating Galician Hasids debated fine Talmudic points and sang psalms between courses. The famous Hungarian folk song attributed to the Tzaddik of Kálló was performed in faultless Magyar by a contingent of *Galitzianers* who could not otherwise speak a word of the language.

When the rabbis started speechifying, the windows were flung open so those outside could hear the proceedings – and so the clouds of pipe and cigar smoke and the smells of the unwashed could dissipate. Outside and in there were men with hooked noses, toothless garblers, gluttons who wolfed their food, louts who misused their cutlery. One tall, erect patriarch called Reb Thaderes with a snow-white beard and a floor-length black caftan beneath which peeped gleaming patent shoes returned year after year; he became, quite inexplicably, the butt of the jokes of the various children who, overcome by excitement and a little too much wine, stifled peals of laughter in the early-morning hours at his expense.

At long last Karl stood up to bestow the honour upon the oldest rabbi of leading the prayer after meals. Then guests dispersed to the barns, tobacco-bunching houses, and specially spruced-up farm buildings after all the more traditional sleeping accommodations had been exhausted. The servants, who worked around the clock during these days, began to restore order; Bertha, the cook, began to prepare the next meal.

In the morning all assembled once more for communal worship. Yakab spread his silver-threaded *talles* over his head, bound his forehead and arms with phylacteries, and began the morning prayer. Similarly garbed congregants followed him in prayer with soft murmurs, yearning cries, and low obeisances as the liturgy required. The brothers once again recited Kaddish and the congregants responded with fervent amens. If the *yahrzeit* fell upon a Monday, a Thursday, or the Sabbath, the Torah would also be fetched by a ceremonious delegation from the estate's synagogue.

After the service, under Róza's watchful eye, the servants spread the table for a breakfast of goose-liver pâté, egg *kichel*, and schnapps. Having pronounced the grace after meals once more, the guests dispersed for a few hours. Farm and village teemed with strolling, chatting, disputing Jews, while in the house preparations were made for the midday meal. Only the obligatory prayer after meals separated dinner from afternoon tea. Twilight began to descend again upon the gathering and with it came afternoon prayers and the final recitation of Kaddish.

There remained one last important but contentious activity: the distribution of money and food to the poor. A previous family conclave had ruled on the contents of each envelope, depending upon the degree of the recipient's need and merit. As each sealed envelope was handed over, Karl requested the beneficiary not to reveal the amount. This request was unfailingly disregarded. The disgruntled clamoured, the satisfied chortled. In the end the grumblers were taken aside in the yard and persuaded to depart with the inducement of an additional envelope or parcel.

Gradually house and yard quietened down. The carriages pulled away with the rabbis. Slowly the aunts, uncles, and cousins took their leave as well. Servants descended upon the house to clean and air it. Leftover food was divided among the village poor, because that which is once destined for charity must not be applied for another purpose.

Absent-mindedly fingering in his pocket the small square box which held the ring he planned to slip on Róza's finger when everyone had gone, Karl Schwarcz stood in the yard watching the departing guests. He was a handsome man, silver-haired but still with a youthful face and bright, intelligent eyes. Standing in front of the low-roofed porch amidst the wheeling carriages, he seemed to radiate optimism and good will by the cocky tilt of his shoulders and his beaming smile. The *yahrzeit*, as usual, had gone off well, the achievement of much forethought and hard work.

Uncle Karl loved both planning and action. An innovative farmer of the same indefatigable cut as his brother Yakab, his fertile mind teemed with schemes for the aggrandizement and improvement of his properties. By means of speculative buying, he and his partner, Albert, had jointly acquired several thousand *holds* of land for farming, grazing, and forestry. No man was better acquainted with the real estate of the southern Nyírség around the town of Nyírbátor than was Uncle Karl. No man was more favourably disposed, more genial, more helpful in providing purchase tips to the family's younger members.

There had been no opportunity to talk business in the solemn hours of remembrance. But as Karl stood waving goodbye to the departing carriages and smoking one of the Havana cigars that were his trademark, he recalled that there was something he had meant to mention to his nephew, Kálmán Weinberger. He beckoned Kálmán's coachman to wait and crossed the yard to poke his head in the carriage window. Ilona and Kálmán looked down at him with polite, inquiring smiles.

"You might be interested in this. The Veres Estate in Piricse is for sale. A very desirable property."

Kálmán asked the price, then shrugged regretfully. "Too much, Uncle Karl, too much for me."

Karl edged closer to the carriage. "Listen here ... Get yourself a partner. You can do more in a partnership. How about talking to one of your brothers?"

It was 1911. Within the year, Kálmán and Ernest Weinberger purchased Piricse in partnership, a depression hit Hungary's agricultural sector, and the banks called in the loans by which Karl and Albert had acquired their properties – loans which great-grandfather Yakab had co-signed and guaranteed. Yakab's fortunes foundered, Karl and Albert sued each other, and Kálmán's little family moved to Piricse.

The First Lieutenant

Face set in grim furrows, Yakab Schwarcz hoisted himself onto the early train bound for Debrecen via Nyíregyháza in the spring of 1916. The white-haired, thick-set old man gazed out on the unpromising landscape speeding by. Torrents of grey rain sloshed against the windows. The April sky poured unremittingly, releasing record and catastrophic amounts of rain. It was the same all over the country, according to the newspaper he clutched in his hands. Planting would have to be delayed. And yet how desperately a good harvest was needed after the imposition of rationing last year. The previous harvest had been only middling, and the present colossal downpour boded ill for the coming season.

How good it would be to talk over such matters with his beloved Belzer *rebbe*! Perhaps the *rebbe* would see a glimmer of hope in even the foul rain and saturated fields, and undoubtedly his wise counsel would guide Yakab in the crisis he now faced. But at this moment such conversation was out of the question, for Yakab did not even know the *rebbe*'s precise whereabouts. Galicia was a no-man's-land for Jews these days, contested and overrun by Russian and Austro-Hungarian armies. The *rebbe* himself was said to be heading towards the Nyírség. Who knew in what village along the way he had taken refuge?

Instead of Belz, Yakab was heading for Debrecen. He had no great expectations of the outcome of his interview with the new *rebbe* he had selected as his stand-in for Belz. Like his father before him and like most of his brothers, Yakab was a *Belzer chosed*. He had had no call to frequent the Komárno *rebbe* before, and surely would not be doing so now but for the fact that the Komárno *rebbe* himself had managed fortuitously to escape from Galicia to Debrecen. But Yakab was desperate for advice, though he did not relish unfolding his life to a stranger unacquainted with his ways. The Belzer *rebbe* knew him intimately, knew the scope of his philanthropy, the strength of his faith, the orthodoxy of his home, the precautions he had taken in the education of his children against the possibility of just such a calamity.

Where had he gone wrong?

The war was responsible for this, the war that had seduced his sons into these errant paths. Still, the war, now in its third year, could not take all the blame. Thirteen years had elapsed since he had arranged the marriage of Ilona and Kálmán, and in that time his sons had shown no signs of voluntarily surrendering their bachelorhood. Yakab had frequently touted likely brides to Andor and Zoltán, the two oldest, but had not pressed them to make use of matchmaker Rezeda's services. His daughter Elizabeth, now at twenty-five pressed hard by the ranks of her unmarried younger sisters who could not fittingly precede her to the *chupah*, persisted in her rejection of eligible suitors for the most spurious reasons. (She had described the latest young man as having the face and intelligence of a sheep.) Out of loving kindness and forbearance, Yakab had not pushed her either.

And this is what came of his love and patience: his two oldest sons engaged to Christian women! With such examples from the oldest, what could he expect of the seven younger ones? What had he done to deserve such a double blow? And what terrible course would this unknown *rebbe* advise in an aging father's treatment of his two grown sons? Must he disown them, his beloved children whom he loved more than his own life, who – as he would write years later in Carlsbad – were the "sweet grape clusters of a carefully selected and carefully tended choice vinestock"? Must he – let it not even be thought – sit *shivah* for them if they persisted in their misguided romances?

Perhaps he ought not to have turned a blind eye to Zoltán's long-standing affair with Margit, the Vaja postmistress. But such liaisons were not uncommon with men who married late, though from this sin he himself had been saved by an early and oh-so-felicitous marriage. As for Andor, Yakab felt he could have forgiven him anything, even the girl's desire for the stage, outlandish as that seemed here in the sodden flatness of the Hungarian Plain. True, she was penniless

– and the Almighty knew that a substantial dowry could be well put to use on the farm right now – but all he really cared about was his children's happiness. Let them forego matchmakers, let them marry according to the dictates of their hearts in the modern way – *as long as their hearts dictated Jewish spouses.*

He sighed, and his face set more grimly than ever. The descendants of Reb Itzig Derzser and of Reb Yankev Fisch, latter-day beneficiaries of the Tzaddik of Kálló's blessing, could not marry gentile women.

Yakab's doubts about Debrecen's new oracle from Galicia and the gist of his thoughts on that depressing train journey were destined to become part of family history. For though my great-grandfather had had modest expectations of the Komárno *rebbe*'s talents, he would subsequently sing his praises with the zeal of a convert. He would repeat with wonderment time and again the *rebbe*'s astonishing, clairvoyant knowledge of his identity and the *rebbe*'s grasp of the intimate details of his predicament. He would dwell on his own moments of suspenseful waiting in the smoke-filled antechamber until the *gabeh* beckoned him towards the inner sanctum. There mystical dark eyes appraised him briefly and a booming voice cut off his greeting.

"I know who you are ... And I know why you've come. You're Reb Yankev Schwarcz of Vaja. And you're beset with worry over the approaching marriages of your two oldest sons."

Yakab was a garrulous man, unaccostumed to being tongue-tied. The *rebbe* motioned him to sit across the table from him. Speechless, Yakab slid into the chair.

"One of your sons has been engaged for some time to a gentile woman of good breeding, the postmistress of your village. Your other son has made an unfortunate connection with a young person in Vienna."

"How do you know this, *Rebbe*?" Yakab whispered.

"I know what I know, that is all that counts. Do not trouble yourself with how I know. The marriages will not take place."

"*Rebbe*," Yakab leaned forward eagerly, "ought I to forbid them? The postmistress is a woman of good family, the niece of a judge.

My son Zoltán has known her since childhood. She is a good woman, an orphan. I like her well enough myself ... My son Andor's fiancée I have not met. She is in Vienna – an actress, they say. The stage. *Films* even, can you believe it, *Rebbe*? He is too old for me to meddle in his life, a headstrong boy but a loving son. So what can I do? What *should* I do?"

The liquid eyes bored into Yakab's faded ones. The deep voice interrupted him again. "Do *nothing*, Reb Yankev Schwarcz. Do nothing at all. *There will be no weddings.*"

The *gabeh* materialized seemingly from nowhere, signalling the end of the audience. In the waiting room Yakab placed an envelope for the *rebbe* in the man's hand, along with some loose coins for his own use. He returned home with hope in his heart.

Shrewd in business, Yakab's acumen stopped short of questioning the methods of a wonder rabbi. But there were some prosaic means by which the Komárno *rebbe* might have acquired his far-reaching knowledge. His *gabeh*'s job included knowledgeability about the affairs of those coming to consult the *rebbe*. Yakab Schwarcz was a prominent-enough Jew in northeastern Hungary for rumours of his troubles to have preceded him. In Yakab's world-view, the *rebbe*'s remarkable insight augured a supernatural intelligence at work; cynics might simply assume that the Komárno *rebbe* kept his ear to the ground.

Nevertheless, the prophecy had the immediate effect of calming Yakab's fears. Reassured by the *rebbe*'s words, he awaited the unfolding of the divine plan.

The outbreak of war in 1914 had foisted choices on Yakab that he never dreamed he would have to make and would have loved to have avoided at any cost. Normally as patriotic as the next man, he was astonished and dismayed when every pore in his body urged him to look for ways to keep his sons out of danger. Yet when his own instincts collided with his sons' desire to serve king and country, it was he who gave way, to the point of making sacrifices to ease their chosen course.

These sacrifices turned out to be as exorbitant as they were varied, from the greasing of palms to keep one child from the front, to the removal of obstacles from the path of another to serve in one of the most exclusive military enclaves of the Austro-Hungarian monarchy.

Thus the recruiting office would find Menyush, the third son (who shuddered at the thought of risking his neck), unfit for active duty on several counts of ill health – without so much as a medical examination. And practical joker Menyush, like the butt of some joke in his own repertoire of comic routines, spent the war years in a sauerkraut factory owned by a Hungarian prince who supplied the armed forces with an excess of cabbage he could not otherwise dispose of.

Yakab's second son, Zoltán, had no greater yearning for the battlefield than did Menyush, but vanity did not allow him to stoop to sauerkraut. Clever, wily Zoltán reckoned that if he had a car with which to enlist, he could parlay himself into a comfortable posting combining maximum personal importance with minimum personal danger. In 1915 his father bought him a car.

Zoltán drove to Vienna in the precious new acquisition and registered his desire to serve the army. He was given the rank of sergeant and immediately seconded for chauffeuring detail between Vienna and other detachments of the army command. Zoltán would spend the war – at his father's expense – happily shuttling messages and high-ranking officers between Austria and Germany in relative safety.

Yakab's greatest sacrifice – a huge financial outlay and the forfeit of his own peace of mind, was expended on behalf of Andor, his eldest son. Andor perfectly epitomized the Hungarian phenomenon of the "gentry Jew" who not only aped the manners and attitudes of the aristocracy but believed in them implicitly. He thirsted for battle and glory in the manner of a medieval knight seeking to win his spurs. Leaping at the opportunity of bleeding for king and country, he was nevertheless unwilling to perform his heroics in the company of Franz-Josef's enlisted foot soldiers. At the outbreak of hostilities, thirty-one-year-old Andor immediately Hungarianized his name to Székács – and let his father know that he had set his heart on serving in the Seventh Hussars.

The Introduction to the Seventh Hussars' *Military Memorial Album*, a massive 300-odd page commemorative volume published in 1923 complete with maps, photographs, and regimental diaries, proclaims the background of one of Hungary's finest military units with telling rhetoric:

The imperial and royal 7th Hussar regiment – or as it proudly calls itself after its renowned regimental patron, Wilhelm II, Emperor of Germany and King of Prussia, the "Kaiser Wilhelm Hussars" – was formed in 1798 during the Napoleonic Wars. Since that day, the Regiment has participated in every campaign of the Austro-Hungarian monarchy, in the course of which it has seen action on all of Europe's battlefields, from Russia to France, from Germany to Upper Italy ... The mobilization of July 14 called it to arms yet again and from then on it fought, struggled, and bled virtually non-stop on every battlefield of the great contest: the bulk of its forces engaged in Galicia, in Volhynia, in Transylvania, and along the Piave; its cavalry division, separated from the Regiment's bosom, in Serbia, on the peaks of Corinth, and even on the ocean shore.

Cavalry held an unrivalled glamour in the consciousness and imagination of Hungarians. The regimental diary boasts, "Our stalwart Magyar Hussars, whose ancestors conquered our beautiful homeland on horseback ... excelled as unrivalled horsemen." It also admits the sad reality faced by romance-seeking recruits in 1914 – "new weapons rendered equestrian fighting almost impossible" – but adds staunchly, "our hussars fought as valiantly and as skilfully with guns, spades, and hand grenades as their comrades in the infantry."

It was the quixotic reputation of the cavalry that attracted Andor Székács: the prestige of the Seventh Hussars with its roster of aristocratic names, its flashy uniforms of red trousers and hats and sky-blue mantles, and the "proud self-consciousness that it wore the famous German Kaiser's name." Within days of the general mobilization the Seventh was heading towards the Russian border where two of its officers harangued the troops in words immortalized in the *Album*: "Hussars: Who among you has not in peacetime dreamt of military glory, dazzling cavalry charges, hussar courage, fame, and heroic death?!"

Thus inspired, on August 15, 1914, the Seventh crossed into Russian territory and won its first battle. "Four pure Magyar light blue hussar regiments, with four thousand Magyar heroes burning with desire for battle, thirsting for glory, upon their whinnying steeds, with flags flying, polished swords by their sides, commands ringing out – a veritable dream come true, an unforgettable picture." It was precisely the dream of Andor Székács, who was not yet of their number but who, by early 1915, was serving as sergeant-up-for-promotion in the Seventh, on the Russian front. There were two hurdles to Andor's acceptance as a reserve-officer trainee in the Seventh Hussars, however: the matter of his Jewishness and his lack of the required educational criterion, a matriculation certificate.

During World War I, Jews served patriotically in all branches of the Hungarian armed forces but (as István Szabó's film *Colonel Redl* strikingly portrayed) in the higher echelons of the service they frequently encountered an impenetrable snobbish disdain all the more painful to endure because Jews too were so thoroughly imbued with the army's inflated ethos. In an attempt to gain social acceptance in the gentile world, many, like Andor, changed their Germanic names to Magyar forms. Many, unlike him, were baptized as well.

The hussar regiments were the service preserve of Hungary's most patrician families. This was especially true of the Seventh and the reason for its attraction in Andor's eyes. If he managed to gain access to it, he would serve with Eszterházys, Széchénys, and Zichys, the historically resonant names of Hungary's great noble families. Even more relevant for him, he would serve with the local notables of the Nyírség, the Vays, the Kelemens, the Padmoniczkys, those families from whom his father and the rest of his family leased their lands and with whom they rubbed elbows, but always with a slight, demeaning deference.

The exact logistics by which Andor gained entry into the Seventh upon his own horse (yet another expense for Yakab) have escaped the historical record. He was certainly not the only Jew to do so, for the regimental roster lists a handful of men with Jewish-sounding names among the officer corps. (There were surely others who, like Andor, had changed their names to Hungarian ones.) More – much more – of Yakab's funds facilitated his access. But the truly odd aspect of Andor's acceptance for officer training was the waiving of the matriculation requirements. This prerequisite was supposed to weed out the bulk of ordinary men who sought officer training. In Andor's case, it failed to do so. According to his sister Elizabeth, the recruiting clerk who processed Andor's application took one look at him and assumed as a matter of course that his elegant demeanour implied a matriculated man. He was never asked to produce a diploma. A more cynical interpretation than that of a doting sister might infer that once again Yakab's money had removed an obstacle.

Andor rose rapidly through the ranks. Following six months of training as a reserve officer in the Rákoscsaba Military Academy in Budapest, he saw action on the Russian front in 1915. The entry of the Romanians into the fray on the side of the Entente in the summer of 1916 gave him the opportunity to distinguish himself. Sixteen months of action – two winters spent on the forbidding, icy peaks of Transylvania cultivating his hatred of the perfidious Romanians (who in their greed for Hungarian land had violated their neutrality and entered the war on the "wrong" side) – saw him promoted to lieutenant in 1916, and to first lieutenant in 1917. The *Military Memorial Album* lists his award for 1916 as the silver medal of bravery, first class. In 1917 he was decorated twice: with the bronze military cross with swords, *signum laudis*, and the Karl company cross. At the end of the year he was transferred to the Tenth Hussars and sent to the Italian front.

To what extent Andor realized his social ambitions within the bosom of the Seventh Hussars depends on how willing he was to delude himself. Certainly his family was inordinately proud of his social and military accomplishments. One of the high moments of my father's childhood was a summer morning when he stepped out on the balcony of the Astoria Hotel in Budapest with my grandfather. It was August 20, the name day of Saint Stephen, patron saint and king of Hungary. Participating in the festive parade below was his uncle's squadron, and there, riding amongst the Seventh Hussars, was Andor in blue-braided cape, the gorgeous plumes of his shako twirling in the wind. "On his own horse," Kálmán observed to his son with a mixture of pride and irritation, for by this time the money squandered on such luxuries was desperately needed on the farm.   .

In the Rákóczi Estate dining room, next to the near-life-sized portrait of the dead matriarch, Karolina, there hung a photograph of her eldest son, the same photograph that is reproduced in the *Military Memorial Album* roster of officers. Andor wears a visored hat – like some railway conductor's – and is trussed in a distinctly uncomfortable-looking high-necked greatcoat collar. He scowls balefully, his expression more suitable for repelling the enemy than for commemoration by posterity.

Another photograph in the *Album* shows Andor in a casual and much more natural pose, half reclining on one elbow, side by side with his squadron commander, George Rakovszky, and three other comrades. The five men lounge in the autumn stubble of a hilly incline, in front of a building that is either stable or barracks. It is October 1916. Rakovszky's squadron has just achieved its baptism of fire, gallantly repulsing the Romanians from a Transylvanian customs house.

Before Rakovszky, Andor's squadron commander had been Count János Zichy, a cousin of the Countess Vay, née Marietta Zichy. There was a snapshot propped on a coffee table in the Rákóczi Estate study of Captain Zichy flanked by his favourite officers: Prince Turn-Taxis and Andor Székács. But while Andor forged these exalted connections in the Seventh, he never served at close quarters with Count Rudolf Vay, the oldest son of the count from whom Yakab Schwarcz leased his lands. Yet arguably it was Count Rudolf's membership in the Seventh that had first sparked Andor's ambition to join this particular regiment.

Andor had always regretted his parents' decision not to take up on Count Adam's offer of the Little Castle some twenty years earlier. He resented the Vays' presence in the village whenever they took up residence there, and he made sure that his own coach and team outshone that of Count Rudolf. When the Vays were elsewhere, out of sight and mostly out of mind, Andor Székács was indubitably the first gentleman of the region, a cut above the rest of the neighbouring gentry in stature, looks, and horsemanship. But on the rare occasions that the Vays graced Vaja with their presence, Andor brooded and fulminated and wished them far distant. Count Rudolf matched his six-foot height, Count Rudolf certainly could handle a horse at least as well as he, and without a doubt the blue-blooded Vays with their historic repute and service to the country were better born than the descendants of Itzig Derzser and Yankev Fisch.

My father would recall many years later how once as a child he had travelled in the same railway compartment as Count Béla, Rudolf's youngest brother. It had been a noteworthy event since normally only aristocrats and members of parliament rode first class. The solid middle classes and the gentry travelled second class; the petty bourgeoisie, peasants, and labourers made do with third. On this particular occasion, for lack of enough first-class passengers to fill up a compartment, a few seats had been set apart at the front of a second-class carriage. In its rear sat Gusti with his aunt Elizabeth who, in a hushed voice, drew his attention to the count.

There were other similar class walls erected between the Vays and the lesser mortals of the Nyírség world. After the railway was introduced in Szabolcs County, Count Adam had a broad, arrow-straight avenue called the Tulip Road cut through his grounds to lead directly from the doors of the castle to the new station. The Tulip Road acquired its name from the double row of poplars the count had planted along its sides, their neatly sculpted tops resembling tulips pushing out of the ground in spring. No one outside the count's family drove along the Tulip Road on pain of a stiff fine, for its *raison d'être* was, precisely, to shield the Vays from the prying eyes of villagers during the few minutes' drive to the station. In later years the count invited Yakab's family to take strolls along the Tulip Road – though never to ride there – if they so desired. Cordial as relations were between landlord and tenant, this particular invitation was issued in a manner indicating that such strolls would be permitted but not welcomed.

Private and reclusive, the count and his family kept the world at bay, cultivating their reputation for haughtiness. When Andor came in contact with Count Rudolf at regimental functions, Rudolf paid him the honour of calling him by the familiar "te." Whereas with other brother officers – even the illustrious Prince Turn-Taxis – this was a reciprocal form of address, the tenant-master relationship of their fathers required Andor to respond to Rudolf with the formal "maga." In Vaja, Andor's family were proud of this one-sided familiarity; one doubts that Andor himself felt the same.

Though the desire to emulate and surpass the Vays fuelled Andor's vanity and ambitions, his envied role models would suffer a most unenviable destiny. When the beautiful countess, Rudolf's mother, began to lose her sight and to require an attendant to lead her by the hand on her daily strolls along the Tulip Road, rumour-mongers speculated that her husband, Count Adam, had infected her with syphilis. The rumours were subsequently borne out by the count's suicide, the countess's eventual total blindness and the madness that afflicted their three handsome sons, Rudolf, Adam, and Béla.

As if lifted out of the bleakest of Greek tragedies, a seemingly inexorable black fate dogged all those related to the Vays of Vaja. After World War I, the three young counts were institutionalized in Budapest, and their cousin, Count László Vay of Berkesz, took over the official management of the Vay estates on their behalf and that of their blind mother. Exemplary relations existed between him and Yakab's heirs. In the nightmare days of April 1944 when the Rákóczi Estate tenants were about to be expropriated prior to their deportation from Hungary, Count László offered to save one of Yakab's young great-granddaughters from the uncertain darkness into which she was headed. A year later Count László himself would lie dead in the hallway of his castle, clubbed to death by the rifle butts of liberating Russian soldiers whom he had tried to stop, vainly, from violating his wife and daughters. At about the same time the blind countess starved to death in Budapest.

Prophecy and Revolution

Andor's soldierly life encompassed a world beyond the battlefield and officer's mess. Between tours of active duty there were pleasurable leaves from the front. At regular intervals he returned to Vaja and delighted his brothers and sisters with tales of his exploits. From time to time he visited Zoltán in Vienna, simultaneously treating a younger sister or two to a special outing in the imperial capital.

In late 1915 Andor brought Elizabeth and Irene with him to Vienna, where they stayed at the Ritz. Zoltán and Andor squired them about, amused by the flirtatious glances the girls cast at the dashing soldiers in grey-blue who milled about the streets. The quartet ate in posh restaurants; they attended the opera. Both girls were present at the coffee house of the Ritz on the afternoon when Zoltán grinned meaningfully at his brother and announced, "I'm about to introduce you to the world's most beautiful girl."

It was the first meeting of Andor Székács and Liane Haid, future star of some forty Austrian, German, Hungarian, and English films. Then aged nineteen, she was poised on the brink of celebrity as an ingénue of the fledgling Austrian film industry. (Her first silent picture would open in 1916 with the timely title *For Emperor and Empire, With God on Our Side*.) True to Zoltán's promise, she was lovely, with finely sculpted Teutonic features and a head of magnificent blonde hair. The daughter of a shopkeeper, her manners were artless and her dress as modest as a governess's.

Andor was immediately smitten. He showered Liane with attention and gifts, and – to the growing dismay of his brother and sisters, well aware of the ramifications of such a romance back home – assumed the attitude of a besotted lover. The young actress, charmed by his attentions and by the self-assurance of a man fourteen years her senior, made no effort to hide the warmth of her response to his overtures. Within days of their introduction, they announced their engagement.

At this juncture Zoltán wrote a letter to Vaja. It was not, as one might assume, a letter alerting his father to family trouble brewing in the imperial capital. It was rather a proposal of marriage to the Vaja postmistress. For years Zoltán had been courting Margit C. at home. In the eyes of his siblings, only the unfortunate fact of her Christian birth stood between the couple and marriage. Plain-featured and kindly, the orphaned daughter of an impoverished gentry family, she had hungered for family life, covering Zoltán's nephews with kisses whenever she visited them in their new Piricse home. The very fact of these visits showed the family's acceptance of the long-standing liaison between her and Zoltán. In Andor's engagement Zoltán quickly recognized the opportunity of wresting his father's approval to a match he had until then lacked the audacity to propose. After all, if his older brother could marry a gentile girl, why couldn't he?

When Yakab got wind of the goings-on in Vienna, the news stunned him with the force of a frontal blow, delivering him into the arms of the Komárno *rebbe* in Debrecen. The Galician wonder rabbi's subsequent assurance that the weddings would not take place gave him some hope, but the absence of any concrete course of action for himself left him edgy with impatience.

During the summer of 1916, as an extraordinary succession of cyclone, whirlwind, and drought followed the spring deluge to produce abysmal conditions for the corn, potatoes, and fodder desperately needed for the war effort, Yakab's third daughter, Irene, developed diabetes. Uncle Saul, the family doctor, shook his head as the girl sickened, and with a downward turn of his mouth advised sending her to a specialist in the Transylvanian town of Kolozsvár (Cluj). Zoltán, home on leave, was dispatched to accompany his sister, and given a letter of introduction to the specialist, Dr János Benedek.

"While you're in Kolozsvár," Yakab told his departing children, "make sure you look up my old friend, Yakab Dick." Yakab Schwarcz's acquaintance with Yakab Dick dated back to the years of their youth when both of them had lived and worked in Kisvárda. Dick, a businessman whose sharp practices had earned him a number of unflattering monikers in Kisvárda, had prospered in Transylvania.

Notorious for the violence of his rages, he was an unpopular character whose reputation was tempered slightly by the influence of his sleek, intelligent, and personable wife. They had two sons who had inherited the father's pugnacious nature *sans* his talent. They had, as well, one daughter.

If not for this girl, Zoltán and Irene would doubtless have found little to induce them to return to the Dick household once they had paid their initial duty call. Outwardly, Gréti Dick resembled her mother more than her father. Pretty, smiling, and seemingly compliant, she was then only seventeen, fourteen years younger than Zoltán. He found her honey-blonde hair, blue eyes, and neat ankles quite captivating, particularly after his discreet enquiries revealed that she would one day be an heiress. While Irene followed a cure with Dr Benedek, Zoltán cultivated his friendship with Gréti Dick and her mother.

Could the Komárno *rebbe* actually have foreseen that this friendship would culminate in a marriage of sixty years? Gréti's smooth, unflappable exterior and soft words masked a nature as autocratic and grasping as her father's. Zoltán, essentially opportunistic but accommodating, might have been moulded under the influence of a woman as benign as Margit the postmistress into a better man. With Gréti he found happiness and also realized his early potential for characterlessness. He became a smooth and amoral man, selfish and self-centred but for love of his wife. The couple faced the outside world with syrupy words and glib smiles, but their essential coldness eventually generated universal dislike in the family.

All this yet lay in the future in the summer of 1916: Gréti's youth, Irene's illness, and Zoltán's service all worked against the marriage for another three years. But Zoltán saw fit to end his engagement to Margit immediately, by the same means as he had couched his original proposal. He wrote the postmistress a letter. In Vaja, Margit blew her brains out with a shotgun.

Zoltán did not attend her funeral. The Székács family was represented at the grim event by his youngest brothers. Margit's uncle, a rctired judge, glared so balefully at the two young men in uniform throughout the service that they almost felt as if they and not Zoltán had brought matters to this pass.

The second half of the Komárno *rebbe*'s prophecy enjoyed a much less tragic fulfilment. From his courtship of Liane in Vienna, Andor had returned to the front, thence back to Vienna, and eventually home to Vaja. There he passed his leave in his customary manner, indulging in his passion for riding, taking considerable interest in the estate, and imposing his brand of tough discipline on the peasants. He did not talk with anyone about his relationship until the eve of his departure when he took his favourite sister, Elizabeth, for a carriage ride. To her, Andor confided his decision to break off the engagement.

He realized, he said, that – much as he loved Liane – their lives ran along tracks that could seldom converge. Her second movie, *Summer Idyll*, had been enthusiastically received, and she was already working on *The Prodigal*, her third. He would be doing her an incalculable disservice to try to win her away from her destiny. To bring her to Vaja would be to bury her alive. But Vaja was his own destiny. He was not cut out to be a lady's man, fawning over film stars in Vienna. He loved the country life. He would have to give Liane back her ring.

Elizabeth freely shed tears that mirrored those brightly banked in her brother's eyes. She praised the wisdom of his decision, while her face spoke regret that the fairy-tale romance she had witnessed beginning in Vienna must come to such a prosaic end.

Such good sense seldom subsequently informed Andor's actions. On his way to rejoin his regiment the morning after he shared his disappointment with Elizabeth, he became embroiled in an altercation with two soldiers billeted on the Rákóczi Estate. In a typical spurt of volcanic temper, he struck one across the face, ordered his batman to disarm both, and dispatched them to Nyíregyháza for further disciplinary action. Such outbursts were second nature to him; he had always been reckless and markedly physical with his farm workers, liberal in dishing out clouts on the head and known as a difficult, if fair, taskmaster. Return to the front now came as a welcome outlet for his aborted passion. He fought valiantly in Transylvania, was decorated and promoted, then transferred to Italy from where he returned in October 1918 to a Vaja abandoned by the rest of his family.

A summer of catastrophic losses for the Axis powers had been followed by an autumn in which huge numbers of debilitated soldiers and civilians succumbed to a devastating outbreak of Spanish flu (44,000 Hungarians perished in October alone). On October 17, 1918, Count István Tisza, the conservative politician most closely associated with the war effort, admitted the defeat of the Axis powers in the Hungarian Parliament.

The trickle of returning soldiers from the front had begun well before this official announcement. After it the stream became a wave. Demoralized deserters, officially demobilized officers, and freedom-fighting nationalists from the constituent ethnic units of the Austro-Hungarian Empire flooded the countryside. In the capital, students and officers demonstrated for peace at the royal residence. On October 25, a left-leaning revolutionary coalition under the presidency of a blue-blooded aristocrat set up its headquarters in the fashionable Astoria Hotel. Less than a week later, on the night of October 31, a mood of euphoria gripped the country as soldiers with bunches of chrysanthemums stuck in their gun-barrels and rosettes of Hungarian red, white, and green pinned over their royal emblems occupied Budapest's strategic strongholds on behalf of the liberal-inspired "Chrysanthemum Revolution." On the same night, a pack of armed men burst into the home of Count István Tisza, the personal embodiment of the old régime, and shot him to death.

As constituted authority fell apart, in the countryside returning soldiers began to loot and terrorize. In the Nyírség as elsewhere, those with land fled their estates to band together for safety in nearby small towns. Yakab's and Kálmán's families ended up in the small market town of Mátészalka where they spent the winter at Menyush's. It was a dreadful winter of Hungarian humiliation. The new liberal-republican government was powerless to halt the territorial disintegration of the old multinational Hungarian state. Spanish flu continued to devastate the populace. Children hardly attended school all year, receiving holidays entitled "Spanish," "coal," and "Romanian" in turn. The first was named after the influenza epidemic, the second after a prolonged fuel shortage, and the last after the Romanian occupation which began in the northeast region of the country shortly after Easter Sunday, April 6, 1919.

Simultaneously with the appearance of the Romanians, power passed from the liberals in the capital to the revolutionary left. A Soviet Republic was proclaimed, the only successful Bolshevik revolution in Europe outside Russia. The fact that about two-thirds of its members were of Jewish origin (all of them having long before severed their links with Jewry) would bode ill for Hungarian Jews in the future.

Like the previous liberal government, the Communist Republic was incapable of arresting Hungarian territorial losses. Hungary lost two-thirds of its land and two million in population to the newly created states of Czechoslovakia and Yugoslavia, as well as to the occupying Romanians. These losses would fuel irredentist movements until war broke out again twenty years later.

Within Hungary, a profoundly demoralized population strove to digest the unassimilable reality that five years of privation, blood-letting, and militaristic fervour had ended in total rout. Trainloads of soldiers and refugees from the territories occupied by the Romanians, Serbs, and Czechs were unloading daily on the railway sidings of Budapest. Russia was disgorging a seemingly endless stream of Hungarian prisoners of war. Diseased and gaunt, their faces purple with cold, they wended their way slowly back to the provinces, despair in their hearts. In their home villages many discovered new, unsuspected grievances.

In Vaja throughout the war years a corrupt village mayor had dealt unjustly with the wives and children of the poorest peasants while fulfilling his official task of doling out rationed supplies. Soldiers returning from the front who had suffered untold miseries were outraged to learn that their families had been apportioned less sugar, flour, and petroleum than the more prosperous smallholder families favoured by the mayor. Seeking redress and revenge, gangs of embittered returnees made the home of Mayor Miklós Kiss the first stop on their round of looting. Since they found him at home, they wreaked no particular damage but vented themselves of some inflammatory language and threatening gestures. Their fury was more readily unleashed on the estates of those who had fled the neighbourhood.

The rallying cry on the lips of the looters heading towards the

Rákóczi Estate was, "Has the First Lieutenant returned?" Some spoke the words a shade fearfully, as if the knowledge of Andor's presence might deflect them from their course. For others, the words were a spur to action, an opportunity to settle scores with Yakab's oldest son.

The confusion that reigned in the village survives in the conflicted and disjointed accounts of its terrible history in the winter and spring of 1919. The common thread running through the disparate, sketchy versions of this chaotic period is the role of Mayor Miklós Kiss. A petty and venal official, he had clearly lost his stranglehold on village life, but was notching up every insult flung at him and keeping score of each inflammatory barb for future reckoning.

Sometime between the return of defeated soldiers in the autumn of 1918 and the triumphant entry of the hated Romanian occupiers the following spring, Andor and his twenty-year-old brother, Sándor, also found their way home. They left the main house uninhabited, camping instead in the office building that had served as Andor's and Zoltán's bachelor digs. A housemaid named Julia cooked for them and shared Andor's bed. In the absence of a labour force, the brothers attempted to fill the most necessary tasks around livestock and fields themselves.

Delegations from the Budapest Soviet were crisscrossing the countryside, promising sweeping reforms. Luckless local peasants would pay with their lives in the approaching White Terror for parroting innocuous propaganda. Once, a communist from Nyírmada addressed a clump of peasants in front of the Vaja village hall. Mounting a wooden table, he harangued the crowd, waxing eloquent about a future in which sinecured clerks at the village hall would be replaced by workers. "Aye, aye," shouted one of the returned soldiers, a father of seven. "Out with the old furniture, in with the new." Standing alone at the edge of the gathering, Mayor Kiss took silent, careful note.

The absent Yakab's popularity and Andor's reputation for severity could not keep looters indefinitely from the Rákóczi Estate. Sporadic acts of violence in the nearby countryside became more and more common. At the family seat in Gyulaj where the ancestors' *yahrzeits* were usually commemorated, Karl Schwarcz's estate was utterly stripped. Then one night, under cover of the commotion occasioned by opening the distillery tap, peasants drove away some hundred heifers and all the draft animals with their tackle from the Rákóczi Estate.

Andor exercised unusual self-restraint and total disregard for his own safety in dealing with the crisis. With Sándor he sought out the most trustworthy villagers and persuaded them to reveal the identity of the looters. Then, without recourse to constituted authority – there was none – Andor called on each of the ringleaders in turn. He ordered them to return the booty not to the estate but to the village commons. "Return everything, and no harm will befall you," he urged them. "Bring back the heifers and the oxen, the carts, and the ploughs. And I promise I'll forget this ever happened."

By sheer force of personality, he imposed his will upon a surly population. Virtually the whole village showed up at its farthermost limit near the straggling Gypsy encampment to witness the sullen procession of returning loot. Sándor herded the heifers apart from the other animals and waited for his brother to speak. When Andor finally nodded his satisfaction, Sándor beckoned to one of the brawniest villagers. Only then, when it was evident that he had been obeyed, did Andor announce that the stolen heifers would be slaughtered. Every family, including the astonished Gypsies, received a portion of meat the likes of which had not crossed their lips in years. Later, Andor would not have to ask for assistance in driving the remaining animals and equipment back to the farm.

The subsequent sweep by the Romanian army of occupation into the Nyírség in early April prior to the drawing up of the Trianon Peace Treaty had a devastating impact on Andor. He had fought in hand-to-hand combat against the Romanians in Transylvania, convinced of the righteousness of the Hungarian cause. Now he had to stand by in bitter uselessness as the line of demarcation between occupied and free Hungary was drawn literally between the tracks of the Nyíregyháza-Vásárosnamény line running under his nose. The bulk of the Rákóczi Estate lay in the occupied zone, while one of his orchards extended on the other side of the track into Hungary, where he was not permitted to set foot. Worse than this, he had to witness the abasement of the village to the whims of a Romanian officer. A time bomb began ticking in his brain. Apoplectic at the best of times, he was unhinged by the new situation.

Although the occupying Romanians were widely disliked, they had some supporters in the village. Their presence certainly reassured Mayor Kiss, who much preferred their rule to that of communists. The commander of the forces occupying Vaja was a lieutenant called Romulus Jovan, a Transylvanian who spoke excellent Hungarian. His favour was courted by the few affluent people in the village, in particular by a distant relative of the Vays, a widow ubiquitously known as Aunt Pityi who lived near the church on Main Street. Aunt Pityi enjoyed a modest reputation as a local hostess. Welcoming the Romanian as a promising addition to the village's stagnating social life, she invited him to a party at her house and, in a balmy spirit of concord, invited Andor as well.

Why Andor, who abhorred Romanians, would accept this invitation is mystifying. Perhaps he thought to prevail upon Jovan to allow him to cross the train tracks into Hungary and tend his own orchard. Perhaps Aunt Pityi, in inviting him, had neglected to mention that Jovan too would be present. Perhaps he simply did not wish to offend the hostess. In any case, both men showed up for supper.

Ample quantities of liquid refreshment preceded, accompanied and followed each course, encouraging the atmosphere of congeniality. From gentle tippling the evening progressed to thoroughgoing drunkenness. Romulus Jovan, transported into a state of sentimental benevolence towards his Hungarian counterpart, reached for his officer's hat on the chair beside him and, with unsteady gait, tottered across the room to Andor, who sat half-reclining on Pityi's sofa.

With a sodden leer, Romulus Jovan clapped his pie-shaped military hat on Andor's dark head and pronounced the warmest expression of camaraderie of which he was capable: "My, but you'd have made a handshome Romanian lieutenant!"

Andor's eyes opened very wide.

"I shaid," – Jovan felt the need to reiterate the compliment – "I shaid ... what a good-looking Romanian offisher you'd make."

"*I* a *Romanian!*" Andor flung the offending hat to the ground and struck the Romanian across the face.

All of Aunt Pityi's diplomatic skills were required to smooth over this deadly insult. "No one saw *anything*," the horrified old woman kept repeating as she trundled the two men out of the house in the early hours of the morning. "*Nothing* happened."

Mayor Kiss had no similar interest in diplomacy. Half the village had insulted him during the revolution; occupation by the enemy would conveniently settle his scores. He accused the villagers whose heckling he had earlier endured of being communists. To Romulus Jovan this charge was like a red flag to a bull. Peasants who had run off at the mouth meaning no real harm, soldiers who had engaged in mild looting, and men innocent of all wrongdoing fell sacrifice to the mayor's spite and the Romanian commander's caprice.

On Saturday night, May 15, Mayor Kiss hauled his drum out to Main Street and, with officious solemnity, beat out a curfew. Overnight, the village was surrounded by a contingent of Romanian cavalry. Some seventy men were rounded up the next morning and taken to the yard behind the village hall. At two o'clock, with the rest of the villages still confined to home, thirteen men were dragged from the yard across a fallow field separating it from the cemetery, to the knoll called Hanging Hill. A shallow communal grave had been dug the night before to receive their bodies. At Romulus Jovan's command, the execution squad pulled their triggers. Among those paying with their lives was the father of seven who had cried out, "Out with the old furniture, in with the new."

The report of gunfire from the village brought Andor on horseback from the estate. Prepared to plead with Romulus Jovan, he discovered that the time for pleading was past. Aunt Pityi, who had been absent from the village, returned that evening by train. She still found a cause to plead with the Romanian commander: at least let the unfortunates be given a decent burial.

The following Wednesday, amidst the keening of widows and cries of children, thirteen coffins on horse-drawn barrows pulled up at the cemetery. Romulus Jovan, his horse hitched to the apple tree of the garden next door, bore unrepentant witness.

Andor Székács did not attend the funeral. A murderous headache was spreading across his skull as he saddled his favourite horse for a canter at mid-day. The horse returned, whinnying softly, hours later. Panic-stricken, Sándor and the maid Julia combed the unsown fields in search of the fallen rider all afternoon.

It was Julia who procured the driver to transport them to Yakab in Mátészalka; Julia who instructed Sándor, bereft as a motherless calf, to remain on the farm; she who cradled Andor's head in her lap, trying to cushion it from the jarring of the wheels on the rutted roads; who helped to carry him to Menyush's little house where Yakab was living; who stammered the news to a disbelieving, anguished father. It was Julia who, under the guidance of a Dr Brody, nursed Andor for the six weeks while he languished in Mátészalka, regaining consciousness for only brief snatches from the stroke that had felled him at the age of thirty-six.

During this time the house remained eerily silent. Yakab sat constant vigil with the servant girl in the darkened room. From time to time Menyush or his young wife admitted the rest of the family on tiptoe. Kálmán and Ilona walked over from the nearby house where they had taken refuge during the year of turmoil; Elizabeth and Irene returned from Kolozsvár where they had been visiting Zoltán and Gréti. The exiled family rallied around their dying oldest brother.

Late at night on July 2 – the fourth day of Tammuz on the Hebrew calendar – all the windows of the little house blazed as a great wailing rose within. The unusual sound and shining windows provoked a fierce knocking outside. Yakab himself walked heavily to the door and scanned the darkness with red-rimmed eyes.

Two Romanian officers stood on the doorstep inquiring about the commotion. Grief and fury suddenly endowed Yakab with Herculean strength. He picked up the first soldier by the scruff of the neck, and bore him wordlessly into the candlelit living room, depositing the man by the uniformed corpse of his son. The soldier stared at the pallid, wasted face, jumped to attention, and saluted.

The next morning Andor's body was transported to Lövő and buried at the foot of his mother's grave.

Yakab would return to the Rákóczi Estate himself only to die. The diabetes that would kill him was diagnosed shortly after the Romanians withdrew from the Nyírség in March 1920. He retired with his daughters to a small bungalow in the county capital, subletting the estate to his son-in-law Kálmán and to his sons Menyush, Sándor, and Ferenc. The cures he sought at the various spas proved futile, and his strength continued to ebb.

Though his energies could no longer be mustered for farming, Yakab's innovative spirit remained unflagging to the end. Confined for longer and longer periods to bed, he resorted to invention: in his will, he left instructions for the patent of a mirror to assist the toilette of the bedridden. He died at the Rákóczi Estate on June 25, 1921, in the narrow little bedroom where Kálmán and Ilona, my grandparents, had once honeymooned.

The Piricse Partners

Ilona and Kálmán's family had weathered the war years in Piricse under considerable strain. The purchase of the Veres Estate by Kálmán and Ernest in 1912 had proved an ill-fated venture, pitting the brothers against each other, and making only too explicit how much old Hersh K'danever preferred his eldest son.

Kálmán had been unable to come up with half the price of the property even though, as Uncle Karl Schwarcz had indicated at the *yahrzeit* in Gyulaj, it was a real bargain. Obliged to borrow from Ernest, Kálmán promised to repay him the sum that would equalize the partnership within a short period.

The Piricse purchase was a speculative venture, undertaken with a view of subdividing the 1,000-*hold* property for rapid resale of the parcelled portions. But the timing of the deal was all wrong for subdivisions and quick profits. A recession in Hungarian agricultural prices brought on by the influx of lower-priced Argentine and Romanian wheat was temporarily offset but not halted by war in the Balkans in 1912-13. Panic-buying on the Budapest exchange resulted in the calling in of bank loans and the plummeting of real estate values. Plans to partition Piricse rapidly gave way to plans – at least in the interim – to farm Piricse. While Ernest's many-pronged business affairs tied him to Munkács and Kajdanó, Kálmán was not similarly bound to Vaja. As Yakab scrambled to salvage a lifetime's work on the Rákóczi Estate, Kálmán prepared in 1912 to move to Piricse to make his fortune.

But the Veres Estate did not lend itself to the making of fortunes. The plaything of three generations of Jewish landowners, it had originally been bought from a collateral branch of the Vay family in the 1840s. On the site of a traditional, seedy-looking manor house the first of the Jewish owners had erected, in the words of the Szabolcs County *Monográfia*, "a smart mansion." Opulently furnished in marble and plush, the house contained ten magnificent rooms of which the largest was a cavernous dining room where, legend had it, an able coachman had once executed a neat turn with a coach and four.

The affluence that had built the manor, however, was not founded upon this particular property. Located in the sandiest, windiest, most barren part of Szabolcs County, its landscape resembled that of the nearby impoverished village where Itzig Derzser had struck root a century and a half earlier. Piricse graphically illustrated the Nyírség aphorism "You plant your seed on one sand-hill and watch it sprout on the next." Gusting winds heaped and shifted the dunes about, in the process wreaking havoc on the pitiful vegetation that somehow managed a half-hearted survival. Tiny quartz crystals scraped and savaged the spindly plants in a phenomenon locally called "sand beating."

Between the sand-hills swept together by the capricious wind nestled a few protected valleys into which the fertile components of the soil had been washed down by many rains. The manor house itself was set in one such basin. Its formal gardens with their undulating lawns, cordon fruit trees in the shape of candelabra, and neo-classical statuary had been inspired by the previous owner's trip to Versailles. Kálmán, who had never expected to farm in Piricse, tried to take heart from the lushness of the landscape outside his window. Soon, however, the very fertility of the gardens became a reproach and insulting reminder of his mistake. From the beginning a pall seemed to hang over the sojourn in Piricse.

Other disillusionments followed. When Kálmán could not repay his loan to Ernest within the specified period, Ernest argued that his younger brother must give up his claim to full partnership. Having paid little more than a quarter of the original price, Kálmán must become a minority shareholder, Ernest reasoned. Ilona, who until now had steered clear of the whole affair, became incensed on her husband's behalf. The brothers, she pointed out to him, had entered into a partnership originally proposed by Kálmán. How could Ernest, who had no urgent need for money, be so petty as to demand it now in order to force Kálmán into an inferior position, when all Kálmán needed was a little more time to repay the loan?

Ernest visited Piricse and heated words were exchanged. Uncle Karl Schwarcz drove over from Gyulaj to arbitrate. By this time Karl was suing his brother Albert over a similar matter, but nonetheless preached the gospel of brotherly love. He suggested putting the matter to Hersh K'danever. "After all," said Uncle Karl, in entirely good faith, "your father loves you both equally." Ernest returned to Kajdanó where he knew himself to be a doting father's favourite.

A few weeks later Kálmán visited his parents. In a private moment with Herman, he began to broach the subject that had been referred to impartial parental adjudication. Herman's right hand sliced the air in front of him as if to chop through unnecessary prattle. The habitual frown of irritation creasing his face deepened. "I've heard it all already. *Ernest es recht.* Your brother is right!"

Cut to the quick, Kálmán came the closest he ever would to criticizing his father: "Maybe he is, *Tate*. But I wish you'd waited to hear my side of things before making up your mind."

My father was a grown man before he heard Kálmán's account of the birth of the minority partnership in Piricse. He was inclined to agree with the legality of Uncle Ernest's original position, and he couldn't help smiling a little over Kálmán's description of old Herman in action. Crotchety Hersh K'danever was a general favourite with his grandchildren. Holidays in Kajdanó were refreshingly undisciplined, with Herman upbraiding his adult children if they played the heavy parent, all the while relishing taking them down a peg or two in the children's presence.

Once, right after the First World War, Kálmán had taken the three boys for a winter visit to Kajdanó. Deeming the conditions too strenuous for a woman, he had not brought Ilona along, although the old man was very fond of his daughter-in-law. The journey, in fact, turned into a nightmare. Passengers were trundled off the train at the Tisza River – the border between Hungary and the newly created state of Czechoslovakia – with casual instructions to cross on foot. Shepherding his sons in front of him on the narrow footbridge that spanned the frozen river, Kálmán congratulated himself on having spared his wife a tortuous trip.

When they arrived to the Kajdanó farm, the jingling of their sleigh bells summoned a beaming, expectant Herman to the porch. But as the old man took in Ilona's absence on the spot, his welcome turned into a growl. "Where's your wife?"

Kálmán made some species of explanation.

"*Bis te putz!*" Hersh K'danever turned on his heel and stalked back into the house, to the stifled merriment of his grandsons and the red-faced discomfiture of his son, at whom he had just flung the epithet for the male member.

And so Gusti smiled a little as, many years later, he listened to the background of the Piricse story. But he too was in the end sucked into the vortex of claims and counterclaims between Kálmán and Ernest. Though the two brothers never quarrelled openly, relations between them became increasingly untenable. It would finally be my father who, in the early 1930s, broke with Uncle Ernest, in a showdown as public as it was unseemly over the disputed responsibility for a wagonload of mouldy wheat. In the offices of a black-bearded grain merchant called Lefkovics, decades of suppurating animosity and jealousy burst open: decades during which Ernest had directed affairs despotically from distant Munkács while Kálmán had to live day to day with the consequences of self-serving decisions; decades of rejection of Kálmán's initiatives; of Ernest's refusal to divide or sell the estate so the partnership could be dissolved.

Now, beneath the titillated gaze of a group that included the three pretty, dark eyed daughters of the grain merchant, Ernest's accustomed *sang froid* and Gusti's clannish solidarity went the way of the wind. Uncle Ernest castigated his nephew as a member of the "Szabolcs gentry." Guszti retorted with the epithet "crooked *Munkácser.*"

"Dare you insult me by calling me a *Munkácser* in that tone of voice," bellowed the hoary-headed dean of the Munkács Chevra Kadisha, "when your own father is from Munkács? I have a good mind to thrash you for impertinence right here in front of witnesses!"

Sucking in his breath sharply, conscious of the glowing dark eyes of the eldest Miss Lefkovics, Gusti drew himself up.

"I wouldn't advise that course, Uncle Ernest. Not at all would I advise it. I'm already holding myself in check *as it is*. Were you not my father's oldest brother, a man with white hairs in his beard,

I don't know what I would have done already. If you lay a finger on me, I'm not guaranteeing the consequences!"

The public tantrum resolved nothing. The Piricse partnership would continue to hobble along, the farm leased to a tenant, with Kálmán and his sons threatening right up to the days of the deportation to take Ernest to court for division of the property. Gusti would see Uncle Ernest from time to time on the streets of Nyíregyháza but would cross the road to avoid facing him, passing by the older man without so much as a tip of the hat or a word of greeting.

Of the two dozen grandchildren resulting from the fertile union of Herman and Sallie Weinberger, only five cousins, scattered over the globe, survived the Holocaust. All had been equally reared in orthodoxy, yet after the Second World War only the two remaining children of Ernest practised Judaism in the manner of their ancestors. Ernest's son, Jenő, who settled in Boston around the time that we came to Montreal, had actually made it through years of labour service without once swallowing *traif*.

My father, on the other hand, while nominally conforming to his upbringing during the lifetime of his parents, had in spirit abandoned orthodoxy long before. After the death of his parents, he no longer pretended. He continued to believe in God, a God who had set the world in motion and then allowed it to operate under the laws of Nature. Such a God, said my father, did not demand submission to the arcane laws that had once been appropriate to a people wandering in the Sinai.

Still, Gusti was not consistent in these theories. I have memories of Hungary – Jewish memories entirely consistent with orthodoxy. Of the *mezuzah* on our apartment door which my father touched with his fingers which he then moved to his lips, each time he left the house or came home. Of being taken to the great Dohány Street synagogue in Budapest on Simchat Torah, a paper flag emblazoned with the Star of David clutched in my hand. Of walking, not taking the streetcar, to *shul* at considerable distance on the high holydays. Of our Seders when my father's college friends and my great-aunts gathered around our table whose centrepiece was a great five-branched candelabrum.

But once we left Hungary, our communal Jewish identity abruptly lapsed. In both England and during our first years in Montreal, we lived as if we were the last Jews left in the world. In our apartment deep in Montreal's east end, our French-Canadian neighbours never dreamed we were Jews. Like latter-day Marranos, we were anonymous.

When I began to attend McGill University, however, my parents fully expected me to blaze a Jewish trail for myself by beginning to socialize with other Jews. To their consternation, I showed no inclination to follow this course. It was at this time that my father accepted an invitation from his orthodox cousin Jenő, and the two of us took an overnight bus to Boston "for a proper *Shabbes* among *real* Jews," as my father put it. During the trip he told me about the old quarrel with Jenő's father. In the dimly lit vehicle his face looked sad and his voice was tinged with regret. All the old rancour had gone.

Embracing Jenő on the platform of the dingy Grayhound station, my father re-embraced for a weekend the old, discarded way of life. He hugged it to himself luxuriantly, passionately even. Transformed from an unremarkable, balding fifty-six-year-old man into a beatific-faced bridegroom meeting the Sabbath bride, he trotted off to *shul* with Jenő on Friday night and Saturday morning, sought introduction to Jenő's *rebbe*, the *Bostoner rebbe* (who dampened the enthusiasm of the moment by refusing to shake hands with a man who did not regularly observe the Sabbath), rediscovered old tastes, old memories, old photographs. In Jenő's French-Provincial living room with its plastic slip-covers, the middle-aged cousins traced the imprint of Hersh K'danever's features on each other's stubbled faces (it's forbidden to shave on the Sabbath), while they exchanged reminiscences of holidays spent together in Kajdanó and Munkács, Vaja and Piricse, always skirting the history of the Piricse partnership which, by unspoken mutual consent, they had decided to avoid. But they spoke, volubly and loudly, of seemingly everything else. My father, in fact, talked himself so hoarse that for the return journey he had no story telling voice left, contenting himself with a rasping summation: "Jenő may look like a Weinberger, but he has inherited nothing of Uncle Ernest's personality. He has the dove-like gentleness of his late sainted mother."

On that first visit to Boston I was not overly interested in Uncles Ernest or Jenő, or in the histories centred on Kajdanó and Piricse. Surprisingly, given my teenaged contrariness, I took to Jenő's three daughters, who tolerated with gentle tact my utter ignorance of orthodox ways. In turn I tried to be open to the strange observances around me, though it must be confessed that the *Shabbes* practices I witnessed seemed as bizarre as customs of moon-dwellers. A huge amount of work had been expended previously – and even more was left to be done – so that none should be performed on the day of rest itself. And the definition of work seemed exceedingly broad, if not downright silly. There were mysterious laws governing the turning on and off of lights; it was strictly forbidden for the oven to be lit, yet food arrived magically hot on the table. We were not allowed to tear toilet paper, or carry our purses if we went for a walk. In a day devoted to refreshment of the spirit, watching television, listening to music, and using the telephone were all forbidden.

Despite differences in our religious lives, Jenő's daughters and I became friends over the years, and I was even a bridesmaid at a Fiddler-on-the-Roof style traditional wedding. On subsequent trips to Boston, I glanced with increased curiosity at a certain photograph in the French-Provincial living room. As I gradually made my peace with Judaism, my interest in Jewish matters increasingly took the form of a fascination with the family's history. Eventually, my obsession took me back to Boston by Grayhound bus more than twenty years after my father and I had made our first journey there.

Beneath the plastic, the green brocade upholstery was still the same, though the apartment was a different one. The girls had left home, and Jenő and his wife, Rozsika, had aged. At eighty, Jenő was still light on his feet and mentally agile, in enviable shape compared to my father, by then confined by paralysis to a wheelchair. Elf-like in old age, with his peaked *yarmulke* and outsize ears like my father's, Jenő was generous in sharing with me his memories of the Weinberger family. Recalling the delicate avoidance by the two cousins of the

Piricse troubles all those years ago, I was hesitant about bringing up my father's feud with Jenő's father.

When I finally alluded to it on the last day of my visit, Jenő stared at me in frank astonishment. "*Apuka* quarrel with Gusti? No, he *never* mentioned it. *Apuka* was very private, like all the Weinbergers. Secretive even, you might say."

Jenő never referred to his father by any other title than *Apuka*, the diminutive of a tender diminutive for "Father." A humble man who, like my grandfather Kálmán, took pride in the fact that he had never once criticized his father, Jenő was himself quite open about his private life. *Apuka* had forbidden him to see the girl he had courted because her family was not a match for the Weinbergers. When Hersh K'danever needed a trusted clerk in the liquor store in Munkács, *Apuka* had earmarked Jenő for the job, even though he had just been accepted at the University of Prague and was wild to go there. "That's the way things were done in those days," he shrugged. "*Apuka* loved us greatly and decided our lives for us."

Late at night, after Jenő and Rozsika had retired, I tiptoed in slippers and dressing gown into the living room and stood beneath the framed photograph of Ernest Weinberger that once had held little interest for me. A charming study of a small family group posed by a baby grand piano, it depicted a seated, smiling woman in an elaborate floor-length gown with leg-of-mutton sleeves, three beautiful, solemn-faced children, and an upright young man, one of his hands resting on the piano, the other on the shoulder of one of the serious children. In 1905 when the picture had been taken, Ernest Weinberger was thirty-three years old. *Pater familias*, with four of his children yet to be born, my father's adversary gazed serenely down at me across the decades.

Three nights in a row I padded silently to pay homage to this effigy, so markedly different from the old tyrant I had envisaged. So *this* was the man his nephews had dubbed "the old Tuareg" and "the great despot," in whose presence conversations had frozen at the table, whom business associates had crossed at their peril, whose children dared not criticize. I saw a short, huskily built, Mongol-featured gentleman, his broad cheeks and slanting eyes three-quarters of a century later faintly reflected in the face of one of his Boston granddaughters – and, by a genetic quirk, in my own slightly Asiatic features. Like his brother Kálmán in his engagement photograph, Ernest wore a brush cut and had a luxuriant moustache; unlike him, he had a full, though elegantly trimmed beard. His round eyes, heavy eyebrows, and dignified bearing, combined with his inscrutable equanimity, gave him the air of an Eastern potentate.

But not of a self-indulgent ruler. Even his detractors admitted that, demanding as Ernest Weinberger was of those around him, he was equally tough on himself. A confirmed chain-smoker who would fill an ashtray to overflowing in the course of drafting a difficult letter, he suffered twice from nicotine poisoning. After the second episode his doctor warned him off tobacco forever. Ernest never touched another cigarette.

And during the final journey of his life, Ernest Weinberger, aged seventy-two, would lie outstretched on the floor of the cattle car rushing its human cargo to Auschwitz, refusing to partake of the meagre rations because, as he kept repeating, one is only allowed to eat non-kosher food on the point of death – "and this is not death yet."

Beneath the icon of an Ernest Weinberger dead now for fifty years, a great-niece playing peacemaker with eternity, I whispered, "Forgive," half-serious, half-mocking about my latter-day mission of pouring balm on a forgotten wound. My father slept his broken, old-man's sleep in a hospital bed in Montreal. The face on the wall, forever young, forever charismatic, forever lordly, gazed back impassively.

The visits to and from Boston were part of a family tradition stretching back to pre–World War I Piricse. In the years that my father was growing up on the Veres Estate, visits from Jenő and his siblings in Munkács and from their favourite girl cousin, Ilush Ullmann, in Debrecen, helped to relieve the blight of Piricse existence. For even to six-year-old Gusti, the move seemed like a banishment from the Promised Land of Vaja. By comparison to the activity fuelled by grandfather Yakab's energy and to the hurly-burly of business and family life on the Rákóczi Estate, Piricse was hopelessly boring for children.

Other than two younger brothers, there were no playmates, and games soon degenerated into scampish behaviour begging for punishment. There was not even school to relieve the monotony: Ilona was too protective to send her sons away to boarding school, and the local schools did not meet Kálmán's standards. In fact, with respect to secular studies, no teacher met his standards until Schoolmaster Sas came along. The first governess, Freda Lichtenstein, was followed by a succession of indifferent young men blown by the winds of war to an isolated farm. Like Piricse's sickly crops, they wilted under Kálmán's withering eye. The one fixture became Reb Schlosser, a brilliant young Polish Hasid with the face of a soulful Christ, who succeeded Miss Freda and became their Jewish studies teacher. Schlosser arrived with a young wife and an ever-growing family, but his position remained secure even after his students reached eighteen and stopped studying with him. From Piricse, he accompanied the family on their travels during the turbulent postwar years, until they all resettled on the Rákóczi Estate in 1920. A dynamic and absorbing instructor, he would eventually replace old "Uncle" Mordechai as the cantor of the family synagogue.

Schoolmaster Sas was a later acquisition who joined the family in 1921 after the move back to Vaja. Wooed away from a Nyíregyháza *gimnázium*, he taught the boys their secular subjects in the morning, leaving the afternoon for religious studies in the large, windowless schoolroom adjoining the "tent" and the glassed-in verandah.

If Schlosser of the molten brown eyes and silky chestnut beard resembled Jesus, Sas with his domed forehead, abbreviated goatee, and piercing gaze recalled a youthful Lenin. He hailed from a small town on the Great Hungarian Plain, and his ways were steeped in Magyarness. Not for Sas a hut on the Weinberger estate like Schlosser: "the Schoolmaster," as he was ubiquitously known, boarded next door to the Catholic church on Nyírmada's Main Street, in the cottage of a widowed peasant woman (who in time gave birth to a little Lenin with the same high forehead and darting grey eyes as the boarder). An uncompromising atheist, his one bow to Judaism was the strict observance of the Yom Kippur fast, based on a deathbed promise extracted from him by his mother.

Despite the religious gulf, Sas found his niche in the Weinberger household. Kálmán delighted in his conversation and the quality of his chess game. As for his three charges, they worshipped him, regardless of his unconventional teaching methods. Throwing the history and geography texts literally in their faces, Sas announced with a shrug, "Memorize these. They require no explanation." Instead, he taught what he liked: Latin, mathematics, and physics. He wanted to stretch their minds, and, over problems during class time and chess games afterwards, he did just that.

But these games of intellectual leapfrog lay ahead during the monotonous Piricse years. For, even as Europe bled and burned and wallowed in mud in the distant background, in Gusti Weinberger's memory a grey sameness framed the six years spent in Piricse. But this bleak mist was pierced for stretches by visits from his cousins and by an inspired gift from his two swashbuckling soldier uncles, Andor and Zoltán.

During the winter of 1914-15, when Russian forces broke through the protective barrier of the Carpathians to within easy reach of Munkács, Ernest Weinberger found it expedient to move his family to the Piricse property. The "smart mansion" strained to accommodate eight permanent house guests. The cousins were overjoyed, their parents patently less so. Both Jenő and Gusti recalled this hiatus fondly, as they recalled the occasional exciting presence of their cousin Ilush from Debrecen. Two years older than Gusti and Jenő, she was not yet playing havoc with their hearts, but the nine-year-old boys already felt stirrings of sexual interest in her company. Decades later, as elderly men at a family wedding, they would chuckle lecherously over recollections of leading her by the hand to witness the mysteries of bovine mating in Piricse. Ilush, whose face now bore few traces of the beauty that had captivated so many, heatedly denied that it had ever happened.

But she recalled the rides in the miniature carriage – among the favourite memories of all of their respective childhoods. A tiny, open four-seater, fully equipped down to its whip in a silver casing, it was pulled by a pair of delightful ponies named Pishta and Yanko, like the carriage, a present from Andor and Zoltán.

The three Weinberger boys shared in the care of the well-matched little team, becoming acquainted with the pair's every idiosyncrasy. As they busied themselves about the animals, brushing and scratching the glossy coats, mixing feed, polishing tackle, cleaning stalls, the boys came to the conclusion that the charcoal-grey Pishta must have been imperfectly gelded. He would whinny and flare his nostrils excitedly in the presence of a mare in heat, while brown Yanko placidly took no notice. Every weekday afternoon all the children drove to the village to drop off the family's mail. They took turns on the box, each having a chance to play coachman. Occasionally the carriage overturned in a tangle of children and ponies, though no great harm ever befell anyone.

The ponies were sold only after Gusti and Paul had married. None mourned them more than Ilona, who wept as they were driven away for the last time as much for the actual loss of the beloved little animals as for the closing of a chapter in her life.

To Walk Straight

In the year 1913, the Hungarian Parliament extended the right of suffrage to include men with secondary schooling over the age of twenty-four (the total electorate now reaching a paltry 6.8 per cent of the population). The Treaty of London ended the First Balkan War; the Second Balkan War broke out between Serbia and Greece. In the Manfréd Weiss munitions factory in Csepel 6,000 workers struck for better working conditions; 119,159 Hungarians left their homeland to improve their fortunes in the United States. The Treaty of Bucharest ended the Second Balkan War. The Hungarian Psychoanalytical Society was founded; the Budapest Ritz opened for business; Gyula Krúdy's brilliant surrealist novel, *The Crimson Stagecoach*, was published.

But for the Weinbergers of Piricse, who read the daily newspapers with avid interest, the most significant development of the year was the fact that seven-year-old Gusti had begun to list slightly to one side as he walked. Ilona and Kálmán began to nag him to "walk straight," when the barely perceptible tilt became a marked curve to the right. Visitors from Kajdanó and Vaja extolled the importance of good posture. But it took irrepressible Andor – as heedlessly capable of mimicking a lame child as he was of spitting at a homely baby – to invent a game commemorating the crooked stance. Between courses at dinner, he crossed to Gusti's side of the table, and, thick lashed violet eyes gleaming with merriment, invited him ceremoniously for a "cripple walk." Grasping the child under an armpit, Andor exaggeratedly twisted his own athletic form to the left, while Gusti naturally inclined to the right. In this manner, amidst laughter and jollity, the mismatched couple made its grotesque progress around the room, the child apparently enjoying the joke as much as anyone else.

The poor posture which Ilona and Kálmán expected their son to outgrow, instead of improving, progressively worsened. Soon, it could not be ignored. In the late spring of 1914 Kálmán took his son to Budapest's foremost orthopaedic paediatric surgeon. Then in his mid-forties, Dr Jenő Kopits was physician-in-chief at the Stefánia Hospital, lecturer at the University of Budapest, and head of a private institute for children suffering from bone diseases. It was at this clinic that he saw my father and my grandfather. A well-built, severe-faced man, Kopits was laconic in giving the diagnosis. The problem was lodged in the boy's spinal column. Since the patient was a growing child, the curvature could be corrected with a corset and custom-made plaster bed.

With practised fingers the doctor palpated Gusti's abdomen until he found the soft growth for which he had been searching. Pointing to a spot below the left hip, he observed with clinical detachment, "This abscess is full of pus, Mr Weinberger. In addition to acquiring the corset and the special bed, you will arrange to come here regularly to have the abscess drained until such a time that no pus forms."

Kálmán looked distraught. "But, doctor, this is an *operation!*"

"Only a very minor one," Kopits said dismissively, setting the date of the next appointment.

All his life, my grandfather harboured a primitive fear of medical procedures. A few years later, when his middle son Feri required emergency surgery for a ruptured appendix, Kálmán folded completely. It was Ilona, bolstered by her simple but all-encompassing faith, who made the arrangements for surgery in Debrecen while Kálmán, in an agony of despair, gave his son up for lost. When he himself required medical attention, he suffered from massive jitters. A confirmed hypochondriac, in any medical emergency he succumbed to an almost pathological fear.

Now in Budapest, without Ilona by his side, he balked at the doctor's diagnosis and treatment plan. He began to search frantically for any alternative to surgery for the child. The following day, he and Gusti boarded the train for Vienna.

Dr Adolf Lorenz was an internationally renowned Viennese professor, one of the founders of the new specialty of orthopaedic paediatrics (and father of future Nobel-prize winner Konrad Lorenz, whose controversial theories on animal behaviour would be used by the Nazis to bolster their racist ideology). Cursorily glancing at the site of the abscess to which Kálmán pointed in agitation, the learned professor pronounced, "There is absolutely nothing to be concerned about here. There's nothing seriously wrong with this little boy. The abscess will be absorbed spontaneously. He will outgrow it."

The doctor's words hung in the air, each one a seeming gift from heaven. Vienna won out over Budapest, the senior doctor's diagnosis carrying more weight than that of the Budapest specialist with the off-hand manner. Hearing the words he so badly wanted to hear, Kálmán jubilantly whisked Gusti out of the office and, like school-boys granted a reprieve from exams, they skipped out of the building hand in hand. Kálmán hailed a *konflis*, a one-horse cab, and treated Gusti to his first sightseeing tour of the imperial capital.

It was the beginning of June, 1914. Later that month, a Serbian student named Gavrilo Princip shot down the Archduke Franz Ferdinand and his wife in Sarajevo. Like moves designated in School-master Sas's chess games, the nations of the world reacted in an inexorable series of ultimatums and actions. Franz-Josef ordered the mobilization of Austro-Hungarian forces on July 25 and declared war on Serbia three days later. Within a week, Russia and Austria-Hungary were at war.

Andor and Zoltán joined up immediately and began officer training. The German army advanced towards Paris, the Russian army towards the Carpathians. By the end of September it had penetrated into Hungarian territory; by the beginning of October it was within 100 kilometres of Piricse, in Transylvania.

Anxiously following every move, Kálmán and Ilona were beset by another, even greater anxiety. Ever since the return from the Viennese professor they had checked vigilantly for signs of the subsiding of the swelling on the child's abdomen. But with the passage of time it became apparent that the abscess, rather than shrinking as Dr Lorenz had predicted, was actually growing. With mounting panic, as the weeks and months passed, Kálmán began to realize that he had made a terrible mistake.

In the fall of 1914, quaking in his lace-up boots, he returned with his son to Dr Kopits in Budapest. Kopits received them, now wearing a white coat over a military uniform. In front of the child, the doctor did not upbraid the father. With economical gestures he motioned to his assistant, an older woman in a long black skirt and snowy apron, to prepare the boy for an immediate treatment in the next room. But as the nurse left the office with the child, Kopits turned on Kálmán with ferocity.

"You call yourself a father, Mr Weinberger? A father? You're no father – you're a *murderer*! Didn't I tell you exactly what you had to do? Why didn't you do it?"

Kálmán dared not speak for fear of further offending the doctor. He dared not say that he had sought out a rival, higher authority, who had given a more pleasing diagnosis.

Kopits continued to berate him. "Your son has spinal tuberculosis! He may remain crippled. He may *die* because of your neglect. Why didn't you bring him back to me sooner?"

Kálmán almost fainted when he heard the word "tuberculosis." "But, doctor, you called it an abscess! You never said 'tuberculosis'!"

"You were scared to death when I said it had to be drained. You would have died on the spot if I had called it by its correct name," Kopits shot back. Then, relenting a little at the sight of the man's tortured, ashen face, he lowered his voice. "Well, we shall do our best even now. Kopits will do his best."

Notwithstanding his massive ego, Kopits was an outstanding physician, a pioneer in the field of orthopaedic paediatrics. Over the next four years he cured my father of the illness whose name Gusti inadvertently discovered only in his thirties. In the child's presence, no one called it anything but "inflammation of the vertebrae"; the exact nature of his illness was a closely guarded family secret. Hungary had the highest rate of tuberculosis in all of Europe. A disease of the lower classes, it carried a marked social stigma.

The child knew that he was sick only because of the strictness of the regime the doctor had imposed on him. He was neither in pain nor restricted from physical activity, as long as he wore his corset. But for weeks in advance of the event, the trips to the capital for the draining of the abscess filled him with dread.

In the absence of antibiotics, a couple of litres of pus would accumulate in the six-week intervals between "puncturings" – the graphic term used to describe the draining process. And so every six weeks, my grandfather and my father came to no. 22 Nyár Street, the child becoming increasingly silent on the long train journey, refusing breakfast in the dining room of the Astoria Hotel, shuddering at the moment the *konflis* was called. When the carriage turned off the bustling, shop-lined Rákóczi Avenue just past the Rokus Hospital into the poky side street, Gusti would tighten his grasp on Kálmán's hand. Mounting the stairs with the wrought-iron balustrade, they would halt at the sign that said "Orthopaedic Institute of Professor Jenő Kopits" and wait after pulling the bell. Aunt Julia, the nurse in the snowy apron, smiled warmly as she let them in, "Now here comes the good little laddie." His fingers by now digging into his father's hand in the lofty hall, he averted his eyes from the sight of misshapen children performing bizarre exercises. Upstairs he undressed and waited for Dr Kopits, who now sported red stripes on his uniform's trousers, denoting his rank of general.

It was always in the instant when the doctor centred the grotesque needle over the abscess, a smile of reassurance on his stern face, that the child's gaze veered towards his father and he implored in a tight whisper, "Please to look only at me, Father. Please to look *only* at me!" Then the needle pierced his skin, searing it for an instant before the yellow arc of pus began to spurt into the basin held ready by Aunt Julia. Two pairs of brown eyes held each other: the child's, fearing some hidden complicity between the doctor and Kálmán should his father look away, and Kálmán's, equally terrified lest he catch a glimpse of the squirting liquid as it gradually became tinged with red and the abscess emptied.

By the early months of 1915 Ernest Weinberger's family had fled from Munkács to Piricse because of the Russian presence in the Carpathians. Three of Yakab's sons had enlisted, and Ilona had begun her twice-weekly fasts for the safe return of her brothers – but with a certain inconsistency. For even as she prayed for their welfare and wished them still at home, her son would overhear her sighing, "Oh, if only I knew that the Almighty would make a soldier of my little Gadi someday, too." All the adults were acutely aware of the prognosis pronounced by Uncle Saul Fried, Yakab's physician brother-in-law in Kisvárda, "The child is under a death sentence. There's no cure for this illness. But death is the better alternative, because if he doesn't die, he will be crippled for life."

The whole household revolved around his care. Despite wartime rationing, every two hours slabs of freshly baked bread thickly spread with butter were brought to him by his aunt Irene who had moved in to nurse him. As for Kálmán, he was so guilt-ridden that his anxiety about the child's well-being robbed him of sleep. He supervised the wearing of the corset at all times, and hovered over Gusti at night lest he roll out of the prescribed supine position in the plaster bed.

As the war wore on, it became increasingly difficult to make trips to Budapest. The army pre-empted trains for the transport of soldiers to the eastern front, the Romanian front, the Italian front. There were unscheduled stops and changes; civilian passengers were ordered off in transit. Infested with bedbugs and other vermin, the trains themselves seemed to crawl along at the pace of insects.

After suffering through yet another of these tortuous trips for the inevitable "puncturing" in Budapest in the spring of 1917, it occurred to Kálmán that there might be an easier way to accomplish the procedure. The city of Debrecen had acquired a university with a medical faculty whose reputation was gradually becoming established. With direct rail connection from Nyírbátor, it was much simpler to reach Debrecen than to undertake a journey four times as long and immeasurably more complicated to the capital. When Kálmán asked Kopits if a surgeon in Debrecen would be able to perform the procedure, the doctor raised a supercilious eyebrow and shrugged. "Why not? If Kopits can do it, why not someone else?"

Six weeks later, in the office of the Debrecen surgeon, Kálmán sat explaining his son's case history and the manner in which the surgery was habitually performed in Budapest. The new surgeon set an appointment for the following day, when father and son once more arrived at the clinic.

The doctor frowned when Kálmán insisted on accompanying Gusti to the examining room. He lowered a curtain at the side of the operating table, a formality with which Kopits, who worked with a minimum of fuss, never bothered. Kálmán penetrated the folds of the curtain and positioned himself behind his son's head. The doctor took out a scalpel, then a larger knife. Kálmán watched with growing unease, for the procedure he had witnessed so many times in Budapest had only required a needle. With nervous movements, the doctor jabbed and prodded at the child's abdomen with his instruments, apparently without success. The little boy searched for his father's eyes behind him, pleading silently and far more effectively than if he had wept or called out.

Kálmán averted his gaze in order to observe the doctor in his difficulties. Despite the nicks on his son's belly, there was still no trace of pus.

Kálmán's voice suddenly pierced the silence. "Doctor, please. Thank you very much. We are leaving now."

"Mr Weinberger, I shall have to eject you if you interrupt me again."

"I am sorry, doctor. This is not the way this operation should be performed. I am not permitting you to continue."

"I am the doctor here, not you, Mr Weinberger!"

"I thank you, doctor. Enough. I will take my son now. What do I owe you? We are going to Budapest on the next train."

Two days later in Budapest Dr Kopits drained the abscess with his accustomed ease. By now Kálmán was sufficiently relaxed in his presence to venture a question.

"Professor, can you tell me why a procedure this simple can't be performed by a surgeon-in-chief in Debrecen?"

Kopits unbent slightly with a frosty smile. "For you, it is a simple procedure, Mr Weinberger. But it is simple only when performed by a Kopits."

Until he was seventy-six and suffered his first series of strokes, my father, as far as I can remember, was never ill. He worked four days a week until he was seventy-three, and in retirement he remained an enthusiastic gardener and a keen walker.

The early childhood illness left no trace. During World War II, when Hungarian-Jewish men were forced into specialized labour battalions demeaningly separate from the rest of the armed forces, Gusti attempted to obtain a medical exemption from a sympathetic physician. With all the good will in the world, the doctor could find no evidence of the early illness. "You have the heart of an ox and the constitution to go with it. I wish I could help you."

Many times Gusti would bid his tearful mother good-bye as he left to join his company. "Why are you crying?" he would tease her. "I remember you asking God to make me a soldier one day."

"Ah, my dear," Ilona wiped her eyes with the hint of an answering smile, "I did not wish for Him to heed me quite so literally."

The end of the illness arrived as subtly as its onset. Trips to Budapest spread out over longer intervals as the abscess slowly subsided. In the galvanized uncertainty characterizing the end of World War I, the journeys became altogether unfeasible.

One day in the fall of 1918, when soldiers began pouring back to the countryside and the Chrysanthemum Revolution was unfolding in the capital, Kálmán held conclave at the Piricse dining table. In attendance were Ilona and Armin Schlosser, the boys' Hebrew teacher, and, as a special mark of favour, twelve-year-old Gusti. Marauding soldiers were terrorizing nearby villages; the neighbourhood was rife with rumours that the National Council was about to divide all large estates; Piricse villagers were returning from looting expeditions with reports that "freedom had broken out."

My grandfather was in favour of immediate flight from the estate, while Ilona was sure that all would be well if they stayed. Kálmán prevailed. He gave orders to the parade coachman, the one member of his household he still deemed trustworthy, to harness the carriage. Still, the family was too numerous for all to squeeze into one carriage.

"Please, Father," Gusti spoke up, "let me drive the other one. A man must know how to do everything," he added self-importantly, highly conscious of the privilege of attending the select family council. His parents regarded him fondly. He stood straight and hale, a little round-shouldered to be sure, though less so than his brother Feri whose health had never given them a moment's concern.

"Run along then, and harness up," Ilona said, almost gaily. Gusti harnessed the team. Taking back roads, the second carriage followed the first into the nearby little meadow town of Nyírbátor where the Weinbergers first took refuge. During the course of the journey, no one saw the young driver aim a small bundle at the roadside bushes. Gusti Weinberger would have no further need of a corset.

PART TWO

Gusti and Feri in Ukraine, 1941. In World War II
Jewish men of military age were assigned to special
labour battalions. One officer said of his
responsibilities to his Jewish labour servicemen: "I
see a good officer as one who brings back few Jews."

The Academy Years

An anti-Semite is one who loathes Jews more than is necessary.
Kálmán Mikszáth

On a September day in 1924, a fiacre emerged from the dappled sunshine of Debrecen's Great Forest into the full glare of the September midday. Cool, spicy forest air gave way to prairie dust.

The Royal Hungarian Agricultural Academy of Debrecen was situated beyond the city precincts in the village of Pallagpuszta. The Great Forest, a precious if anomalous stand of woodland stretching between the academy and the city, was a fitting transition from the world of town to country. City tramlines ended abruptly at the forest, and commuters continuing on to the village were obliged to transfer to trains for the six-kilometre ride – or to walk.

The fiacre with its three passengers wheeled past the offices and outbuildings of the model farm. There were still few students. The academy was still quiet, although on the following day scores of young men would hustle and elbow their way to classes. A broad two-storey building of the yellow stucco ubiquitous in the Austro-Hungarian Empire rose out of impeccably groomed grounds. Kálmán Weinberger instructed the driver to stop by the main entrance and wait in the shade. Gusti and Feri followed their father into the building, their faces masks of resolution. In fact, they looked downright grim, far more solemn than is customary even embarking on the first term of one's first college year.

It was not a good time to be coming of age, not a good time to be going away to school, not a good time to be Jewish. A quarter of a century after Kálmán had matriculated in the cosmopolitan liberalism of Nagyvárad, it was now nearly impossible for Jewish students to gain university placement. But all three of Kálmán's sons badly wanted to be the family's first college-educated farmers. Though poor Latin scholars, they could quote Horace with conviction: *Omnium rerum, ex quibus aliquid aquiritus, nihil est agricultura melius, nihil dulcius, nihil uberius, nihil omine dignimus* – "Of all things with which we may occupy ourselves, nothing is better, nothing more pleasant, nothing more worthy of man than the practice of agriculture."

The two older boys, just a year apart in age, had always been instructed at the same grade level. The question of their eligibility for higher education arose in 1924, two years before that of Paul, the youngest. Gusti's and Feri's great fortune in being accepted at the Debrecen Academy derived from the exceptional liberalism of its director, Kálmán Ruffy-Varga. Though by 1924 a quota regulating Jewish enrolment in higher education had been in place for four years, the academy in Debrecen was the only one of three such colleges in the country still willing to accept Jews. It was to meet the director responsible for this distinctive and honourable stance, and to entrust him personally with his sons' welfare, that Kálmán Weinberger had accompanied them at the beginning of term.

A flat town of the steppes, baked in the sun in summer, buffeted by keening prairie winds in winter, Debrecen was (and is) the largest city of the Great Hungarian Plain. Quintessentially Magyar, its seven centuries of proud and troubled history were emblematic of much of Hungarian life. In medieval times the town had attracted runaway serfs and itinerant artisans who laid its foundations as a centre of agriculture, crafts, and international trade. During the Reformation it turned stalwartly Protestant and soon won the unofficial title of "the Calvinist Rome." Only Calvinists were allowed permanent settlement, a fact that drew upon the town the ire of its staunchly Catholic Habsburg rulers. Neither a devastating sixteenth-century fire nor the ravages of Turkish occupation could quell the spirit of the city's dourly puritanical inhabitants. During the Counter Reformation the town remained a haven for persecuted Protestants throughout Europe.

In 1693, as a reward for its neutrality in the Rákóczi Uprising, Debrecen was accorded the status of "free royal city." In return, it was obliged to allow Catholic settlement and toleration. Nevertheless, the city elders still maintained their unyielding anti-Habsburg stance. In 1849 Louis Kossuth's revolutionary government fled Budapest to establish itself in Debrecen's famous Protestant College, which bore on its pediment a motto pleasing to any good Calvinist: *Orando et Laborando* – to pray and to work. The revolutionary declaration of Habsburg dethronement was proclaimed from the city's Great Church.

Debrecen's reputation as a haven from persecution did not, however, extend to Jews. Jewish merchants participating in the town's famous fairs had to sleep beyond the city limits until the 1840s when Jewish settlement was first permitted within. For the balance of the century, however, the Jews of Debrecen flourished and made their mark; by the end of World War I, some 10,000 Jews lived there, about ten per cent of the population.

Debrecen had been a centre for higher education since the Renaissance, its College frequented by learned Dutch and Swiss prelates. It boasted several fine boarding schools, both Catholic and Protestant, for girls and boys. In 1868 it was also granted 400 *holds* of land in the village of Pallagpuszta on which to operate a Hungarian-language institute of agriculture and forestry.

A smile lit Director Ruffy-Varga's face as he extended his hands in welcome and ushered his guests into the high-ceilinged, leather-upholstered office on the ground floor of the academy. He was a man of about fifty with an impressively tended black moustache, florid colouring, and dignified bearing. His welcoming words were tinged with the *palóc* dialect of the Mátra mountains of his origins, accents that a generation of botany students had grown to love. Yet aside from his country speech, there was nothing countrified about Ruffy-Varga.

A sound scholar and brilliant teacher whose career would be capped by a seat in the Hungarian Upper House, he ran the academy on principles of academic excellence and human decency. Defying the prevailing anti-Semitic climate, he argued that since other agricultural colleges would not accept Jewish students, Debrecen was obliged to go beyond the official six per cent permitted by the *Numerus Clausus* quota. While he could not physically prevent anti-Semitic demonstrations at his school in a period when they were the norm throughout the country, he spread the mantle of his protection over his Jewish students. On his meeting with the Weinberger boys, he made a solemn promise to their father.

"Mr Weinberger, nothing but a poor scholastic record will hinder your sons from thriving in this school." Ruffy-Varga would take that promise very seriously.

It is difficult to grasp the dimensions of the revulsion against Jews that seized Hungary after World War I. Five years earlier, in the autumn of 1919, Admiral Miklós Horthy had entered Budapest on a white horse as the symbol of victorious counter-revolution. An archetypal reactionary and director of the White Terror, Horthy was shortly to appoint himself Regent of Hungary. From the royal castle on Buda Hill he would preside for the next quarter of a century over a sham monarchy without a king and a parliamentary system without democracy.

In the immediate aftermath of the Hungarian Bolshevik Revolution of 1919, being a Jew in Hungary was transformed from mere social liability to life-threatening hazard. The abortive and unpopular Communist Revolution with its markedly Jewish leadership had created an association between "Jew" and "communist" in the public mind. This association was the surface rationale for the military units that sprang up and attached themselves to Miklós Horthy's National Army in the late summer and fall of 1919 to purge Hungary of communists and to punish those allegedly guilty of crimes committed during the rule of the Soviet. Beneath this apparent reason simmered the broader issues of the loss of the war, social and economic dislocation, and the dismemberment of the country.

Jews were accused of not having shared in the burdens of the war, of profiteering, and, paradoxically, of wanting to do away with private property. In the new ideology that began to emerge with the counter-revolution of 1919, the principle of Jewish integration into Hungarian society ceased to be regarded as a positive value. Jewish prominence in industry and finance, which had contributed so markedly to modernization in the second half of the nineteenth century and had formed the basis of the post-Emancipation "Golden Age of Hungarian Jewry," now faced harsh rejection.

The most important political and military body behind the White Terror which unleashed itself upon the country after the overthrow of the communist regime in August 1919 was the Society of Awakening Magyars. Formed late in 1918 by chauvinistic university students in Budapest, it had gone underground during communist rule; it was now resurrected, and became in the Twenties the strongest and most visible of the organizations of the extreme right. Anti-Semitism constituted the principle tenet of its ideology and activities.

White Terror gangs ran loose over the villages and small towns of Transdanubia and the western slice of the Great Plain. A member of the American military mission in Vienna described their activities as veritable pogroms, and listed in his reports the desecration of Torah scrolls, the mass murder of Jews of entire villages, and the rape of little girls whose violated bodies were thrown into wells.

Israel Cohen, a British Zionist official and journalist, described other atrocities: "Jews were dragged out of their homes, abused, flogged, robbed, tortured, and driven or deported to some other town ... They were compelled to sign fictitious confessions of penal offenses, and if they refused at first they were flogged until they submitted. They were accused of illicit trading, of war-profiteering, of unemployment – of anything that could serve as a pretext: the real accusation was that they were Jews."[3]

The intensity of the pogroms reached its peak in August and September of 1919, but there were fresh outbreaks of violence in the spring of 1920 after the election of Horthy as regent and provisional head of state. By the middle of 1920, the Society of Awakening Magyars had a national membership of some 80,000. In partnership with the national army, it acted at will throughout the country. This strong-arm policy had the acknowledged approval of the regent and rested on a wide base of popular support because of what was perceived to be the "Bolshevik danger."

The counter-revolutionary forces placed the blame for the collapse of the old régime and the convulsions of the two revolutions in its wake squarely on the shoulders of the country's intellectuals. And there was no disputing that the Hungarian intelligentsia included a preponderance of Jews, and that Jews had been prominent left-wingers. The punishment devised for these "crimes" lay in the abrogation of the rights of Jews to further educational opportunities.

In September 1920 the Hungarian Parliament became the first European legislature of the twentieth century to pass anti-Jewish legislation. The law, commonly called *Numerus Clausus*, was passed in response to the generally held attitude that Jews – and particularly educated Jews – had caused the fall of the old régime. The terms of the law dictated that the proportion of various races and nationalities in the student population must not exceed the percentage of such groups within the general population. As Jews constituted six per cent of that population in 1920, the quota of Jewish university students must not rise above that figure either. The law's most vocal proponents were university students and faculty: the previous year, students had initiated such a campaign of violence against their Jewish classmates that the universities had had to be shut down.

By the autumn of 1924 when Gusti and Feri Weinberger and six other Jewish young men began to attend first-year lectures at the academy in Debrecen, the abuses perpetrated by the Society of Awakening Magyars were pale shadows of the White Terror's first atrocities. Acts of organized terror had gradually subsided during the premiership of Count István Bethlen, who enjoyed the reputation of a moderate. Although his political bedfellows were Horthy and the military, the new prime minister viewed the restoration of political and economic stability as paramount. As a result, Jewish lives and property were once more secure.

Still, it is difficult for someone of my own generation, coming of age in the 1960s in a part of the world where campuses bubbled with the yeast of left-wing ferment and faculty was overwhelmingly liberal, to project myself even imaginatively into the stultifying atmosphere of interwar Hungarian university life. When my father and his two brothers attended the academy, student protest movements, backed by anti-Semitic teachers, did not aim at pushing administrations towards the left, but towards the right.

In the five years since the beginning of the White Terror, the Awakening Magyars had become, if anything, stronger, and their influence on university life all-pervasive. Jewish university students in Debrecen attempted to defuse their feelings of fear and inadequacy by ridiculing their enemies: since members of the Society referred to one another as *bajtársok* (comrades) amongst themselves, Jewish students alluded to them by the same term, although in tones of dripping sarcasm. While the *bajtársok* poisoned their lives in countless petty ways, Jewish students tried to shrug them off as a passing nuisance; their quasi-military organization, silly uniforms, and pompous airs made good butts for satire.

But with the hindsight of history, the Society of Awakening Magyars cannot be laughed off as a bad joke. The organization was a harbinger of enormous evil. In the early Twenties it forged ties with Austria and Germany where it was in close touch with the fledgling Nazi Party. In 1923 a plot was discovered against the Hungarian government to be carried out in co-operation with Bavarian nationalists led by General Ludendorff and Adolf Hitler. The project included a plan to eliminate the Jews of Hungary. In the same year, Gyula Gömbös, leader of the Race Protection Party and a future Hungarian prime minister, attempted to establish rapport with Hitler. Within a decade both men would rise to power in their respective countries.

In Debrecen, during the White Terror, even the academy's liberal director had been obliged to bow to public pressure. For two years before my father's arrival there, the academy's doors had been firmly bolted against Jews.

Anti-Semitic feelings ran high at the academy where the Awakening Magyars had the strongest organization in the city. In 1921 a gang of gentile agriculture students had ambushed several of their Jewish classmates near the railway station. In the ensuing mêlée one of the Jewish students had pulled out a gun and shot his assailant in the stomach. Luckily for all concerned, the young man had lived. When the case came to trial, the judge acquitted the Jewish student on grounds of self-defence. The judgment elicited such a vehement anti-Semitic reaction that, for their own safety, Ruffy-Varga chose not to admit Jews to the college until 1923.

When Gusti and Feri Weinberger and six Jewish classmates began attending lectures at the academy a year later, the days of Jew-beating, if not Jew-baiting, were over. The most common form of persecution now came in the guise of a "warning off," the term used for advance notice given to Jewish students by the Society to steer clear of classes. Far more humiliating were the spontaneous barrings from class. Sporting navy-blue jackets and pie-shaped hats trimmed with the yellow ribbons of their branch of the Society, the *bajtársok* guarded lecture halls and prevented Jewish students from entering. On other occasions, Jewish pupils had to withdraw from class in mid-lecture to boisterous choruses of "stinking Jew."

At eighteen and seventeen years of age, my father and my uncle were ill-equipped to bear the brunt of such malice. They had never been away from home before. As private students, they had never been hardened by an earlier apprenticeship in public school against the daily stigma and petty hurts of classmates' taunts. Armed only with their brains and a high sense of purpose, they arrived in Debrecen absolutely dedicated to the ideal of learning. Their cosy relationship with Schoolmaster Sas, a fair and sympathetic taskmaster, had hardly prepared them for professors who deliberately quizzed Jewish students on material they knew them to have missed because of being barred from class.

Anti-Semitism did not indiscriminately taint all of the academy's professors. None overstepped the bounds of civilized disdain marked out by the novelist Kálmán Mikszáth's aphorism that an anti-Semite is "one who loathes Jews more than is necessary." Most were exaggeratedly correct in granting the *jeles* or "outstanding" grade when it was deserved. Some made no secret of their sympathy towards Jewish students. Yet not one took the courageous stand of certain professors at the University of Debrecen who refused to teach classes from which Jews had been barred and who would not lecture until Jewish students were recalled. And not one of the academy's professors was himself a Jew. Professor Mihály Rácz, the academy's foremost scholar, had been born one, but had converted to Christianity while a student in pre–World War I Budapest.

Most of what I know about the indignities endured by my father and his brothers has come to me from my uncle Paul's best friend, László Weisz. By the time I knew him he was László Vincze, a noted agricultural researcher, practitioner, and author in post–World War

II Hungary. But he still recognizably merited the affectionate nickname conferred on him by his college chums: even in his eighties, "the little Yorkshire" retained the pink cheeks, round blue eyes, and well-stuffed form that had put budding farmers in mind of a Yorkshire piglet. László spoke freely about all aspects of their college life; my father, on the other hand, had a deep-seated reluctance about dwelling on former indignities and humiliations. He preferred recalling only good times. Gusti emphasized Ruffy-Varga's generosity rather than the events that had necessitated its display. But László too was scrupulously fair in trying to unveil for my benefit the nuances of decency towards Jews in the academy's vicious atmosphere.

About three-quarters of the more than 300 students were members of the Society of Awakening Magyars. Yet only a small minority, László maintained, a dozen or so in each of the three years, had joined the Society out of conviction. Most of the rest were swept along by their peers or motivated by financial pressures. Wealthy patrons of the Society offered stipends to students willing to join the organization; for many, such support made the difference between being able to attend the academy or not. Such pragmatic *bajtársok* often acted honourably towards their Jewish classmates within the framework of existing conditions.

László recalled an assembly during his second year when extremists from the law and medical faculties of the main campus vigorously heckled Ruffy-Varga for being soft on Jews. Upstairs in the second-year lecture hall, László, Paul, and their two fellow Jewish classmates heard the beginning chords of the *Hymnusz*, the Hungarian national anthem, the signal that the assembly would shortly disperse. They were the only Jews in the building. Scenting trouble, those in the other years had stayed away, but my uncle Paul, a single-mindedly conscientious student, had insisted on turning up for a lab. Unwilling to leave him on his own, his three Jewish classmates had come along to protect him.

As the strains of the anthem floated upstairs, Endre Erendics, one of the *bajtársok*, materialized on the threshold of the laboratory. "Boys, get out of here, pronto!" he said breathlessly. "The trouble-makers from the university want to search the building."

The four young men tiptoed downstairs. The doors of the *Aula*, the great auditorium, were wide open as 300 students stood at attention, patriotically in song. Hats in hands, László Weisz, Paul Weinberger, Emery Moskovits, and László Bader stole silently past the open doors and out of the building.

On another occasion, the leader of the Society's academy branch came in person to "warn off" László and his classmates. Ernest Nics, by then a reserve lieutenant in the artillery, was slightly older than the other students and felt a sense of responsibility even towards Jewish classmates. "Boys, don't come in tomorrow," he said. "Please. There'll be foreign elements here from the university over whom I have no control ... I promise to send for you when it's all right to come back."

The many political metamorphoses Hungary has undergone in the seventy years since that particular "warning off" have not diminished László Vincze's gratitude to Ernest Nics. Without a trace of irony, he said to me, "He was a real gentleman from a truly distinguished family. Really decent to us Jews."

In their first year, Gusti and Feri had little cause to be grateful to any of their classmates. Their excellent marks only targeted them for extra unpopularity. By mid-year, the two young men who had set out with such high ambitions decided to withdraw from the program. A particularly ugly incident had sparked their decision.

The chairman of the Department of Agricultural Practice, Professor Halász was a general favourite on campus. He owned a fashionable villa in back of the main building and held fashionable opinions; his team of white Arab stallions was much admired by his students. He treated the Jews in his classes with elegant disdain, yet, because he prized diligence, he frequently held up the work of the Weinberger brothers as an example to the rest. At one of his demonstration classes after he had singled out Feri's work a *bajtárs* threw a lit cigarette down the neck of the prize student. Feri jumped up in consternation and performed a minor St Vitus dance. As the class roared with mirth at his plight, he and Gusti left the room with bowed heads.

The next day the two turned up at the director's office, dressed in the customary garb of the academy, spruce bow ties and jackets over knickerbocker breeches and lace-up ankle boots. Ruffy-Varga greeted their announcement to withdraw with astonishment. They refused to divulge their reason, although the director pressed them repeatedly. He praised their performance and called them assets to the school with promising careers ahead. Finally, Ruffy-Varga reminded them of his promise to their father that "nothing bar your own performance would hinder you from graduating from this establishment."

At this Feri impulsively exclaimed, "With all due respect, sir, forfeiting my self-respect is too high a price to pay for any diploma!"

Bit by bit, Ruffy-Varga extracted from them the history of the humiliations of the past few months. When he heard of the burning cigarette, his normally high-complexioned face flushed an unhealthy crimson. He slammed his open hand on the mahogany desk. "Name me the ringleaders this minute and I'll call them in straight away. If *one hair* on your heads is hurt again, I'll not only expel them from this place but I'll make sure they won't find another school anywhere else in this country!"

He was as good as his word, and Gusti and Feri stayed on. No one dared to tangle with any Jewish students again that year. And although some who had harassed them continued to dart poisonous glances at the Weinberger boys, they did so from a distance. Eventually Gusti, Feri, and Paul all earned *jeles* diplomas from the academy – a record for three brothers in the annals of the college.

First Loves

Perhaps no one else took as much pleasure in the brothers' academic achievements as their new uncle in Debrecen, Charlie Békés. A lawyer, voracious reader, and armchair philosopher, Uncle Charlie peppered his speech with Latin phrases and literary allusions. He was a pedagogue *manqué* who loved to instruct and pontificate. The presence of his nephews in town gave him a ready-made audience.

In 1920, well past the first flush of youth, my great-aunt Elizabeth had finally found an acceptable suitor in Charlie. Whether from the point of view of family background, physical appearance, or personality types, it was a clear case of the attraction of opposites. Charlie was the pampered only son of an assimilated Debrecen family whose lack of Jewish observance Yakab had overlooked only because of his delight that frivolous Elizabeth was finally serious about a man. Tall and dark, Charlie cut a handsome figure next to his dun sparrow of a bride. Yet they made excellent foils for one another: she looked up to him for his bookishness and his string of war decorations, while her shrewd intelligence and efficiency would stand them in good stead when it became clear that Charlie had no head for business.

It took a decade for him to realize that he was not cut out to practise law, although he had graduated with honours from law school. Elizabeth, on the other hand, had considerable business acumen and launched several successful cottage industries. Eventually Charlie found a niche as a salaried bank official, while Elizabeth in turn ran a cooking school, a lingerie salon, and a boarding house. They were never well off, yet she managed to graft a patina of affluence onto their straitened circumstances. Her one pregnancy drew the couple especially close. She almost died giving birth to twins by Caesarean section in 1921. One baby was stillborn; she and Charlie doted upon Aggie, the surviving child.

When her big cousins began attending the academy in Debrecen, Aggie Békés was a mop-headed, precocious toddler. As she grew to lanky childhood, a warm friendship developed between her and Gusti and Feri. The Békéses' modest flat at 61 Piac Street was much too small for boarders even had Elizabeth kept a kosher home, so she found lodgings for her nephews in her apartment building with a certain Mrs Blasz, the widow of a rabbi. Despite the boys' studious habits, there were many opportunities for them to pop downstairs to gossip with Elizabeth, be quizzed by Charlie, or tease the little cousin with the huge brown eyes. In particular, Aggie and Feri developed a special bond as she matured. She grew into a bright, ambitious girl who had inherited her father's bold features, stature, and love of culture, and wedded them to her mother's enterprising nature. As an only child, she was fond of adult company. She and Feri became mutual confidantes.

Feri would confide in her the details of his long string of love affairs; Aggie in turn told him about her academic dreams and struggles. Whereas her mother's ambitions for higher studies had been frustrated by an obstreperous parent, Aggie's path to university would be blocked by a discriminatory educational system. Eventually it was her father's plodding research that found a loophole by which she managed to squeeze into university in 1940. In one of the last letters written from the Rákóczi Estate in April 1944, my grandfather would refer to her as "the pride of the whole Family." The first of its women to attend university, she received her doctorate in English and Hungarian comparative literature wearing a Jewish star, two weeks after the arrival of Uncle Kálmán's congratulatory letter, two days before moving into Debrecen's ghetto.

Directly across Piac Street from the Békéses' narrow-faced greystone apartment building, across a double row of acacias edging the sidewalk and the steel tracks along which yellow streetcars rattled the length of town, stood the bungalow of Solomon Ullmann, Debrecen's largest wholesale grocer and the husband of Kálmán's sister Toni.

At the end of the winter of 1925, as the vendors of snowdrops and violets began to supplant those hawking roast chestnuts and baked pumpkin along Piac Street, as the bitter winds sweeping off the plain softened to breezes aromatic with the promise of acacia and lilac blossoms, Gusti and Feri Weinberger's inconsequential stock was rising at the academy. Several times a week one or both young men might be spotted along the Korzo, strolling among the well-heeled youth of Debrecen.

The Korzo was the elegant promenade along Piac Street's west side which began at the Casino on the corner of Kossuth Street and ended almost exactly at Solomon Ullmann's house. Here on sunny Saturday and Sunday afternoons and balmy spring evenings, Gusti and Feri Weinberger, a pair of studious grinds, might be observed in the company of a willowy, beautiful girl. Envious-eyed *bajtársok* sauntering on the steps of the Casino or escorting other young women craned their necks to ogle the progress of the two brothers up and down the street. Who was the girl with the deep-set eyes and full mouth, long hair cunningly arranged under a saucy hat? How had those two finagled an introduction to her? And which of the two did she actually favour with her affections?

Gusti and Feri were not about to divulge that the leggy ash blonde who swept so alluringly up and down the Korzo in their company was their cousin Ilush, daughter of Toni and Solomon Ullmann. Both brothers were thoroughly besotted with Ilush of the enigmatic smile and keen intelligence, the same Ilush who had once brightened their Piricse exile. A couple of years older than the Weinberger boys, she was equally fond of both. They were a welcome respite from the string of admirers who besieged her in person and through the intermediary of marriage brokers. Within a year her parents would choose a wealthy Belgian diamond merchant who would take her away first to Antwerp, and then to New York. In the meantime, her cousins squired her along the Korzo, fancied themselves in love, and basked in the reflected glory of her company.

For the first time since the petty jealousies of childhood, a wedge entered the relationship between the two brothers. They were inordinately close, twins in all but chronological age, who formed a tight unit that shut out everyone including Paul, the youngest brother. They were united by an almost telepathic understanding – often a shared glance sufficed instead of words, whether they were in the farm's schoolroom working at identical sums, struggling together for acceptance at the academy, managing the estate in partnership, or serving side by side as forced-labour soldiers in Ukraine.

As they grew older, they even seemed to look alike. In the last picture taken of them together in 1941, this impression is reinforced by the military uniform they both wore. The identical peaked caps, army fatigues, and round wire-rimmed glasses imposed an illusion of uniformity on two patently dissimilar faces. For they were not nearly so alike as my father was fond of recalling, either in appearance or personality. In the Twenties when they were both chasing after Ilush Ullmann, only Gusti wore the round goggles that later Feri also adopted. Without the glasses, the surface similarity disappeared. True, both were of the same medium height and build, my father not yet having assumed his later rotundity. They also had similar colouring and heart-shaped high foreheads carved out by prominent widows' peaks. But otherwise there was little resemblance. Gusti had the round, full-lipped face of a bespectacled cherub with outsize ears. Only one of his snapshots of this period captures his benevolent smile and sweetly naive nature; usually in these academy shots he frowns stolidly, affecting a Napoleonic stance, his arm self-consciously tucked behind his lapel. Feri is more poised before the camera and before the world at large. With his arched eyebrows, high cheekbones, sardonic smile, and thick chestnut hair, he cuts a dashing and worldly figure next to his ingenuous older brother.

"When I saw how much Feri cared about Ilush, I withdrew my suit" was the quaint way in which my father summed up his first disappointment in love. Nearly a decade later, another girl of beauty and charm powerfully attracted both brothers, and again Gusti felt bound to leave the field clear. A certain passivity underlay both withdrawals, a passivity perhaps attributable to his six long years of illness.

Only one academy friend was privy to Gusti's delicate confidences about Ilush, as he was similarly privy to tales of Feri's many amorous adventures. In a later incarnation he would be my "Uncle" Siggie, one of my father's three intimate friends from the academy days. Uncle Siggie was the rake, Uncle László the sage, Uncle Willie the mystic. László had been Paul's best friend at the academy. Siggie and Willie were slightly older than Gusti and Feri. After graduation the six young men kept in touch, but the full flowering of adult friendship would unite only four of them. After the Holocaust, Siggie, Willie and László drew almost as close as brothers around my father, trying to cushion for each other the terrible losses they had all suffered.

In their student days it had been with Willie that Gusti and Feri shared their first religious doubts. An ardent Jew and indefatigable community worker even as a youth, Willie's religious life embraced eclectic principles. Though Gusti and Feri had begun to be irritated by the many restrictions of orthodoxy, they were still shocked when Willie announced he was as comfortable praying in a church as *davening* in *shul*. Already dabbling in spiritualism in Debrecen, he spoke passionately about the contacts he had made with "the other side" and the séances he attended. The brothers were unswayed by these reports, but their regard for Willie's intellect and liberalism encouraged them to question the tenets of their own faith, even as they continued to endure Mrs Blasz's kosher but unappetizing dishes.

In middle and old age when I knew him, Siggie was a handsome man, the picture of a sparely built aristocrat with a proud aquiline nose and splendid blue eyes. Yet in his youth he had been positively homely, skinny and awkward, with gangly limbs and a shock of dark hair that fell over his brow. Yet despite his looks he was irresistible to women, to the envy of both his friends and foes.

That envy was still an element in his friendship with László Vincze sixty years later. "I have *never* been able to understand Siggie's magnetism to women," shrugged the eighty-year-old "little Yorkshire," his face both baffled and wistful. "Whenever Sig entered a room, the whole scene seemed to *ignite,* as if by magic. In a bank, or a post office, or a ball, the most beautiful women were completely bowled over when he appeared."

Siggie was generous about sharing his secret with his friends. He interspersed tales of conquests with advice to the less fortunate. "Find something to compliment about a woman – just make sure it's *true*. If she's plain, find the one thing about her that's exceptional – her fingernails! her hair! It's really quite simple." But it never worked for the others in the way he prescribed. For them it was a question of technique, for him something elemental. Siggie loved women, literally could not live without them. It was this vulnerable dependency more than the flawless manners, the well-cut clothes, and the air of urbanity that accounted for his magnetism.

The son of a landowner and, at twenty-four, older than his class-mates, he had applied to the academy for pragmatic reasons, to take advantage of a recently passed law that exempted the estates of college-trained farmers from a measure of compulsory land-division. When he entered the academy, he already had considerable farming experience behind him and called himself "an old man." He also took his studies more lightly than the Weinberger brothers who, straight out of secondary school, treated every word uttered by their professors as sacred and gave equal weight to each subject, whether it was likely to be of use to them or not. Siggie instead partook of the varied social life of the big city: in the company of one attractive woman or another (generally all were married), he attended balls, concerts, *jours fixés*, the theatre.

Consequently, as spring began to hint of summer, Siggie's thoughts began to turn to catching up on a year's worth of lectures. And so it was originally for Siggie's benefit that Gusti's and Feri's "Saturday morning lecture tours" came into being.

There were compulsory Saturday morning classes at the academy, a fact of life difficult to come to terms with for observant Jews. The campus lay nine kilometres from the centre of town where most of the Jewish students lived. It was a journey of no consequence when made by public transport; students who took their meals at the kosher cafeteria in town made the trip several times a day. The problem was Saturday, when travel by moving vehicle is prohibited because of the Sabbath. Of the score or so of Jewish boys at the academy, only my father and my uncle still respected this prohibition. Every Saturday morning through the four seasons, rain, sleet, or snow notwithstanding, they trekked across town and through the forest, sat through lectures without taking notes (writing being also forbidden), and once again trudged back to town for a late mid-day meal at the Ullmanns.

As mild spring mornings became milder, Siggie Morvay was faced with the grim reality that *his* academic performance might bar him from a return to the academy the following year. Reluctantly he accepted Gusti's suggestion that he join them for the walk on Saturday mornings for some much-needed tutoring. Thus Saturday mornings began to find him – having detached the arms of some woman or other from his neck – pacing in front of 61 Piac Street, waiting for the weekly walking tutorial which he hoped would obtain him a passing grade.

Upstairs on the third-floor walkway overlooking a rectangular inner courtyard, the two brothers tipped their hats good-bye to a bewigged Mrs Blasz before descending the glassed staircase two steps at a time, passing on the ground floor a door that bore the engraved motto "Dr Charles Békés, Lawyer." Outside, they exuberantly clapped Siggie across the shoulders and began to quiz him about the adventures of the previous night before tackling the academic subjects that were the reason for his company.

Their progress along Piac Street towards the Great Forest took them past many of the city's landmarks. The street well deserved its name, which meant "market." On its east side, sedate bourgeois apartment buildings housed large stores on their ground floors. The city's best shops were located along this stretch of boulevard, including the wholesale and retail emporium of Solomon Ullmann. Set between the prosperous greystone buildings were the smaller-scaled stucco homes of an earlier era in gay rainbow shades. From the balcony of a forget-me-not blue dwelling at Széchenyi Street, Louis Kossuth had roused Debrecen's populace with his stirring vision of freedom in 1849. Across the street loomed the rococo First Savings Bank bedecked with sculpted balconies; on its first floor the Debrecen Casino attracted the patronage of many a student of the academy. Next was the neo-classical city hall with its massive columns.

These showy buildings dwarfed the shadowed, winding side streets arising from the east side of Piac Street. Simonffy and Crown Prince Jozsef Streets were the two most concentrated locales of Debrecen's Jewish community. Paneth's kosher salami *bodega* did a brisk business in tongues, cold cuts, and smoked meats to a clientele as often gentile as Jewish. Should they happen to glance to their left, the Saturday-morning walking tour might catch a glimpse of the Jewish *gimnázium*, the orthodox synagogue and congregational centre along

144

Crown Prince Jozsef Street. They would have to possess the gift of clairvoyance or singularly dark imagination, however, to catch a glimpse of the future of both streets, which, twenty years later, would formally be declared part of Debrecen's ghetto. In the spring of 1944, 10,000 Jews would be squeezed into these narrow houses and community institutions prior to deportation from their town.

Up ahead stood the grand, grey-turreted Golden Bull Hotel with elegant shops facing the street and a spacious coffee-house where Jewish and gentile smart society mingled on equal terms, although at separate tables. Here Charlie Békés would beam with pride some four years in the future as Debrecen's socialites honoured a visiting English nobleman at a glittering banquet. The son of a London publishing magnate, Viscount Harmsworth reaped the adulation of Hungary after his father published an article in the *Daily Mail* denouncing the Treaty of Trianon and calling for the return to Hungary of part of the territory and population ceded by the peace treaty. In its gratitude, Debrecen's Chamber of Commerce commissioned Elizabeth Békés, renowned for her culinary skills, to produce an appropriate dish for the illustrious visitor.

Elizabeth obliged with a map of Hungary fashioned of *paté de foie gras* and coloured aspic. Its rivers flowed in bluc, its original boundaries were marked in red, and the borders of Rump Hungary in black. No one appreciated the English visitor's wit more than did Charlie Békés. Asked whether he wished to sample the Transylvanian or Czech parts of the delicacy, the English lord replied, "I'd like to eat from all of it because I wish to devour all of Hungary's enemies."

But now the trio of Saturday morning scholars reached Debrecen's most famous landmark, the monumental twin-spired Great Church on Calvin Square, three of its nine clocks stamping its front like features on a stern face. Fourteen years hence, Gusti Weinberger would tear as if pursued by demons out of a birthing clinic up the street, the clanging of streetcars insufficient to drown out in his skull the shrieks of his labouring wife. Tears coursing down his face, he would embrace the trunk of a massive oak in the park by the Great Church, seeking solace from nature against the cruelty of birth as his first daughter made her way into the world.

But now, his future unwritten, he veered with his brother and friend to the right towards the residential part of the city where gracious villas alternated with schools, hospitals, and university departments. These streets already held the astringent scent of pine from a park tamed out of the Great Forest marking the city's boundary. Children's shrill cries and the songs of revellers in the nearby Vigadó restaurant floated on the strains of Gypsy music into the woods.

The road now led arrow straight through six kilometres of virgin oak, olive, willow, and pine. It took an hour's brisk march to reach the academy. But then, the curriculum was also long and Siggie Morvay had much to make up for in chemistry and technology, botany and physics, agro-geology and gardening. At last they reached the clearing where sunlight once more warmed their faces and the model farm lay revealed with its orderly fields of grain and tobacco, meticulously pruned orchards, and pristine barns and stables. Past these was the administration building with its lecture halls, where it seemed that of late the atmosphere towards them had somehow assumed an aspect as balmy as the weather.

As the school year approached its end, Siggie Morvay was not the only first-year student to feel at an academic loss. Anti-Semitic outrages no longer livened dull classes, partly because of Ruffy-Varga's disciplinary action, partly because picking on Jews was a mid-year sport before the spectre of final exams roused indifferent scholars. One Saturday morning as the brothers emerged through the iron gate of 61 Piac Street, a classmate who had laughed most heartily when the lit cigarette burned Feri Weinberger's neck stood outside their apartment, textbook in hand.

"Hello, boys," he greeted them with a sanguine smile. "I wonder ... Could you explain something to me that isn't entirely clear?" His fingers rifled through the pages of the book, his eyes avoided contact.

"By all means," answered Feri after a short pause. "Absolutely. Except we're in a bit of a hurry now. Did you know that we Jews don't take the tram on Saturday? No? Well, that's the way it is, so we have to really step on it to make it to class."

"But if you'd care to join us on foot," Gusti added, "we'll explain whatever you like."

The young man fell in step, asking hesitant questions that revealed a foggy grasp of the subject. He was only the first of several such disciples. Each subsequent Saturday until the end of term, Gusti, Feri, and Siggie were joined by an ever-increasing contingent of *bajtársok*, until Charlie Békés, who had once studied at the Piarist *gimnázium* up the street, quipped that his nephews resembled a couple of priests expounding the doctrine to a following of seminarians as they strolled across town.

Later that spring Siggie received the first of many invitations issued by Ilona and Kálmán to their sons' friends to come stay at the Rákóczi Estate. Recalling for me his first stay in 1925, the old Don Juan lowered his voice to a whisper of complicity.

"When I stayed at the Rákóczi Estate," he arched a graceful white eyebrow speculatively, "I had the opportunity of meeting *Anny Schutz*. In person." And then he recounted for me my father's would-be romance with the Austrian governess of his uncle Zoltán's children.

"She was very beautiful," Siggie said in the manner of the very old, his eyes gazing past me into regions fathomable only to himself. "I see her before me now. I even recall that she said she lived in Johann Strauss Street in Vienna ... Very beautiful. Golden hair, large dark blue eyes, like a china doll."

Zoltán and Gréti had recently moved back home from Transylvania and taken up residence in the former bailiff's house which had served as the synagogue in Yakab's time. Anny Schutz was the first of a long line of governesses for their two children, for Gréti was so exacting and temperamental that staff rarely lasted. Unlike those who followed in her footsteps, Anny was a real looker, with the varnish of Vienna on her clothes and flirtatious manner. After Anny, Gréti's choice of the plainest women for her household became proverbial.

Unknown to Gusti who came home only on holidays, the young governess was simultaneously the mistress of two of his bachelor uncles. These attachments, however, did not prevent her from allowing the naive newcomer to drive her about the estate and village, or to plant a few fervent kisses on her lips. Within short order of having relinquished his chaste, cousinly pursuit of Ilush Ullmann, nineteen-year-old Gusti fell in love with the freewheeling Anny. He resolved to marry her.

Anny never had a chance to respond to his proposal, so that her feelings in the matter remain in the shadow. Generally regarded as a species of intellectual proletariat, governesses held a nebulous social position midway between their employers and domestic servants. To an opportunistic young woman in such a situation, a proposal from the wealthy nephew of her employers might have been tempting even if she didn't care a jot for him. But even when head over heels in love, my father was first and foremost a good child. He could not avow his honourable intentions to Anny before asking for his father's permission. Kálmán's reaction was swift and predictable. At nineteen Gusti was too young to marry, even if the girl were not a gentile of blemished virtue. Kálmán bluntly informed his son of Anny's other liaisons.

The lesson of Gusti's bitter disillusionment was as long lasting as anything he learned that year. For the next two decades he would apply the sexual double standard as strictly as if it were defined in some Talmudic ruling. Until he married, physical love remained the domain of the office building or tobacco-bunching shed with farm girls and chambermaids. And he would be most cautious in his selection of a wife. When he finally brought himself to a decision more than ten years after Anny Schutz had left Vaja, his choice was as appropriate as if it had been arranged by a marriage broker. He picked a woman of exemplary character and breeding, Mancika Mandula, a woman he would care for and esteem for all eternity, without being in love with her for one moment.

Only the cataclysm of the war and the total devastation of his personal life shook the lesson of Anny Schutz out of my father. At forty, when he had lost everything and given up on everything, he fell in love with the blind rush of romance that he had barely tasted as a young man. He would never quite understand how the ability to love again was restored to him nor why a startlingly beautiful woman who looked young enough to be his daughter should reciprocate his feelings. Her name was Anikó (it would take him years to stop calling her "Anny"), a child-woman with coal-black hair tumbling to her shoulders and the long, slender legs of a gazelle. My mother.

Apprenticeship in Varsány

A good farmer eats from the bread of many ovens.
Hungarian Proverb

Lifting aside batiste curtains, Gusti Weinberger, recent graduate *cum laude* of the Debrecen Academy, smiled to himself, thinking he could well have been on a landed estate almost anywhere in Europe. Rose bushes lined walks beneath the high windows of the dining room; beyond the terrace, spiky yuccas pointed skywards in the landscaped grounds. Everywhere rows of hedges and tidy fences screened the ivy-clad manor house from the nearby stables, barns, and industrial buildings.

Gusti was in fact not far from home at all, but a mere twenty kilometres from Vaja in Nagyvarsány (Varsány for short, in family parlance). And he was pinching himself at his good fortune, for he was not here at the largest and wealthiest farm in the extended family as a weekend guest of his mother's cousins, the Rochlitzes, but on a long-term working stay. Back home, his new diploma notwithstanding, his father and uncles had not seen fit to trust him with any real responsibility in the family business; his suggestions at meetings had met with chilly silence. So when the position of bookkeeper had suddenly opened up at Varsány, he had jumped at it. It was an ideal way of soaking up practical experience: when he returned home in due course, he would be armed with practice to match his theoretical knowledge. At future discussions at home with his elders, he hoped one day to stand his own in the fray.

The two years Gusti spent on uncle Zolka Rochlitz's estate in Varsány were formative ones. He hero-worshipped Zolka, admired Zolka's wife, Yanchika, and doted on their two small children, Zsuzsi and Péter. He felt privileged to be received as an intimate among the best-educated, most progressive, and richest branch of the clan, where the winds that blew the sand about were not of orthodoxy but of freethinking rationalism, freemasonry, and feminism.

My father would often say in his postwar life that, next to School-master Sas, Uncle Zolka was the smartest man he had ever known and the one from whom he had learned the most. This learning was not restricted to farming, for Zolka also exerted a powerful moral and secular influence on an impressionable young man. In 1928 when Gusti arrived in Varsány, he was twenty-two to Zolka's forty-five (he called him "Uncle" without similarly calling Yanchika, who was only thirty, "Aunt"). Head cocked in deference, my father tagged by his side making the rounds of the estate. Varsány was the biggest agricultural enterprise in the whole family, "a regular industrial establishment," as my father would later say. It consisted of two full-fledged farmsteads connected by a private horse-drawn train, a distillery, oil factory, and generator on site, and fields stretching into the territory of five villages.

Although Gusti had learned the rudiments of bookkeeping at the academy, Zolka retrained him to his own exacting standards, thereby enabling Gusti to make a living in his Canadian life more than thirty years later. When we arrived in Montreal in 1959, my father began working in earnest as a bookkeeper. For the next twenty years, this would be his livelihood, a far more important skill than he had deemed it to be during the old apprenticeship.

In fact, keeping the books was a mere pretext for his presence in Varsány. Why he was really there was to see how things were done elsewhere than at home. And, as record-keeper and favoured junior cousin, he was ideally situated to learn the ins-and-outs of running a big estate. Uncle Zolka, who was expansive by nature – what we would today call "a good communicator" – made an ideal teacher. Skilled with his hands and with an excellent head for mathematics, his first love had been engineering, but the early death of his father had pushed him into the family business of farming. His precision was stamped all over the estate, which ran with the exactitude of a Swiss watch. At a time when electricity was rare in Szabolcs County, even its pigsties were electrically lit. Each field was itemized in my father's books by name, area, the crop with which it had been planted, and its yield. As pig-fattening was the estate's chief focus, swine were likewise listed by herd name, species, and other variables.

A legacy of Gusti's Varsány apprenticeship was the subsequent introduction of pig-breeding and fattening – one of Szabolcs County's most lucrative agricultural specialties – at home. The biblical proscription against the eating of pork by Jews applied by extension to pig farming, and Kálmán and Ilona recoiled from even the hint of such an undertaking. But when Kálmán retired from active farming in the mid-Thirties, Gusti and his brothers would purchase several herds which they fattened and bred to advantage.

Gusti's conversion to the benefits of pig-raising was emblematic of a larger conversion he underwent during his Varsány stay. His parents' continuing concern about his observance of the dietary laws had not let up despite his maturing years. As in Debrecen, he had to board apart from his religiously lapsed relatives. Yanchika's kitchen could pass muster no more than did Elizabeth's in Debrecen, and Gusti took his meals and lived in the home of the estate's unimpeachably kosher head distiller.

But the disaffection with orthodoxy, to which he had barely given name in Debrecen, was now emboldened by the example of the Rochlitzes. After all, Uncle Zolka's religious upbringing has been equally strict as Gusti's. And Uncle Zolka, for all his being a freethinker and a Mason, never denied his Jewishness and took considerable pains not to offend the sensibilities of other Jews. Though he did not keep the Sabbath or attend synagogue, he never set foot in a moving vehicle on a holy day for fear of shaming his people. Within his household, however, Zolka's rules were very much of his own making. A tree in the living room was a fixture at Christmas once Helga, Zsuzsi's and Péter's governess, arrived from Vienna – not because Helga demanded it, but because Zolka pronounced that "someone so far from home ought to be able to celebrate her holiday the way it's meant to be." Hung in Hungarian style with flaming candles, angel hair, and candies wrapped in silver paper, the tree became a treasured Rochlitz tradition long after Helga's departure.

Not even a pretence of keeping the dietary laws was made in the kitchen with its larder hung with home-cured bacons, hams, and sausages. Zolka would pointedly remind his young cousin at mealtimes of his parents' desire that he eat at the distiller's. For several months Gusti reluctantly left Zolka's side at mid-day, although he would much rather have stayed to eat with the family. Finally, he made a formal renunciation of orthodoxy to his cousin. "I really see no necessity for binding myself to archaic rules established for reasons that have long ago lost any validity they might have had," he declared pompously, but Zolka nodded a brisk approval.

"You are certainly old enough to make an independent decision about religion," the older man replied. "It's hardly incumbent on me to enforce the rules of your parents against your adult will." And so Gusti's relations with the Rochlitzes grew even closer, as he took his place among the three generations who gathered at the dining-room table. At its head sat "Klara Mama," Yanchika's mother, a short, dark woman with a shapeless body, who always wore a blue enamel brooch on her breast with the gilded word "Pax" proclaiming her political views. Pacifism ran high in the Rochlitz family, and for good reason.

At the age of thirty-two, Zolka had sustained a tragic and ironic accident. Encamped in a forest trench one moonless night during World War I, his regiment had been beset by fellow Hungarian troops who mistook them for the enemy and jumped upon them with open bayonets. In seconds Zolka's right eye had been gouged out. Years later, Gusti would note on his tours of the Varsány estate by Zolka's side that his uncle saw more with the piercing blue gaze of one eye than most people did with two. But the loss of that eye left not only an empty socket and a legacy of murderous headaches; it triggered a crisis in Zolka which only his marriage, eight years after the accident, had begun to heal.

By the time Gusti knew him well, Uncle Zolka talked rarely about the depression into which the injury had plunged him. But, as outgoing and gregarious as he was by nature, he had lost interest in everything. Convinced that no woman could possibly find him attractive again, he had vowed never to marry.

It was his oldest sister, Gisela, a widow then in her forties, who set out to prove him wrong. Gisela was the family's most commanding female. An author, feminist, and philanthropist, she was bossy, stubborn, formidably intelligent, and an inveterate meddler. After hearing Zolka declare his intention of remaining single, she determined to find him a wife. In 1923, she set up an Italian holiday for herself and Zolka, taking along as guide a well-travelled young bluestocking teacher from Budapest, the niece of the founder of Hungary's feminist movement. Marriage was as far from the intentions of Yanchika Kozma as it was from Zolka's mournful withdrawal from life. But against the romantic backdrop of Venice, Gisela looked on benignly as Zolka shed his depression and Yanchika's professionalism gradually thawed. By the end of the holiday, the match was a foregone conclusion; the wedding took place a few months later.

Two children followed in quick succession. Both were delivered in Budapest by "Doktoressa" Sarolta Steinberger, the first woman to practise medicine in Hungary, part of the coterie of Hungarian feminists to which both Gisela and Yanchika belonged.

My father loved Yanchika every bit as much as he loved Uncle Zolka. Quiet as Zolka was garrulous, she was self-contained without being self-effacing. He liked the way she held her own in the discussions at the table and stood up to Zolka when he erupted into one of his rages which came on as quickly as summer squalls. Yanchika would interrupt these outbursts with quiet intensity. "Don't yell, Zolka, please don't shout."

Zolka's favourite whipping boys were the wandering Jewish scholars who met such a welcome at the Rákóczi Estate. Often a well-meaning phone call from Kálmán commending a certain Hasid as a candidate for Zolka's philanthropy would result in quite the opposite effect than the one my grandfather had intended. By the time the hapless man arrived in Varsány, Zolka would have worked himself into a state of outrage, ready to deliver himself of a tirade the Hasid would not soon forget.

"Every man should do an honest day's work," Zolka thundered, "and I don't mean poring over useless texts to determine the precise meaning of a word that hasn't been used in speech for a thousand years. That's not work, that's a pastime!" He would quiz the unfortunate man on the number of his children (invariably large) and denounce him witheringly for living off the labours of his wife who not only had to bear and nurture the brood but must support the whole family.

Witnessing these diatribes, my father would have cause to reflect on both his own father's support of impoverished Hasids and Zolka's point of view. The concern of his uncle for the Hasid's wife was of a piece with the Rochlitz household's general feminism. My father, who grew up in a home where men's and women's roles were markedly separate, became an egalitarian husband long before his economic circumstances made that necessary and certainly well before that was a societal norm. Even in his first marriage he was a notably hands-on father, sharing in the care of his little girl out of principle and love.

Child-rearing among the Rochlitzes was also something out of the ordinary. In a household where there was no shortage of servants, the two tots made their own beds and polished their shoes as soon as they were big enough to fold a blanket and wield a brush. Zsuzsi and Péter were much younger than Gusti – by eighteen and twenty years respectively – but my father loved children, and he dandled them on his knee when they were small and took interest in them in a doting, avuncular way during their adolescence when the Varsány apprenticeship was long behind him.

After the war, Gusti and Zsuzsi, each the sole survivor of their large families, grew as close as brother and sister – first in Budapest and later in Canada, after we settled in Montreal and Zsuzsi and her daughter in Toronto. Our families visited back and forth; on Sunday mornings my father and Aunt Zsuzsi conducted lengthy tête-à-têtes by telephone while my mother, a bit jealous of their intimacy, huffed as the long-distance minutes ticked by.

But for all their closeness, Gusti and Zsuzsi could never bring themselves to share their respective wartime experiences. Zsuzsi and her family were taken to Auschwitz on the same train as my father's family. Yet he never asked Zsuzsi about the details of that journey – or about that arrival.

On a cool day in early June 1944, a boxcar carrying thirty-four members of one large Hungarian-Jewish family pulled up at the selection platform of Auschwitz-Birkenau. Zolka's sister, Gisela, always the leader, was the first one ready to disembark. Now seventy, but still observant and commanding as ever, Gisela did not comment on the scene below her perch on the train step. But some sort of momentary glut on the platform gave her a chance to study the selection process taking place.

A tall, immaculately uniformed man standing at insouciant ease was pointing left or right with white-gloved hands. Gisela did not breathe a word of this, but with matching sang-froid called over her shoulder three times to Zsuzsi and Yanchika behind her.

"Yanchika, hold on to your daughter's hand."

"Yanchika, hold on to your daughter's hand."

"*Yanchika, hold on to your daughter's hand.*"

Yanchika looked much younger than her forty-seven years and passed as her daughter's sister when she held Zsuzsi's hand. Dr Mengele selected them both for work, sending them to the right. Among the men, Zsuzsi's brother, Péter, and my father's brother Paul were also ordered to the right. The rest of the huge family was despatched to the left and perished that day.

During the four and a half months that they spent together in Auschwitz, while Zsuzsi succumbed to illness and apathy, her mother kept her alive through force of will and loving ministration. The two were separated on October 7, 1944, the twenty-first anniversary of Yanchika's and Zolka's marriage. That day Zsuzsi was selected for shipment to Germany and Yanchika kept in Auschwitz. Zsuzsi tried to run after her mother, but the girls in her work gang held her down. The train that sped her to a German bomb factory, howling, she says, "like a calf taken from its mother," guaranteed no salvation, but remaining in Auschwitz meant almost certain death.

Of all the houses in the extended family, the gracefully proportioned manor which Zolka Rochlitz built for his bride and to which my father arrived in 1928 for his apprenticeship was the only one built to last. And last it has. Zolka, the engineer *manqué*, knew how construct something properly and had the means with which to do it. The house has withstood the neglect of the intervening decades to the extent of remaining recognizable today. Once remote from the village, it now stands at its heart, practically swallowed by corn fields and the boxy peasant dwellings which have sprung up around it. But it's a house of ghosts, used for almost nothing. In summertime, at least, the laughter of children echoes inside the cavernous rooms as small peasant girls play hide-and-seek in the abandoned chambers and by the kitchen's unfired open stove.

My father, third from left in knickerbocker pants and bow tie, learning to fatten pigs on uncle Zolka Rochlitz's estate.

The Rochlitz mansion, built by Zolka Rochlitz in 1923 for his bride, Yanchika. The three tiny figures at the table on the terrace are Yanchika and Zolka with baby Zsuzsi between them. Twenty years later, of thirty-four family members dispatched to Auschwitz in one cattle car, only Zsuzsi would return.

Zolka's sister Gisela and brother Béla tending grapevines on the Rochlitz Estate.

The Agricultural Academy of Debrecen where my father and his two brothers graduated with distinction. Taken in communist times, this picture shows the red star of the state emblem on the pediment.

Great-uncle Zoltán's and great-aunt Elizabeth's two families in front of
Zoltán's house on the Rákóczi Estate in the early 1930s. Left to right:
Zoltán's daughter Magda, Zoltán, his son Lacika, his wife Gréti (an avid
gardener, holding a bouquet), Aggie, Elizabeth, and Charlie Békés.

Family gathering in Zoltán and Gréti's garden in the early 1930s. Standing:
Feri, Zoltán, Mancika, Paul, Ferenc Székács, Kálmán, Gusti (in favoured
Napoleonic pose of his youth). Seated: Mancika's sister Ervzsébet, my
grandmother in a relaxed version of her wimple, with a few locks of hair
showing, and Gréti, raffish in leather jacket and cap.

In the garden at the Rákóczi Estate, August 19, 1936. The wedding of Paul (standing, with flower in his lapel) and Mary (beside him in white) that caused such consternation in the family and countryside.

My father, Gusti, with Mancika, his first wife, February 1937. The two wedding attendants, Mancika's niece and nephew, would perish a day before liberation in Austria.

Three generations. Standing: the three brothers, Paul, Feri, and Gusti. Seated: Mary (pregnant with Marika), my grandmother holding Évike, my grandfather, Mancika.

Gusti, Mancika, and my half-sister, Évike, aged three, by the glassed verandah on the Rákóczi Estate.

Évike, aged four, in the yard. Note in the background thatch-roofed stables and barns and the distillery chimney, the tallest landmark in the neighbourhood.

Évike and Marika, aged five, in white-rabbit winter garb, as they appeared in a picture on my bedroom wall in Budapest when I was their age.

Aggie Békés whom my grandfather referred to in his farewell letter to her parents in April 1944 as "the pride of the whole Family." Aggie would receive her doctorate in comparative literature from the University of Debrecen wearing a yellow star days before being forced into Debrecen's ghetto in May 1944. Here, in happier times, with Marika and Évike on the estate where she spent every summer vacation.

My grandfather Kálmán holds Évike on his lap; my grandmother Ilona holds my cousin Marika. In April 1944 Count László Vay, the aristocrat from whom the Weinbergers leased the estate, offered to hide Marika at his castle in Mohara. Had my uncle Paul agreed, she would almost certainly have been saved.

My mother, Anikó, in a snapshot similar to the one in which my father first saw her.

Our family shortly before our departure from Hungary in 1957.
I am on the far left.

Me, in front of No. 22 Nyár Street, Budapest 1995. "The Orthopaedic Institute of Dr Jenő Kopits": a tablet still marks the building where more than seventy years ago my father went for treatments to the surgeon who cured him of spinal tuberculosis.

The Rákóczi Estate railway station built by great-grandfather Yakab still stands at the foot of what was the old estate, apparently in use in 1983.

The state emblem of the Hungarian national education system tops a doorway at what used to be the Rákóczi Estate, 1983. When I returned three years later, lilacs had grown over this part of the ruins of the old farmhouse.

Working Days

On an exceptionally cold September morning in the early 1930s, veterinarian Ferenc Balla shared a compartment on the north-bound train out of Nyíregyháza with a farmer by the name of Grosz. The subject of the weather dominated their conversation. The temperature had dropped steeply overnight, endangering the bulk of the tobacco crop still standing in the fields.

As the train pulled into the Rákóczi Estate station, the vet observed that nowhere in the country would frost wreak greater havoc than here at Hungary's largest producer of tobacco. Grosz clucked assent, and both men peered out at the gradually lightening landscape as the train lurched forward. The tracks curved sharply to the north past the house and kitchen gardens, and the engine began gathering speed through fields densely planted with tobacco.

But there was more than tobacco in these fields. The two men gaped in surprise at the scene that met their eyes. Since the previous morning when a weather warning had gone out, draft horses and oxen had pulled wagons of dampened straw to the fields. Men, women, and children had spread it beneath the plants, and now at dawn, with the air at its coolest, were setting fire to the moist straw, then quickly extinguishing it in an attempt to stave off the frost. As the train sped up, the vet and farmer could just discern the performers of this strange rite: peasants crouched around barely smouldering fires, while Gusti and Feri Weinberger in white knickerbocker suits flitted nervously among them, thermometers clutched in hand.

"Doctor," nodded Grosz, an orthodox Jew with a reputation as a wag, "I guess *this* here tobacco isn't about to freeze! I'll bet you old Kálmán Weinberger's in his synagogue reciting psalms, sure as you're sitting opposite me ... And those two young whippersnappers in the field are up to some magic they picked up at the academy. Who'll say what saved the tobacco, his prayers or their tricks?"

Several years had passed since a crisis brought Gusti home from Varsány and Feri from the University of Budapest (where he had been working towards his doctorate), and since old Hersh K'danever had died, and in death finally bestowed on Kálmán the blessing that had long eluded him.

The decade since Yakab had left the lease of the Rákóczi Estate jointly to his three youngest sons and to his son-in-law Kálmán had begun with postwar runaway inflation and ended with the Great Depression. Economic uncertainty had scared the three youngest brothers out of the business, but had attracted Zoltán, whom Yakab had deliberately left out of the estate's management. It had seemed to the dying but vigilant Yakab that Zoltán's fortune was the most secure in the family. Zoltan's bride had brought with her as a dowry a substantial hotel in Transylvania, where the young couple had settled. It would have taken a more cynical parent than Yakab to predict that his snobbish, gentrified second son would quickly tire of innkeeping and pine for Vaja's horses, farm smells, and peasants to order about. In 1924 Zoltán liquidated the hotel and entered into partnership with Kálmán. Many years later he would comment ironically, "I came into the business with a fortune in hand and withdrew with nothing but a walking stick."

It did not take long for the friendship between the two brothers-in-law to sour. The first hurdle was an ambiguous relationship that began between Kálmán's teenaged son Paul and Gréti, Zoltán's attractive young wife, almost as soon as the couple moved to the estate. The partnership itself unfolded like some morality play about the perils of mixing family and business. No sooner was Zoltán ensconced on the estate than he began to miss the hurly-burly of town life and the thrill of turning a tight deal as much as he had earlier missed rusticity. He dabbled in shady deals on the side, dipping into common funds without Kálmán's knowledge. By the end of the decade Zoltán's losses and the stock-market crash had reduced the business to candidacy for the auctioneer's block. It was then that old Hersh K'danever died and left a fortune which – even when divided among his eight surviving children and with a double portion for Ernest as the oldest – would salvage Kálmán's affairs.

Overcome by shame, Kálmán blamed himself for excessive credulity as much as he blamed Zoltán. At fifty, he had suffered a crisis of confidence from which he would never completely recover; for the first time in his life, he leaned on his children. From now on he would view his sons, particularly the two oldest who had returned to help him take charge, as adult equals and professional superiors. Did they want to declare bankruptcy and start a new business with the inheritance? Or would they rather pay off the debts while maintaining the partnership with their uncle?

Recoiling from the prospect of bankruptcy, Gusti and Feri chose the latter course. Undeterred by the precedent of the blighted Piricse arrangements, Zoltán was demoted to the status of a junior partner with twenty-five per cent of shares. The legacy would pay off his debts. Armed with an arsenal of accounting skills acquired in Varsány, my father took over the books. It took months for him to untangle the mess as outstanding bills that Kálmán had no prior knowledge of continued pouring in.

The new partnership was born under a cloud and remained under one for the rest of its days. In the mid-Thirties the acreage of the estate was formally divided by an arbitrator in a futile attempt to resolve differences. Finally, at the outbreak of World War II, Zoltán gave up farming altogether and moved to Budapest. The firm then underwent its final reorganization. Paul, who had gone to Vienna to obtain his doctorate, returned home. Kálmán, long semi-retired, now took only an informed back seat in the management of the estate. Under the new name of Weinberger Brothers, the business operated at its most successful level since Yakab's death.

The compatibility and professionalism of the three young partners only partially accounted for this sudden spurt of prosperity after years of languishing profits. War once again favoured the agricultural sector. And, for the first time, the fact that the estate was leased and not owned became an advantage. Anti-Jewish legislation passed in the early 1940s led to the expropriation of land owned by Jews, but left many tenants untouched. While the Rochlitzes, for instance, were driven out of business, the Weinbergers thrived.

Feudalism was abolished in Hungary in 1848, yet, almost a century later, the labour and social organization of Nyírség farms was still by and large feudal. In the 1930s, the sickle and scythe and the horse-drawn plough continued to reign supreme in the region. More than 300 peasants crowded the whitewashed, straw-thatched mud hovels scattered around the estate, providing its work force. That number included married women and children who, although not officially employed "on the domain" (as the peasants called the estate), supplemented its labour force whenever needed. The adult males worked under a yearly contract called the *convention*, by which they received payment in agricultural produce, usually potatoes, flour, and bacon. In labour-intensive periods such as harvest or tobacco-stringing, additional hands from the village were hired either on a monetary or a similar "conventional" basis.

To the resident peasants the master owed customary services in addition to his contractual payments. He supplied them with a roof over their heads, a small garden for their private use, transportation for their children by cart to the village school, adjudication of their quarrels, and house calls from the family doctor in case of illness.

Yet the master automatically took far more than he owed or gave. An informal but very real version of *droit du seigneur* rendered the sexuality of young women his natural preserve. On the Rákóczi Estate, where two generations of men cast their questing eyes over the ranks of field and domestic servants, girls retained the prerogative of at least refusing these advances with impunity. On many other farms they did not.

The unmarried young men of the Weinberger family – who were addressed by the title "honourable young master" as opposed to "honourable master" after they married – lived in the office building, a primitive bachelor preserve separate from the main house, where they could carry on their liaisons without the explicit knowledge of their parents. While playing out their formal roles on the farm, master and servant might consort on many intimate levels. For instance, Gusti's one-time wet-nurse, Lizzie D., a robust peasant woman, had originally been named to this desirable posting in the manor house because, before her marriage, she had been Zoltán's mistress. When he became a partner in the firm, Zoltán always kept an eye out for her interests, promoting her husband first from field hand to foreman of the oxen workers and later to foreman of tobacco.

Tobacco was the mainstay of the Rákóczi Estate's diversified agriculture. Potato and grain farming, the production and refining of alcohol, cattle and swine breeding all played important roles in the successful reorganization of the family business in the Thirties. But tobacco was indisputably the estate's most lucrative crop. Like alcohol, it was a highly regulated state monopoly in interwar Hungary. The nature of this sensitive annual required careful handling and exact timing, and gave work the year round. Seeds had to planted in hotbeds in February, then transplanted to fields in late spring, just before the last of the so-called "Frosty Saints" on May 25. The plants matured until mid-August or early September (but no later than "Young Ladies' Day" on September 8) when, having reached just the right shade of ripe green, the broad leaves were broken off, loaded onto carts, and strung on ropes in airy barns to dry. In the dead of winter, after the tender leaves had softened, the strings were carried to the huge bunching house where they were graded by Yosef D., the tobacco foreman. Tied into bales according to category, they were finally driven to the tobacco exchange where revenue officers checked the grading, and the state took charge of the leaves.

Share-cropping accounted for 115 of the estate's 150 *holds* of tobacco fields. For a half share of the profits, twenty-three tobacco farmers were each allotted five *holds* of land to farm at their own expense, making free use of the farm's equipment and materials. The remaining thirty-five *holds* were farmed directly by gangs of peasants under the direction of the foreman. These workers, having no expenses, received only the *convention* as remuneration. Generally, share-cropping was more profitable than "conventional" farming, and peasants vied with each other to join the ranks of croppers.

Cultivation and sorting of tobacco was a highly social enterprise involving every member of the tobacco-farmer's family. After the leaves were harvested and taken to the five big barns, stringing went on amidst singing and much banter. Over the next few months the stored tobacco mellowed from green to yellow to brown. When it came time to sort and grade, the lighter the shade of brown, the more valuable was the leaf.

Though the young partners had no involvement in the supervision of stringing and grading that took place in the vast bunching house, they were drawn there by the singing of the pretty tobacco girls and the jolly atmosphere to which they contributed their own share of teasing as they made the rounds of the tables. There were no less than twenty-three of those tables, one for each farmer, at each of which sat four or five workers. Long strings of tobacco were brought in one by one from the five tobacco barns on winter mornings when it was still dark outside. Girls and boys worked by lamplight until eleven at night; they sang not only to while away the time but also to ward off sleep. The foreman circulated among the tables, making sure that roughened fingers did not mis-sort fragile leaves assigned to their category a leaf at a time. When a bale was large enough, the farmer carried it back to the barn where it would await shipment to the exchange.

In the summer of 1932, Kálmán was suddenly taken ill and underwent emergency surgery. Though in time no trace would remain of a thrombosis in his leg beyond the looser lacing of one ankle boot, his protracted convalescence prompted some intense personal stock-taking. He decided henceforth to give his sons free rein to run the farm, all the while keeping abreast of their most minute moves.

Gusti and Feri shared an amusing idiosyncrasy – they could not thrash out business matters without pacing. Each took a side of the long dining-room table and, as if controlled by some invisible puppet master, took measured steps in tandem. Of identical height and identically clad in white summer suits or grey winter breeches, they strode the length of the table and then reversed direction: on one side Gusti, bespectacled and slightly pigeon-toed, hands locked behind his back, on the other Feri, round-shouldered yet rakishly handsome, a cigarette dangling from his lips. And leaning against the tile stove in the corner of the room whether it was summer or winter ("supporting" it, the family joke ran), their father listened attentively, occasionally asking a question or offering an aside, but for the most part a mere observer.

Kálmán raised no objections when his sons began to tamper with age-old farming practices. The resistance came from the farm workers whose senior ranks Gusti and Feri frequently consulted for practical advice. When the young masters introduced some of the surveying

techniques they had studied at the academy, consolidating each tobacco farmer's plots in one location rather than the far-flung patches
that until then had equitably divided both rich and poor soils for
each man, those who had received inferior plots grumbled at the
unfairness of the new practice.

And when the brothers decided to introduce horse-drawn mechan-
ical hoers into fields traditionally hoed by hand, grumbling turned
to vociferous protest. The idea of horses tramping between the fragile
protruding tobacco leaves alarmed peasants trained from childhood
to bestow loving care on a fussy crop. They muttered under their
breaths at the first experimental hoeing when the distance between
rows was still wide. But at high season when the plants had grown
both tall and bushy, there was more than grumbling to be faced
by the horse teams when they arrived in the fields. Barring the path
of the hoeing machines stood ranks of tobacco women. Wringing
their hands and wailing loudly, they accosted the culprits responsible
for this outrage.

"Your honours mustn't!"

"Your honours'll ruin the tobaccey!"

"The horses'll trample the leaves, you'll see!"

"It's you who'll see," Gusti and Feri tried to placate them. "You'll
see what a fine job the horses will work for you." Amidst high-pitched
laments, the horses entered the lush fields and within a day accomplished a task that otherwise took a week.

The following year, the women approached Gusti after the first
spring rain that traditionally heralded the first hoeing.

"And when will it please your honour to send in the horses?"

The life of the estate revolved as much around the house on the
little hill as it did around the work of its fields. And the central
figure in that house in the years after Yakab's death was my grandmother Ilona. The entire family, including Kálmán and her siblings,
called her "Mama" – as its matriarch, she commanded enormous
respect. Within the household this was by dint of authority, among
her sisters and brothers because of seniority, and in the extended
family by sheer force of personality. Yet she herself was modest and
understated. A plump pigeon of a woman with the ever-present white

wimple over her thin brown hair, she defined herself as wife of Kálmán and mother of three sons. Devoted to the care of others, she was the heart of the farm and of the family.

Ilona's own heart beat in equal measure for her children and for her God. She signed all her letters to her sons "your passionately loving Mother." In those same letters she called her religious faith "convulsive." It was the shining sincerity of that faith that accorded her her unique clout in the extended family. Her intelligence and education might fall far short of a Gisela or a Yanchika Rochlitz, yet they doted on her. While the Rochlitzes regarded her obsession with heightened forms of observance as nonsensical, they honoured her piety as much as they loved her fondness for laughter and her encompassing thoughtfulness. She was a cherished guest whenever she visited Varsány, even though she insisted on bringing along her own food and cooking utensils.

At home, the spheres of Ilona's responsibility were the house, the garden, and the kitchens. She was assisted by a staff of four full-time domestic servants: a cook, chambermaid, washerwoman, and "weekly." The parade coachman and the night-watchman – who were, properly speaking, farmhands – also lent a hand in the house when their other chores allowed.

As befitted a household in which food played a paramount role, the cook was the mistress's second in command. In the 1930s two sisters, Blanche and Helen B., took turns in the post. Both cooked with delectable flair but neither could take the frenetic pace of the kitchen for more than a few months at a time.

In Blanche Ilona met the sole spiritual match of her life. Behind her back, Ilona's sons mocked Blanche's saintly ways as they would never have dared their mother's. Mistress and servant shared a dedication to a stringent observance of *kashruth*; Gusti's future father-in-law, a pillar of one of Hungary's largest orthodox congregations, would joke, "Tell your mother to send me any of her discarded *traif* dishes, they'll be kosher enough for me." A long line of Jewish girls had preceded Blanche to Vaja; after her arrival, only her sister ever replaced her.

Ilona owed this golden pair to Rezeda, the family's ancient match-maker. Rezeda had a flowing beard that reached his waist and a following of village urchins at his heels making great show of sniffing the air, a play upon his name, synonymous with that of a common wildflower. He was unctuous and insinuating in manner, and his claim that "you can sooner look into the sun than into her eyes, she's so blindingly beautiful," tended to wear thin after indiscriminate repetition. But he was a true professional, making meticulous notes on marriageable females over the age of puberty and keeping tabs on good Jewish families in the whole northeast of the country. In the early 1930s, while trying to interest Ilona's younger brothers and adult sons in accounts of matchless beauties, Rezeda learned of the need for a cook on the Rákóczi Estate. Making a show of consulting his notes, he observed, "There's a decent carpenter in Kisvárda, a very religious man. His father was a rabbi and he has many mouths to feed ... The two oldest girls ought to have married by now, but they've stuck. They're hard up enough to go into service."

These were grim times, the early Depression years, when qualified secondary-school teachers took jobs as governesses for Gréti Székács, and Blanche and Helen entered service in the house on the hillock. It meant an irredeemable social disgrace: women who accepted household employment in exchange for pay lost claim to belonging to the middle class. They sank into near chatteldom; even their relatives avoided public contact with them.

Vestiges of this stigma survived in communist Hungary through world upheavals, as I discovered when I met Blanche in Budapest in the 1980s. My parents had kept in touch with her over the years, looking her up each time they visited Hungary. Describing these encounters to us afterwards in Montreal, my father invariably raved about the old-time delicacies she had concocted for them. So much had happened in the intervening years that I assumed she was now more friend than faithful family retainer.

A chunky old woman with a nimbus of grey hair pulled the door of the basement apartment open and pressed me to her ample bosom. Her smoky eyes were opaque and lashless; her face, despite its great age, was smooth with benevolence. Before sitting me down, she took me on a tour of her tiny place to convince me that she lacked for nothing. She had been ill and moved with effort, yet everything gleamed in readiness for the approaching Sabbath. Her kitchen had room only for a two-burner range and a little white table covered with a cloth edged in Hebrew letters. Four brass candlesticks waited to be kindled at sundown, next to a prayer book open at the Sabbath benediction and two small, braided *barkeses* under a snowy cloth. Glowing with pride, the old woman opened up her kitchen cabinets to reveal sparkling glasses on shelves edged with lace runners.

Plying me with cherry cake, espresso, and fruit, Blanche lamented that she had had no chance to prepare fittingly for my coming. But she had important matters to impart to me, she whispered, and had saved her energy for that purpose. For a moment I wondered if she would confide in me a secret she had once divulged to my mother and that others had hinted at. But no – this serene, saintly woman (who had struggled through the war without once touching *traif* and who, even in Auschwitz, made a distinction between the Sabbath and weekdays by hauling loads on the holy day on one arm only), was not about to bare her soul to the granddaughter of her former employers.

Instead she would set the record straight for posterity. She had been no ordinary servant.

Taking quick, shallow breaths, she struggled to muster her forces for a long speech. "Your grandparents were such good people, I'm convinced they sit at the Almighty's right hand in heaven, at this moment ... They loved me like I was their own, and I loved them as my own parents. Even today I light *yahrzeit* candles for them two days after I light for my family because their train left for Auschwitz two days after ours. On *Shavuoth* our train left, and how it grieved your grandmother that I would travel on a holy day!

"People can't conceive how good they were. Your grandmother would give me presents, she would kiss my hand even! When something I made turned out especially well – don't get me wrong! everything was always good – but if something was extraordinary, she'd look for me in the kitchen and say, 'Let me kiss those little hands of yours, you're a wonder.'

"And I'd give her presents, too. I'd crochet runners and embroider tablecloths to give her. Because, you know," the opaque eyes suddenly sharpened, "I didn't *have* to cook. I was an expert seamstress. I could have sewed for my living! I'd never have cooked for them if they hadn't treated me like a member of the family."

There was an unexpected knock at the door, and Blanche's young neighbour popped in to give her the day's mail. For a moment the old woman seemed disconcerted, caught somehow between two incompatible truths. Then, with a warning look towards me lest I contradict her, she introduced me as her niece from Canada.

Until she was widowed, Blanche's sister Helen, who had married after the war, did not pick up the thread of acquaintanceship with my family lest her husband learn from us of her years of service at the Rákóczi Estate. Blanche, too, despite her insistence on her status as family intimate, was ashamed of her past.

The way the house and gardens of the Rákóczi Estate were designed underscored differences between master and servant. The dining room's high windows gave onto a dozen walnut trees and Ilona's flowerbeds and shrubs; the view from the servants' room was of an ice-pit, dung hill, and outhouse. A network of neat paths marked out by hedges led down to the train station for the family and its guests; a dusty trail where geese, ducks, turkeys, and chickens ranged untrammelled took peasants and servants to the same destination. At the back entrance to the house stood a shed where freshly killed poultry from the ritual slaughterer in the village waited in heaps to be plucked and cleaned. At the masters' entrance, an elegant terrace was furnished with wicker tables and chairs. But the cook and chambermaid who shared the servants' quarters had little time or energy to lavish on the view or to ponder questions of social justice. The chambermaid's sphere of work extended to the whole house, while the cook virtually lived in the kitchen.

The kitchen had originally been a vast room which Ilona, on her return to Vaja in the 1920s, divided into two compartments, one for dairy, the other for meat, "lest the cooking vapours mix." It was the site of a staggering amount of work. Seldom did fewer than twelve sit down for a meal in this house where business visitors had to be entertained during the week; on Sabbath and holidays so many extra mouths arrived that an additional table had to be set in the second dining room called the "tent," and some two dozen diners might present themselves at the family table. And this was a household without electricity or labour-saving devices, with wood and coal heating and only rudimentary running water, yet with elevated standards of cleanliness, comfort, and religious observance. Care was even taken of finicky taste preferences and digestive foibles, so that Kálmán's food came without onions, Ilona's without garlic and onions, while a third platter bore regularly prepared dishes for everyone else. One can begin to understand why, with these standards and variables, Blanche and Helen could work only for short periods at a time before needing to be spelled.

The two cooked and baked and dished up and planned menus, but were both too grand and too busy to do anything else. The "weekly" boy (in fact he worked by the *convention*, not by the week at all) set the fires and hauled in fruit and vegetables from the garden and meat from the ice-pit. He and the chambermaid washed the dishes, although in a pinch the mistress thought nothing of rolling up her sleeves and doing them herself. Ilona was no *grande dame* dispatching commands from the dining room; she had inherited her father's prodigious energy and the levels of her physical output often surpassed the servants'. She cleaned, dried dishes, planted, weeded, and hoed at the same time as she supervised the servants and kept a master plan in mind of their daily tasks.

If the cook was the mistress's right hand in the establishment, the chambermaid was her left. Up until the mid-Thirties, local peasant girls filled the post, although for reasons of security as the political storm clouds gathered, only Jewish domestics would be hired. Assisted only by the young "weekly" who gave a hand with the more daunting tasks (at night, for instance, everyone placed shoes and boots outside their bedroom doors and magically found polished footwear in the morning), the chambermaid was no less overworked than the cook.

By country standards, the Weinbergers were late risers. In the morning, before the breakfasters trooped in, the chambermaid had already finished with the dining room and the "tent," the first two of the dozen rooms she would attack each day. She dusted, swept, and washed down surfaces, in the summer throwing the wet rags to dry on the bed of petunias in the yard. In those days before vacuum cleaners, once a week she hauled the carpets out with the "weekly" to the carpet stand in the yard where she beat them with a cane, raising great clouds of dust.

Kálmán was the first of the family up, unbolting the iron cross bars on the double doors of the dining room which led to the outside world. Ilona and the boys put in an appearance by eight for the self-service breakfast of morning pastries which the chambermaid brought in. Blanche baked twice a week, with the main baking on Thursday night into Friday morning. The breakfast table was loaded on Fridays with raised and folded pastries, cheese and jam squares, crescents stuffed with braised grated cabbage, or cocoa, or cinnamon. Friday morning saw bread-baking of dozens of loaves for the week – white *challah* called *barkes* and a dark sourdough rye with caraway seeds. By mid-morning the *lángosh*, a delicious flat-bread, came out of the oven and was served cut in squares and swimming with butter.

Set for 7:30, the breakfast table could not be cleared until all the late risers had partaken of the meal some three hours later – a custom devised for the convenience of guests, not servants. Dinner was not served until two o'clock. Once again the chambermaid set the table, this time more elaborately, although in summer at least the meal was served in the less formal "tent." She then scrubbed her face and hands and slipped on a fresh apron to serve diners one by one from warmed serving platters in the French manner. The meal lasted until late afternoon and was followed by dish-washing which in turn gave way to preparations for a light evening meal. Supper seldom ended before nine o'clock, followed by at least an hour of clean-up.

The chambermaid's day was formally over at this point (although she might have further services to offer a young master in the office), but Blanche was left with one final task: the selection of the next day's menu with the mistress. Blanche cherished these evening exchanges by the tile stove in the dining room in winter, on the terrace in summer. She took joy in the fact that Ilona called her by the familiar "te" whereas she was more distant with Helen for whom she used the formal "maga." The number of geese to be sent to the slaughterer the next day, the choice of desserts depending on who was currently visiting (Ilona kept track of guests' favourites) were often mere excuses for the companionship which was Blanche's truest satisfaction in her job.

"I loved them both greatly, your grandparents," she told me half a century later, "but your grandmother was my soul mate. I loved her best of all."

Sometime during this decade the day arrived when Ilona's level of activity superseded her own record for prodigious output, when after the late-evening discourse with Blanche she continued working with a manic speed for which there seemed no external reason. Days and nights blended together; she might start dusting the dining room at midnight and be out weeding the salvia beds at dawn. Inevitably, there came the day too when the frantic busyness suddenly stopped. Ilona's body and will ground to a halt, and she sat in utter stillness in an armchair in the dining room, oblivious to the pall that her silence cast over the house. My father named these periods "the quiet times," and they became more marked and frequent in the mid-Thirties, causing increasing concern in household and family.

The house continued to run with precision during these periods, but with an uneasy sense of something lacking. The merry peals of laughter from the mistress were stilled. Nothing would tempt her to leave her chair, not even accounts of her flowers, usually a passionate source of interest. Blanche continued to come in at night to the dining room, day after day, in hope that the bout of silence had run its course this time and Ilona would greet her with a broad smile displaying her one vanity – her pearly teeth. But in response to the ritual question, "And what shall we have tomorrow, madam?" Ilona responded listlessly, without turning her head, "Oh, you know, Blanche ... Make a dinner."

Holidays

Despite the lavishness of their hospitality to business guests and to the poor, the Weinbergers liked best of all to socialize among themselves. On weekdays business visitors outnumbered the family at the table, but holidays were almost exclusively family affairs. On national holidays like King Saint Stephen Day, extended family such as the Rochlitzes would be invited. But on holy days the house on the hillock welcomed "immediate" family only, the children and grandchildren of Yakab and Karolina.

Of the religious holidays, Yom Kippur was the most solemn, Purim the most jolly, and Passover the most labour-intensive. Passover preparations invariably turned the household upside down; the build-up to the Day of Atonement almost as invariably turned the heads of the household inside out. The hours immediately before this most sombre of the festivals (when, it is believed, the Almighty decides upon the fate of every being for the year to come) were filled with tension, until a quarrel finally erupted between a testy Kálmán and an overwrought Ilona.

As the feast preceding the long fast must end before sundown, the family gathered around the table when the sun was still high in the sky. To signify a state of purity, Ilona wore white slippers over white stockings and put on a richly embroidered white silk kimono, a formal garment very distinct from her usual clothes. On her head, her trademark white wimple was on this day silk rather than batiste. During Yom Kippur prayers she draped her shoulders with an additional white-fringed shawl reminiscent of the *talles* worn by men. These ceremonial garments, like the white *kittel* worn by men on the Day of Atonement, she intended one day to wear before her Maker as her shroud.

"It's a *mitzvah* to eat heartily before Yom Kippur," Kálmán, himself dressed in an impeccable dark suit, urged the family gathered around the table. The first course always featured the *kappori* fowl. A vestige of the ancient animal sacrifice, this custom required a separate bird for each person – hen for woman, rooster for man, chicken for child – as a form of expiation. The day before Yom Kippur, everyone said a prayer during which they held the birds aloft, swinging them around three times, while the unfortunate creatures stared back with beady, terrified eyes and squawked vociferously.

"This is my expiation, this is my redemption. This bird will be killed, and I shall enter upon a long, happy, and peaceful life," went the prayer. But little Aggie Békés failed to see the connection as she held her chicken in the air, and sobbed at the thought that afterwards it would be taken to the ritual slaughterer. The adults tried to console her with the explanation, "This is the chicken's fate. It will be the one to die, instead of you."

At the festive table the *kappori* was supplemented by roast goose, cracklings, chopped liver, and beef – a variety of rich food that caused enormous thirst the next day when neither food nor drink could be partaken. Traditionally the menu also included tomato sauce and sweet carrots, and *barkes* dipped in honcy to symbolize a sweet year. Sponge cake and quince compote followed as Kálmán continued to press food upon the assembled company.

When the meal had been cleared away, all mourners lit candles in memory of the dead before the women kindled and blessed the holiday candles. Then came ceremonial good wishes for an easy fast, and the invocation "Let all that is good be brought about by prayer." The men then adjourned to the estate's synagogue and the women to an adjoining room for prayers. The voices of the men floated in from next door, but the women had their own leader, Gréti Székács, who, like Ilona herself, prayed with sustained concentration throughout the long holiday. Half a century later, Blanche told me that her most cherished reward for her back-breaking work in the kitchen was to pray alongside her mistress on the holidays and Sabbath.

That evening all the family, with the exception of Kálmán, retired early after services. Kálmán did not sleep on Yom Kippur, but stayed up all night reciting Psalms. He took the injunction for self-mortification further than anyone else by praying upright, never sitting down for even a moment, during the entire night and day. Garbed in his *kittel*, his prayer shawl almost totally covering his face, he faced the Ark – which also wore a festive robe of white for the occasion. On this long holy day, Schlosser was spelled in his cantorial duties by old Uncle Mordechai, who had been coming to the estate synagogue since Yakab's time. My father and his brothers, other family members, and visitors all drifted in and out of the synagogue, but at the front of the room, my grandfather swayed back and forth and beat his breast and succumbed to no distractions.

The ancient melodies were chanted, the litanies of sins repeated over and over, the petitions for mercy invoked, the Torah portions read. The long day eventually drew to a close. The younger worshippers peeked out to search for the first star which signalled the recitation of the concluding prayer. Finally, when it was quite dark outside, came the long blast of the ram's horn, the *shofar*, and the end of the holiday.

Purim, by contrast, was a merry carnival of practical jokes and epicurean feasting. Since the festival celebrates the foiling of Haman's plot to destroy the Jews of ancient Persia, in the light of Hitler's comparative success in doing away with the Jews of Europe, the holiday has been somewhat downgraded in the diaspora. But in the 1930s, the last decade before the Holocaust, it was still possible to celebrate Purim with heedless and wholehearted abandon.

The Purim meal began mid-afternoon and continued until dawn, but preparations for the holiday had begun weeks, sometimes months in advance. A Purim tradition consists in the sending of gifts, customarily of baked goods, although any household specialty may be substituted. Thus Purim preparations were two-pronged: the year's most lavish feast had to be assembled for the party at home at the same time as gifts of food were dispatched both to the scattered members of the extended family and the customary beneficiaries of its charity. In addition, a steady stream of beggars presented themselves at the door for this holiday synonymous with the act of giving.

At this time Blanche worked day and night. Extra slaughtering of poultry had to be organized, with several wagons of turkey and geese being sent for gifts to the poor. Trays upon trays of delicacies were baked for weeks without cease. Blanche kneaded the largest annual braided *barkes* – so long, she subsequently claimed, that it took up half the table. She sliced and poached enormous carp, and when the pieces had jelled, reassembled and decorated them; the fish, now with bunches of parsley stuffed in their gaping mouths, seemed larger than life.

Course followed rich course, to the accompaniment of Gypsy music – afterwards, the Gypsies too would have to be fed. Wine flowed freely and in the normally sedate household, wild dancing, outlandish costumes, and practical jokes were the order of the day. Menyush grabbed Blanche by the waist and whirled her around the room. Armin Schlosser, now the cantor of the farm synagogue, entered into the carnival spirit with a marked religious fervour. To the strains of the Gypsy's violin, the Polish Jew organized a circle of male dancers. Centre-circle, eyes closed, and sweat trickling into his beard, Schlosser belted out the lyrics of Magyar folk songs with the accents of his native Poland.

On Purim everything was fair game for frivolity – even prayer. Sometime after midnight Feri rounded up the children, whispering mysteriously for them to follow him to the "tent." They tiptoed out in anticipation of a joke, leaving the din of the smoke-filled dining room. In the cool quiet of the adjacent room two candles burned on the table, framing between them the form of Schlosser at prayer. Or rather it appeared to be Schlosser (but was he not dancing next door?), for he wore Schlosser's suit, his square skullcap, and even his phylacteries. Yet even from the rear the figure seemed too substantial for the cantor. Turning at the sound of their whispers, his face half-covered by a prayer shawl, "Schlosser" beamed Gusti's beatific smile.

Immediately after Purim preparations began for Passover, only a month away. In the frenzied onslaught that now took place to rid the house of products that contained leaven and associated forbidden foods, it was entirely possible to forget that this was a holiday celebrating freedom. In fact, from the point of view of work, this was the hardest time of year for everyone in the household.

Ilona's zeal in hunting down each speck of *chometz* (the foods prohibited during the eight-day festival) rose to new heights each

173

year. Starting from either end of the house, every room was scoured and aired until her forces finally converged on the kitchen. She then neatly solved the logistical problem of not being able to give this room its final cleaning while *chometz* was still being prepared by simply eliminating the consumption of bread and other forbidden foods in the house well before the time prescribed by rabbinic law. The distinction between Passover and the rest of the year was so stark that even the farm dogs were aware of it, learning to hide away husks whenever a great pile of bread was thrown their way.

When Ilona was pleased with the status of the kitchen, she shut it down and moved the freshly scoured Passover dishes, cutlery, and pots to the outside summer kitchen, used between Passover and the high holydays. This screened-in airy structure in the yard was divided in two like the winter kitchen, but made a more pleasant working space during the fly-infested summer months – although it was still rather chilly in early spring when Passover arrived.

It was here that the enormous quantities of food required for the holiday were prepared. Well before, Ilona began storing up the supply of eggs required (in lieu of yeast and chemical leavens) to raise the finely ground matzoh-meal prepared in-house with mortar and pestle. One thousand eggs – over one hundred a day – were consumed during the holiday. Eggs were featured during the Seder meal and in the *knaidlach* and Passover pancakes floating in the fragrant meat soup among islets of yellow fat; scrambled eggs sprinkled with paprika quivered in hot goose fat when served at a break from services to the congregants who faithfully turned up for worship from neighbouring farms and villages. Passover *chremslah*, a square, doughnut-like specialty, potato pancakes and stuffings, airy, flourless tortes – every traditional food depended on eggs. Even at snack time, hard-boiled eggs served as filler with thick slabs of home-made brown matzoh. Such indulgences were unshadowed by even the slightest foreknowledge of the perils of cholesterol.

Images forever frozen in the memories of those who were there: the dining room with its high windows and glass-topped doors, its long table set with white damask and laden with silver, candles, and ceremonial foods. Beneath the photographs of Karolina, with her sparse bun and multiple chins, and her son Andor in his first-lieutenant's uniform, the family grouped itself in the spring of 1941 to celebrate the Seder, the ritual meal that ushers in Passover.

The entry in Charlie Békés's diary – a diary that would travel with him to Bergen-Belsen and to the German village of Hillersleben where he perished five weeks after liberation – reads: "April 1, 1941. Midnight. The Seder has just ended. Led by Brother-in-Law Kálmán. Participants included Ilona, Gusti, Mancika, Évike, Feri, Paul, Mary, Augusta, Elizabeth, Aggie, Blanche, Irene, and the other domestics.

"The table was beautifully set for twenty-four with silver candelabra and candles and presented an impressive sight. Kálmán recited the Haggadah in the Hebrew language which, regrettably, I don't understand. There was excellent wine from the Foothills which Augusta brought, the prescribed four glasses, although I did not drink. Excellent supper. The magic of a hospitable home. Well-heated rooms ... If only the threat of the loss of the estate didn't hover over Vaja as well, and if the three boys, Gusti, Feri, and Paul were not in danger of having to join up at any moment."

It was at this particular Seder that the remarkable memory of twenty-year old Aggie Békés absorbed a few words uttered by her uncle Kálmán which were quite unconnected with the prescribed ritual:

"My dear child, I firmly believe that the Hungarian peasant ought to be cast in gold for his tolerance. Because, if after all the provocation he hears from above, the Hungarian peasant doesn't take a pitchfork and turf us out of here with it, he is a remarkable creature indeed."

What my grandfather meant by "provocation from above" was the steady diet of anti-Jewish propaganda that streamed forth from radio, newspaper, and pulpit during the Thirties and Forties. While he might praise the goodwill of the Hungarian peasant at his table, Kálmán did not take it for granted. He devised elaborate rituals for locking up the house at night, bolting the double doors of the dining room, and unlocking them himself in the morning. A night-watchman was hired for a show of security (but as he gardened by day, he mostly spent the night dozing in one of the stables).

Kálmán's jitteriness infected the rest of the family. Feri ordered miniature "Lilliput" pistols from the capital for himself and his brothers, which they occasionally fired in the air as gestures of might. But such security as these measures offered was purely symbolic. For the true threat to the Weinbergers and their way of life was not posed by a downtrodden peasantry. No act of self-protection – save perhaps for emigration – could ward off the menace posed by the increasing influence of the political right.

In 1932 Gyula Gömbös, formerly leader of the Race Protection Party and convenor in Budapest of the World Anti-Semitic Congress in 1925, had become prime minister of Hungary. Ferenc Szálasi, a discredited army officer who would become Hungary's führer in 1944 (and would subsequently be executed for war crimes), began to formulate his ideology of "Hungarism," out of which the Arrow Cross – the Hungarian Nazi Party – would eventually evolve. Szálasi called for "the final constitutional settlement of the Jewish question ... the constitutional definition of the Jews as a race ... the suspension of Jewish immigration for all time; the expulsion of those Jews who ... received settlers' permits [after August 1, 1914] ... [and] those who were not at the Front during the World War ... We demand the relentless obliteration of the Jewish mentality manifested in all directions, and demand the practical fostering of the inflexible Christian spirit."[4]

By 1938 propaganda translated into legislation, and the First (Anti-) Jewish Law restricting participation by Jews in economic life and the professions was passed. Yet, as Kálmán had marvelled, despite the propaganda and the punitive legislation, peasants on the Rákóczi Estate remained loyal to their masters to the end. After the day in March 1944 when the village mayor beat out on his drum on Main Street the proclamation, "Herewith let it be known: No one owes further service to any Jew," peasants ran in pathetic incomprehension to my uncle Paul. Home on leave from labour service, he was the only one of the three brothers to witness the dissolution of the estate and of a way of life. "What does it mean, your honour?" they asked him over and over. "What are we to do about this proclamation?"

No, Hungarian peasants did not turf out their Jewish masters. It was not the peasant who brought about the 19th of March – the German occupation of Hungary in 1944 – nor the 15th of October

– the date of a putsch that signalled the triumph of Hungary's fascist Arrow Cross party.

But neither did the Hungarian peasants lift a finger to stop these events. They stood by and watched in impassive silence, with neither the wherewithal nor the will to intervene.

In the summer of 1981, as part of a school project, teenagers from Budapest's Kálmán Könyves *Gimnázium* travelled to Vaja to compile an oral history of old peasants in the village. The subjects were men and women in their seventies and eighties who had survived two World Wars, the Great Depression, the Communist takeover, and the collectivization of Hungary's agriculture. Entitled *Castle in the Village: Conversations in Vaja*, the exhaustive interviews won a prize in an oral-history contest mounted by Hungary's prestigious national historical magazine, *História*.

Clearly delighted by the interest of the young, the old condemned the harshness and inequity of the old system in cold and dispassionate words. "Székács[5] leased over a thousand *holds*, but the poor had no land, not even to lease we weren't allowed. The count wouldn't lease to a peasant," said one man.

"I was only nine, in the second grade, when I first went out to the field," said another. "This was in 1913. You had to scramble because it might even happen that you wouldn't get a job. My sister had signed a contract [to work on the estate], but then she emigrated to America and my mother had to go instead of her, and I went with my mother. If there was a contract, you had to go or send someone in your stead."

One man recalled the summer of 1926 when he had harvested for Zoltán, gregarious, boastful Zoltán – who had given up hotel-keeping a couple of years earlier to return home to farm. "There's a flat piece of land in these parts called the Brickditch. In 1926 we planted this field with peppermint, which makes a very good tea. Ten, fifteen *holds* we planted and then hoed ... So then the Jewish tenant says to our leader, 'What do you think, Hodi, how much did I make from this peppermint?'

"Hodi answered, 'I don't know, your honour.' (That's how we had to address him, 'your honour.') 'Imagine,' he says, 'I could pay off the whole lease out of what I made.'

"Fifteen hundred *holds* of land they leased, half of the Vaja limits! And one year's peppermint harvest paid off their whole lease! ... They didn't originate from here, these Székácses. But when they settled here, they built a house on the Rákóczi Estate. It is still here. You could call it a castle ... That's where they took them away from in '44."

In Montreal, where Aggie Békés sent me a typescript of the Vaja interviews, I cringed as I read these accounts. I had not yet been to Vaja, but my nostalgia for it was already evaporating. Perhaps Itzig Derzser had struck root in the wrong place when he settled in the Nyírség. Or perhaps all the effort his descendants put into that land was doomed because it was built on the exploitation of others.

Lust and Love

Shielded from view of the manor house by the summer kitchen, the office building marked the boundary between house and field. Great-grandfather Yakab had constructed it a plain, square building windowed on each side to give a commanding view of the comings and goings of his servants in yard and meadow. It was a bare-planked, functional room, spartanly furnished with two big desks, a typewriter, a telephone, filing cabinets and, in one corner, a massive, grey-tiled stove.

Over the entrance hung a wreath of drying wheat trailing paper streamers, the gift of the harvest hands to the master at the previous year's harvest festivities. Every evening through this door filed the men who held positions of responsibility on the estate: Dániel, head of the farmhands; D., the tobacco foreman; Mislai, the head coachman; the distillery manager; the bailiff; and so on. Feri sat behind the desk in the middle of the room with his notes spread in front of him. The men ranged themselves before him, holding their sweat-stained hats. This was "posting of orders," when the foremen reported on that day's events and received instructions for the next.

From this room there opened up an even more utilitarian chamber, the so-called "big boys'" bedroom, the private preserve of the senior bachelors of the household. Andor and Zoltán had slept here in the days before World War I; Sándor and Ferenc, their youngest brothers, in the years after. In the Thirties the room passed to their nephews Gusti and Feri. Long, narrow, dank, and cold, with a view of the coal ditch outside, it contained two beds regimentally aligned along opposite walls, a couple of wardrobes and chairs, and a washstand. To this room by night stole a changing array of women, even the occasional whore from Nyírmada escorted here by the night-watchman. Generally they visited the younger of the two young masters, but to this room as well came the more constant paramours of the elder.

It was no secret that the sex lives of the family's young men were conducted in this cell. Nor could there be much doubt as to the object of their attentions. On such a self-contained locale, their choice of bedmates was restricted to the domestic staff, the field-workers, or the governesses of Zoltán's children. Today we would justifiably call it sexual oppression. But – at that time and in that place – sex with the local supply of women was viewed, by the master class at least, as the normal discharge of a male impulse, as much a matter of convenience as desire. With the farm girls there was little attempt at the preliminaries of courtship. A gruff "How about it, then?" sufficed, and the girl, if willing, would know to present herself at the office after the posting of orders had run its course.

Despite the apparently matter-of-fact acceptance of these changing liaisons, at times, beneath the tightly woven fabric of family, work, and religious life, the household seethed with jealousy and intrigue. For instance, when Gusti and Feri returned home in 1930 after serving their respective apprenticeships, their uncle Sándor, a bare ten years their senior, was still living at home. Sándor, a slight, self-effacing man in his mid-thirties, moved out of the office bedroom to make room for his nephews, withdrawing to a little windowless room tucked away like a cupboard between the kitchen and the synagogue in the main house.

Sándor's mistress was Sári the cook, a capable girl endowed with a ready tongue and an independent mind. When young Feri, newly returned from doctoral studies in Budapest and always in search of variety in women, began to besiege the girl in the kitchen with his attentions, Sári's head was easily turned. Sándor, however, stood firm in his proprietary rights and forbade her to flirt with his nephew. A girl with less spunk might have heeded him, but Sári quarrelled noisily with her lover and that night materialized on the threshold of the office. Informing Feri that she had left Mr Sándor, she arranged herself on his bed, while Gusti in the other cot rolled over discreetly and turned his face to the wall.

The next morning, Sándor dealt Sári two ringing slaps and ordered her back to his room. Their affair resumed seemingly as before, but

Sári was plotting revenge. A few months later she left the estate triumphantly behind for America.

Feri's seduction of Sári was only one in a seemingly endless succession of affairs. Promiscuous since early adolescence, he once told my father that he didn't want "the reek of any one woman to cling to me for too long." He found fair game for dalliance everywhere. While studying in Budapest in his early twenties, he carried on a clandestine affair with his elegant, demi-monde aunt Cirmi, the much younger wife of his uncle Eugene. He would later confide to his cousin Aggie with whom, despite a considerable age difference, he was fast friends, "Cirmi and I spent Yom Kippur in bed together while Eugene was in synagogue." Fourteen-year-old Aggie was pleased with her own blasé rejoinder: "Really, you could have chosen a more appropriate day."

For all his many flirtations, Feri fell in love only twice. There had been his early, hopeless teenage passion in Debrecen for his cousin Ilush; there would be another more mature love a decade later. Quite separate from these affairs of the heart and equally so from his inconsequential string of fancies, two women stood out in his affections.

In the early Thirties, Gréti Székács hired the last governess her children would require before going away to school. Aggie remembered Blanka E. as "the cream of governesses." A high-school teacher specializing in modern languages, she was universally loved in the Székács household and treated as a family member during the three years she spent on the estate. Afterwards, the Székácses always kept in touch with her, even in wartime Budapest where she suddenly disappeared during the siege of the city.

Vain to the point of ridiculousness, Gréti would not hire a woman in her household with any claim to attractiveness. Blanka was intelligent, cultured, witty, and good-tempered, but painfully plain. She had a large nose and poor skin, short mousy hair, and a wry posture, one shoulder higher than the other, which quite camouflaged a nice figure. "But you forgot it all," Aggie recalled, "when she opened her mouth. Her voice was like music, her conversation sparkled."

Seemingly as ageless as she looked colourless, Blanka was probably a good five years older than Feri. An unusual openness characterized their liaison. Feri did not hide the connection even before the children, and Blanka's regard for him was obvious. To Aggie and the two Székács children it added romance and piquancy to farm life.

But there was little romantic about the setting of this affair. Like the field-workers or chambermaids singled out by the young masters, Blanka must have picked her way to tryst in the dreary office bedroom after the farm headmen had left for the night. Blanka, as had all the governesses in the household before her, shared the children's bedroom. It was a lovely room with two enormous windows, one of which looked out on Gréti's wonderful garden of palms and ferns growing improbably in the Nyírség sand. Yet it was also a room crammed full of furniture – couches and overstuffed chairs, wardrobes and chests, cupboards and commodes, even a freestanding blackboard. For three years this "cream of governesses" lived in the same room as her two charges, an adolescent boy and girl, while down the hall a spare room stood empty save for an annual week's visit by Gréti's mother.

Jealousy seemed an ingredient totally missing from Blanka's make-up. When Feri fell in love the second time, she befriended his new flame and kept up the friendship long after. By her manner Blanka made it clear that she regarded it as only natural to be supplanted by a young, captivating girl, lacking though she was in Blanka's refinement and accomplishments. There were no scenes or recriminations.

Kálmán and Ilona maintained an admirable tolerance and detachment towards their sons' intimate lives as long as they remained centred on female servants in the office bedroom. The selection of wives, however, was fraught with high tension. Accommodating though the young men were to most of their parents' expectations, they all balked at even the hint of calling in Rezeda, the family's marriage broker. In turn, Ilona and Kálmán objected to all the prospective life partners their sons chose. Ultimately, Paul defied his parents, Gusti disappointed them, and Feri gave in to them – but then never married.

In the summer of 1934, a young woman who wreaked havoc with virtually all male hearts on the estate was introduced to the household through the unimpeachable entrée of family connection. Ferenc, Ilona's youngest brother, who replaced Gusti as bookkeeper on the Rochlitz Estate, had married a woman from Budapest. Sofia, the new bride, had a niece in the capital, a gym teacher called Márta, whom she invited to Varsány for the summer holidays. The new marriage and Márta's visit further enhanced the warm relations between the Weinberger and Rochlitz families, and Ilona invited Sofia and her niece for an extended stay on the Rákóczi Estate.

Márta was athletic, chic, and high-spirited. Despite an engagement to a young man then in military service, she was also flirtatious. While diligently dispatching letters to her fiancé, within a matter of days she had thoroughly captivated both Gusti and Feri. An attractive young woman made a likely diversion, and the young men vied to take her on outings to Piricse and the Vay castle. Márta chirped with delight at every attention, playing off the two suitors. Suddenly, as he had done earlier with Ilush Ullmann, Gusti withdrew from the chase: no woman seemed worth the coolness that arose between himself and Feri.

When Márta returned to Varsány, Feri became a daily caller there. Even today, Zsuzsi Rochlitz's hazel eyes brighten with the recollection of the clip-clop of the hooves of Feri's magnificent grey mare, Diamond, on the Varsány carriage drive on late mid-summer afternoons. After a decent interval in the living room with the family, the young lovers would withdraw to the privacy of the shaded grounds.

Ilona and Kálmán objected strenuously to Márta as a daughter-in-law. Not only was she engaged but vague rumours about her virtue disqualified her altogether. It was hinted that she had once taken an unchaperoned day trip to Lake Balaton with her fiancé from which the couple had not returned that night. An escapade such as this carried the same weight with Ilona and Kálmán as it would have with the parents of the hero of a Victorian novel.

There were secondary black marks against Márta as well. Her family was neither religious nor wealthy. Kálmán in particular longed for his sons to marry well: in the early Thirties, the Rákóczi Estate was still not out of the financial woods. A girl with a fortune, a girl from an orthodox home, a girl from a solid local family –

Kálmán's aspirations ran in these channels. Yet these worldly considerations might have been overlooked in so charming a girl as Márta if not for the blemish on her reputation.

At the end of the summer, Márta returned to Budapest. Varsány was rife with expectations of a broken engagement and the announcement of a new one. Feri spoke with his parents who, though careful not to alienate him, put their case against the girl forcefully. Whether from a desire to please them or because Márta's charms lessened in absence, he eventually gave her up. Márta would marry the young man to whom she was originally engaged, bear a son, and survive the war in Budapest, where she would meet my father after it was over. By then she was living apart from her husband with another, much-younger man, and obesity had covered all traces of her former good looks. Perhaps with Feri she might have found the happiness that eluded her without him.

Towards the end of the decade, Ilona began to hire only Jewish domestic staff: in the era when the Race Protection Act outlawed sexual relations between Jewish men and gentile women (although not vice versa), Ilona sought to protect her last bachelor son from falling foul of the law. A Jewish girl called Olga from the Highlands met the approval of both mother and son. When Olga subsequently became pregnant, Feri arranged her abortion at the same excellent birthing clinic in Debrecen where both his nieces would be born. There was little to be seen of the insouciance of the gay bachelor in the no-longer-quite-so-young man who sat by his girlfriend's bedside, head in hands, in the dim and functional servants' room. The staff saw him come and go several times during Olga's days of convalescence, assuming by her bed the same dispirited pose. But by the early Forties, private losses were not the only cause for Feri's dejection.

If Ilona and Kálmán had disapproved of Márta, Paul's choice of bride made the former positively glow with eligibility. Paul's romance, in fact, offended more people than his parents. Ripples of consternation spread from the Rákóczi Estate to the extended family, little waves of gossip titillating even the wider Nyírség community.

It is instructive to keep in mind that Paul Weinberger wooed Mary Ratzesdorfer in the days when Edward VIII courted Wallis Simpson: in the parochial eyes of Szabolcs County, Paul's love interest seemed as outlandish a choice for him as the twice-divorced American adventuress was for the king of England. For the criteria by which Ilona and Kálmán judged their sons' prospective wives were as rigid as those binding the British royal family.

In the spring of 1936, the veterinarian Ferenc Balla (that same Dr Balla who had observed the curious stratagems to save a tobacco crop some few years earlier) echoed the opinions of the countryside when he bumped into Elizabeth Békés in the waiting room of the Nyíregyháza train station. Balla knew the Weinberger family well and was on especially familiar terms with Elizabeth, since his son boarded in her spare room in Debrecen throughout his university years.

"Tell me," Balla whispered conspiratorially after they had exchanged greetings, "*is it true?*"

"Is what true?" Elizabeth feigned ignorance.

"Paul? Is he really getting married then?"

Elizabeth nodded.

"And is it true," Balla asked more boldly, "that he's marrying a *Viennese* woman?"

"Quite so."

"And is it true that she's many years *older*? And is it true" (the vet was practically roaring with delighted disbelief by now) "that she has a *fourteen-year-old daughter?*"

The diminutive Elizabeth Békés drew herself up to her full height with great dignity. "*That* is not true ... She has a fourteen-year-old *son.*"

Paul Weinberger died more than fifty years ago and – unlike most of the people in this story – his secrets died with him. He was a loner with very few confidantes; nearly everyone I spoke with about him commented at some point in the conversation, "Of the three boys, I knew him the least."

He grew up in the shadow of two slightly older brothers who formed a tight and impenetrable bond. Two years behind them in school, Paul was the baby of the family, shunned from the games and studies of the two older boys. In three years' rapid succession in the first decade of the twentieth century, my grandmother had given birth to three children; after the first two boys, she and Kálmán had longed for a little girl. Instead came another son and, when no other children followed, she kept baby Paul's hair in long ringlets well after the age of three when it was customary to shear the locks off little boys. The close attachment between Ilona and her sons was tightest between her and Paul. As a toddler crying at night, Paul could be comforted by no one else; as a grown man, his mother's bouts of melancholia caused him almost physical anguish.

He was, however, in all respects a manly man, the handsomest of the three brothers, with broad shoulders, a splendid brow, and thick brown hair. In the ways of the world, too, he was the most polished of the three, as befitted one who had obtained his doctorate at the famous University of Vienna. The only one of the brothers to break out of the conservative mould in which they had been raised and espouse left-wing opinions, Paul had beautiful manners beneath which he maintained an iron self-control and unflinching loyalty to those he loved. This discipline and loyalty he taught himself in the crucible of a forbidden adolescent infatuation.

There were three women whom Paul loved intensely and in whom he confided where he otherwise did not confide: his mother, his aunt Gréti, and his wife, Mary. At an age when his older brothers were chasing farm girls in the fields or stealing kisses in the tobacco barns, Paul spent every free moment "at the other house," the former bailiff's dwelling just beyond the distillery that had once been the synagogue and afterwards became Gréti's and Zoltán's home.

In 1924, with the departure for Debrecen of their older sons, the newly emerging relationship between sixteen-year-old Paul and his aunt assumed centre stage for Ilona and Kálmán. Gréti and Zoltán had only recently moved to the estate from Transylvania, but the strikingly pretty young matron soon alienated her husband's whole family. Stories abounded about her laziness, her selfishness, and the airs she gave herself. The servants in both households gossiped about her extravagant wardrobe (on an isolated farmstead, she changed her stylish clothes some four or five times a day) and her bad temper. If displeased, she might as easily slap a coachman twice her size as an errant chambermaid; in a fit of anger, she was known to fling her heavy bunch of keys at her hapless husband's head. After an initial period of grace, the two households maintained only distant contacts other than through the business connection with Zoltán, itself a fraught affair.

Then an unaccountable amity sprang up between Paul and Gréti. In later life Gréti would earn the nickname by which Zoltán called her from the beginning and, for most of their sixty years together, she was indeed his "golden-hearted little bunny." After they moved to Budapest, she became sleek and round, as even-tempered as she had once been hysterical. But she detested the farm and the close proximity to Zoltán's family. While he turned himself inside out to please her, she made little effort on his or anyone else's behalf. She took minimal interest in her two small children; household tasks bored her; cooking she never mastered. She spent much of her day in long, solitary walks or in directing work in her fabulous garden of ferns and yuccas. She shunned Zoltán's family, with the sole exception of his youngest nephew.

As soon as Paul completed his lessons with Schoolmaster Sas or Armin Schlosser, he bolted from home to "the other house." If anyone asked Gréti what he did there, she shrugged and tossed over her shoulder that he came to talk. The servants whispered that he had access to her closely guarded keys. If, in her indolence, she could not be bothered to take out the locked stores for them, she sent the young master to the kitchen instead. They hinted at far worse indiscretions as well.

By the strict standards of the Rákóczi Estate, the affair, if such it was, constituted a scandal. Marriage vows were sacred and, once taken, the code of marital fidelity was absolute. There was no tolerance for indiscretions after marriage even for men, and no hint of such indiscretion had ever touched anyone until now. Kálmán and Ilona spoke of little else between themselves during this period and finally, at his wife's instigation, Kalman confronted Zoltán about the matter in white-lipped sternness.

Zoltán's response incensed my grandfather so thoroughly that it became a family byword: "Gréti says evil is in the minds of those who talk, not in what she does with Paul. There's nothing more than friendship between them. And even if there is, I'm powerless to stop it." Eventually the relationship died a natural death. In 1926 Paul left for the Debrecen Academy and the opportunities for contact with his aunt became restricted to holiday visits. Paul never said anything about it to László Weisz, his best friend at the academy. Yet even years later in Vienna, when Mary Ratzesdorfer already dominated his life, Gréti's photograph still occupied the place of honour on my uncle's bedside table.

At the academy, Paul maintained the standard of excellence set by his older brothers and after graduation set out for the University of Vienna. He arrived in 1929 with only a smattering of German; four years later, having obtained his doctorate and mastered the language, he was offered a position as lecturer in the department of agriculture. In those pre-Anschluss days and in that city, it was quite an achievement for a Jewish boy from the backwoods of Hungary.

Like Feri with Márta and Gusti with Mancika, Paul's second love interest opened up through the medium of a family introduction. On leaving Debrecen where he had boarded with the Ullmanns, he was given the name of a niece of his uncle, Solomon Ullmann. Médi Ratzesdorfer, his uncle's niece, had married a Viennese businessman; doubtless Paul would find the Hornsteins a congenial couple. How this humdrum introduction evolved into a taboo romance no one can say now. Paul did not confide its details to anyone. All that the family saw on his summer visits was that at the end of each vacation he seemed very cheerful to be returning to Vienna.

During the seven years between their first meeting and their engagement, the woman to whom the family had unwittingly steered Paul divorced her husband and thereby forfeited her respectability in the eyes of the Rákóczi Estate. When Paul wrote his parents of his desire to marry "Médi," as he still called her then, the letter produced a crisis.

Even the thought of a divorced woman was repugnant. That the woman was thirty-five, seven years older than their son, that that son was the epitome of eligibility, newly graduated from Vienna, that on top of everything else, the woman was saddled with a teen-aged child – it was all, in the vernacular of the Nyírség, "a dumpling they couldn't swallow." In the end Kálmán and Ilona had three choices: disowning Paul, accepting his bride, or dissuading him from his course. Putting their hope in the last, they dispatched Gusti and Feri to Vienna to talk the couple out of their plans.

The brothers scheduled an evening and a day for thwarting a seven-year romance. The engaged couple in turn had devised a strategy to keep opportunities for discussing sensitive issues to a minimum. Immediately upon the guests' arrival, they were whisked off for a gala performance of Léhár's grand opera, *Giuditta*, conducted by the great composer himself. Decidedly unmusical, Gusti spent the evening fretting about his mission and dozing off.

The next day they were invited for luncheon by Médi, who then still used the (now unfortunate) childhood name derived from the German word for "maiden." Between beautifully presented courses, in the presence of the hostess, the brothers gingerly outlined their parents' opposition. The couple stonewalled to good effect. Paul said that he had given his word to marry Médi, but if she had changed her mind, it was up to her to say so. Médi countered that she loved Paul, but if he regretted his proposal, she would free him instantly.

Eventually the three brothers returned to the hotel where Gusti and Feri delivered an unexpurgated version of the family's objections. Poker-faced, Paul heard them out. Then, looking at first one, then the other, he observed quietly, "I wonder ... If you were in my shoes, and had promised marriage to a woman if she divorced her husband for you, wouldn't you honour that promise when it came time to do so?"

Gusti's and Feri's eyes locked in one of those exchanges of te-lepathy so common to them with a surge of sympathy for their brother's plight and recognition that he was undissuadable. Paul seized his advantage. "Go back home and, for heaven's sake, stop working against me. Tell them that their blessing means a great deal to me, but I'll marry her even without it. Either way, I promise you the marriage will go ahead."

On the morning of August 19, 1936, the day that his youngest son would marry over his stated objections and the day before his oldest son embarked on a journey to secure a bride of his own, Kálmán Weinberger paced disconsolately in front of the verandah behind his house. His sister-in-law Elizabeth, busy with last minute preparations for the wedding feast, watched him from the summer kitchen. His unhappiness seemed so palpable that it made her own heart heavy. She put down a tray of hors d'oeuvres, wiped her hands on her apron, and headed for the yard. Finding Kálmán by then seated with bowed shoulders on a bench, she sat down beside him.

Kálmán seemed oblivious to her presence. As if talking to himself, he mused in a voice laden with bitterness, "I don't wish upon a single parent in the world the feelings in my heart on what should be a joyous day."

Closer proximity with Mary – she had arrived in the spring having renamed herself, the association with maidenhood being best forgotten – had made the match seem even more baffling. The first meeting was painfully awkward. Mary had travelled from Vienna through Debrecen where the train stopped long enough for Charlie Békés to perform one of his gallant courtesies. Carrying a bouquet of flowers, the handsome middle-aged gentleman walked the length of the train, stopping at each compartment to ask, "Excuse me, is there a lady here bound for the Rákóczi Estate?" In the last car sat two women in opposite corners, one exceedingly pretty and the other plain and blunt featured. Smiling benevolently at the good-looking woman, Charlie asked once more, "Are either of you ladies bound for the Rákóczi Estate?"

"Why, yes," the other woman spoke up cheerfully, "that's where I'm headed."

Recovering quickly, Charlie introduced himself to her as Paul's uncle and handed over the flowers. Charmed by the gesture, Mary travelled on to Nyíregyháza where Paul met her and they continued the rest of the journey together.

At home the atmosphere awaiting them was electric. Everyone was well acquainted with Kálmán's habit of meeting and greeting every cherished visitor in person at the station at the foot of the house. But as the moments ticked by before the arrival of the night train, Kálmán remained planted in the three-legged armchair by the tile stove in the dining room. First Gusti, then Feri pointedly eyed their watches and left the room. Fifteen-year-old Aggie Békés, visiting for the Easter vacation, hung back to see what her aunt and uncle would do. From below there sounded the shrill whistle and then the rattle of the train itself. Ilona hoisted herself slowly out of her armchair.

"I don't care what you do," the old woman flung at her husband. "*I'm* going down." She took a little flashlight to light her way and prepared to face the unwanted bride.

Supper had been postponed in honour of the guest and they supped at ten. To Aggie, the newcomer did not appear *so* unattractive. Mary was tall and had a good figure (Blanche would later characterize her for me as "regal") which she showed off to good advantage in an elegantly cut checked suit and green suede pumps. But the seven-year age difference which so bothered the old couple was unmistakably stamped on her face, particularly after a fatiguing journey. She would prove a woman of superior intelligence and sharp wit, yet she never attracted a following in the family. An abrasiveness of manner and an assertiveness that at times verged on the aggressive did not endear her to those predisposed to dislike her. That night Mary's highly praised talents as a conversationalist were put sorely to test. An awkward silence reigned in the dining room which Aggie tried to enliven by kicking Feri under the table to prompt him to speak. Eventually a strained discussion about mutual acquaintances in Vienna was broached. The rest of the pre-nuptial visit elapsed in a similar oppressive atmosphere.

There were no other visits until the wedding day in August. Both the civil and religious ceremonies were held on the farm. The civil marriage was performed by the village notary in the leather-appointed study, a particularly agonizing business because of the public proclamation of the couple's vital statistics. In front of the assembled guests, the notary sonorously announced that Dr Paul Weinberger of the Rákóczi Estate, born in the year 1908, would wed Mary Ratzesdorfer Hornstein of Vienna, born in the year 1901. This unpleasant chore accomplished, the wedding party withdrew to change into formal attire. The guests gathered in the garden where the wedding canopy had been erected. In a festive gesture, each of the guests was given a taper to light before the bridegroom arrived.

Departing from tradition (and underlining the unstated but obvious feelings of the parents), Gusti and Feri instead of their father escorted the bridegroom to the *chupah*. Arms linked, faces uniformly wreathed in smiles, the three brothers approached from the office building where Paul had changed into a tuxedo. The bride arrived next in a suit with fashionably padded shoulders, on the arms of her mother and her aunt Toni, Kálmán's sister. The traditional ceremony proceeded without a hitch. A sumptuous feast followed, but there was little revelry and no dancing. The bride and groom left by the afternoon train for a wedding trip to Lake Balaton.

Despite the frosty reception, despite the exile that followed, Paul found happiness with his Mary. At first they returned to Vienna, fleeing the city just before the Anschluss, in time for their daughter, Marika, to be born in Debrecen in July 1938. For Ilona the child healed any rift that had existed, but Kálmán continued to ostracize the couple for years. Paul was kept out of the business until Zoltán withdrew from it in 1941; until then he was awarded the thankless Piricse sinecure, farming in so-called partnership with the impossible Uncle Ernest. Paul and Mary rented a little house in Nyírbátor from where Piricse was readily accessible. Mary, thirsting for company, soon led a busy social life. Their best friends were a local doctor, Béla Mandel, and his wife, a pretty socialite from Debrecen.

After the outbreak of war, Paul's bouts of labour service alternated with long periods of home leave. By then Zoltán and Gréti had moved to Budapest and the youngest brother then came to occupy "the other house," the setting of that long-ago attachment that had caused his parents so much grief. In the absence of his older brothers in labour service, he finally had a chance to prove his abilities on the farm, and they were every bit as formidable as his academic qualifications implied.

It was upon Paul that the terrible task of handing over the estate in April 1944 to Hungarian authorities devolved, and it was he who supervised the end of three generations of solid effort by his family. Like his parents, wife, and child, and the wife and child of his oldest brother, he was on the same train bound for Auschwitz as the Rochlitzes, the wagon from which only Zsuzsi Rochlitz would return.

But the subsequent fate of Paul Weinberger, unlike most of the others in that cattle car, is not mercifully anonymous. I quote below from a letter in my father's collection written to him after the war by Dr. Béla Mandel, Paul's friend in Nyírbátor:

February 6, 1946

Dear Mr Weinberger,

Of your brother Paul, my dear and good friend, I must now dredge up the painful and soul-lacerating memories, because you desire to know what happened to him during the time we were together, or rather when he was in the hospital where I worked as doctor.

Poor Paul was first transferred from Auschwitz to Buchenwald and from there to our death camp (Commando Troglitz, Camp Buchenwald) sometime in the second half of January 1945. Despite his weakened condition, he could take the work to the extent that he could make it out daily. The food was so bad however that within a few weeks he became emaciated to skin and bone. Only his legs, abdomen and face were swollen, this is called hunger oedema. They admitted him to the Schonung block [sick bay] where, although he rested, the deterioration of his cardio-vascular system was so pronounced that no medical intervention could have saved him.

This he knew as well as I. I talked to him a great deal in the absolutely apathetic state that he had by then reached, when nothing interested him, when he already waited for death to redeem him.

It was I whom he forced to give to his cousin Péter Rochlitz his valuables, the fearfully guarded knife and some other trifle item. I could not urge him to hold on. His high level of intelligence made him see everything with perfect clarity and I can honestly say that he waited for the end with miraculous calm.

This however did not occur during our stay there. By the cruel edict of our commanding officer, our camp was evacuated. They threw everyone, including the sick and dying, into open wagons where, because of the total lack of food, virtually all our sick perished. Those with still some vestige of life in them, were destroyed by the bullets of the SS on detrainment. My dear good friend Paul was among these last.

That a few of us escaped from this hell is a miracle of God in the literal meaning of the word. He had no special words of farewell.

This is all I can write of Paul, the destruction of a truly valuable, noble-hearted man by executioners. The heart and flower of Hungarian Jewry is gone. Of those of us who have come back, very few can be compared to them.

Sincere respects,
Béla Mandel

Marriage and Liaison

The day after Paul's wedding, Gusti embarked on a journey all in a dither. Though his destination was Miskolc, northern Hungary's commercial, industrial, and manufacturing capital, he did not have business in mind. His head was teeming with matrimonial matters, both because of the previous day's ceremony and a certain letter burning in his breast pocket.

In the summer of 1936, my father was thirty. He had known the woman towards whom he was travelling for thirteen years; in a sense he had been journeying towards her for a decade, for he had toyed with the idea of marrying her for at least that long. Yet he might have continued indefinitely the internal debate over the pros and cons of the married state had not news of another suitor for Mancika Mandula's hand been leaked by her parents just prior to Paul's wedding.

Gusti instinctively associated Mancika with the idea of marriage. His first glimpse of her all those years ago had been on his way to a wedding. Framed like the subject of a portrait by a large window, she had gazed down at him, her face charmingly propped on slender elbows, the sweet but wistful face of a fourteen-year-old girl left out of the festivities he was about to attend. Soon afterwards, another wedding would unite their respective families when her oldest sister, Erzsébet, married a brother of Ilush Ullmann.

At the time of these earlier marriages, the Mandulas were a wealthy family. Although their lumber firm had failed during the Depression, when Mancika was growing up no expense was spared on the schooling of their large family. The youngest of eight, she had received as fine an education as was then deemed appropriate for a girl from an orthodox family. She attended a local *polgári* – the non-classical secondary stream for those not heading to university – and was then sent to finishing schools in Frankfurt and Montreux to acquire the accomplishments of a woman of good breeding. She spoke perfect German, good French, and a smattering of English. She played the piano, sang, and was a good dancer. She knew how to run a household and was adept at all kinds of handwork. In schools where girls of many nationalities mingled at close quarters, she learned diplomacy and tact.

When Gusti attended the academy in Debrecen, he had many opportunities to observe Mancika. He was a frequent visitor of his Ullmann cousins; Mancika often spent weeks at a time at her sister Erzsébet's, particularly after the birth of Erzsébet's two children. A family tradition evolved of inviting the young Ullmanns to the Rákóczi Estate for the holiday of Shavuoth; often Mancika was included. In return, Gusti and Feri were also invited by Mancika's parents; clearly the Mandulas approved the prospect of a match between their daughter and either of the brothers.

Soft-spoken and even-tempered, Mancika hardly seemed the type of woman to attract Feri. Except for her fine, thickly lashed eyes, her looks were unprepossessing, and her manners modest. Short and round with pleasant but unremarkable features, she spoke with a breathy lisp that some found annoying but Gusti thought endearing. He frequently found himself thinking that Mancika Mandula would make an excellent wife, yet this realization did not lead him to single her out in any way. Only once was he moved to a discreet press of her fingers under the spell of a beautiful night.

In those days, Shavuoth, the Festival of Weeks, which marks God's gift of the Ten Commandments to the Jewish people, was Gusti's favourite holiday. It usually fell in May, the Nyírség's most delightful month, a time of hope and fledgling growth. Spring planting was over, and in field and garden everything burgeoned with new shoots and tendrils, while the acacias in bridal white suffused the countryside with honey-sweet fragrance. During the Shavuoth visit of 1936 when Mancika once again accompanied the Ullmanns to the farm, a balmy spring evening enticed the party outdoors. Cane chairs from the verandah were carried to the garden, and young and old settled beneath the walnut trees. A lovely moonrise silvered the sky and inspired the young people to sing.

Gusti sat beside Mancika. Generally devoid of musical sensibility, he felt moved by the girl's clear soprano which soared effortlessly above the other voices. The moonlight, the scent of spring, and the seductiveness of the song all worked a mysterious alchemy. He reached in the dark for Mancika's hand. She did not pull it away.

In retrospect, he always regarded that moment as the one when he decided to marry her. Yet the inner resolve still did not translate into action. He continued to entertain a bachelor's fear of losing his freedom, of being tied down by family responsibilities. In no way was love of Mancika a matter of urgent pursuit.

One wonders what Mancika thought as she allowed her hand to rest in his. In 1936 she was twenty-seven, on the cusp of spinsterhood by the standards of her circle. Her father's bankruptcy had not helped her marital prospects. Still living at home were two older brothers and a retarded sister. Besides the centrally located, imposing home, the Mandulas were left with so little in the way of financial resources that Mancika's trousseau would eventually be ordered and paid for by her future mother-in-law.

The moment under the walnut trees passed. The couple did not meet for three months. In July Gusti received an invitation to Miskolc for the weekend following Paul's wedding. He accepted willingly but with no intention of declaring himself. Shortly before his departure, his father took him aside and showed him a letter from Mancika's father. Mór Mandula requested information from his friend Kálmán Weinberger about Kálmán Fried, the son of a nearby landowner who had been proposed as a possible match for Mandula's youngest daughter.

Churning with impatience and indecision, Gusti arrived in Miskolc before the Sabbath. He was ushered into Mór Mandula's study where he handed the older man his father's letter of response and, in answer to further questions, gave his own succinct, unenthusiastic account of the Frieds of Nyírmada. He had in fact always disliked Kálmán Fried, a sly-looking man with the irritating habit of grilling him about the running of the Rákóczi Estate, but clamming up when asked the most innocuous question about his own business. The thought of Mancika having a suitor was disturbing; the thought that she might marry Kálmán Fried of all men – as a consequence of his own procrastination – was particularly galling.

Gusti's visit was to last until Monday afternoon, but the question of whether, where, and when he would declare himself weighed heavily upon him. Mandatory synagogue attendance on Friday night and Saturday morning and mealtimes *en famille* left no opportunity for private *tête-à-têtes* for the first two days. On the Sunday a sightseeing trip to the nearby Bükk Mountains proved more promising. Climbing alongside a mountain stream, Gusti stuck close to Mancika, waiting for the right moment. In lieu of romantic opportunities, an August squall drenched the party to the skin. Wet and bedraggled, he managed to sit next to her on the bus taking them back to Miskolc, but instead of broaching the all-important subject, he continued to agonize internally: should he marry or not? Mancika was the right woman, yet marriage was a serious undertaking. If he didn't speak up, Kálmán Fried might win her, but if he did, his days as a carefree bachelor were over.

Mancika broke the silence with a casual query. "I wonder when I'll see you next, Gusti."

He was astonished by the ease with which his answer popped out. "That all depends on you."

Startled, she looked straight into his eyes. "How do you mean?" she asked without a trace of archness.

"If you wish to see me, you can always spend the rest of your life with me ... I mean, I'm asking you to come to me as my wife."

For a moment Mancika was too astonished to speak. "But Gusti, you've never spoken to me of such things before!" she gasped.

"I'm speaking of them now," said the newly eloquent suitor. Then he added, a little fearfully, "Tell me, am I too late?"

Mancika hesitated – and then she said, "No."

And with that "No" their partnership was sealed. Though the official engagement did not take place until two weeks later, though he would not kiss her until that official engagement, "the bus finally shook the proposal out of Gusti," Charlie Békés subsequently noted in his diary.

The next morning, with everyone still in the dark about their changed status, the betrothed pair strolled through the park facing the Mandula house, towards the pretty Catholic cemetery that was one of Mancika's favourite haunts. Amidst the gravestones and crosses, they mapped out their future lives: how they would rent the house in Nyíregyháza that Gusti's uncle Ferenc Székács had just bought and for which he needed a tenant, how Gusti would commute to the farm three times a week and the rest of the time run the legal side of the business from the county capital. Mancika saw him off at the train on Monday afternoon. Their hearts welling with affection, they made no move to touch; he had too much respect for her, and she was much too proper.

The wedding took place six months later in February 1937, in a suburb of Miskolc. The bridal couple travelled the same day to Budapest where they were to stay the night in the Astoria before travelling to Italy for their honeymoon. In fact, they stayed two nights at the Astoria. Mancika, who had received a sheltered upbringing worthy of any Victorian maiden, was so terrified on her wedding night that she pleaded with Gusti to give her more time. Though terribly disappointed, his courtesy did not falter. He would wait until she was ready, he assured her. Years later, Mancika confessed to him that his patience on their wedding night bound her to him in everlasting gratitude far more than any passionate embrace might have done. But – as my father shyly admitted – in time, they enjoyed their share of passionate embraces.

Beneath the conventionally domesticated and modest shell there lived a strong woman. Among the Mandulas soft words frequently cloaked strong wills. Sitting in the window seat of the Rákóczi Estate dining room, crochet hook in hand, Mancika's mild face clouded over as the Weinberger men harangued each other in the midst of a stormy business discussion. By sheer force of will she compelled Gusti to look her way, then raised a quelling finger to her lips.

"It's nothing at all," he waved back. "It's only our usual noisy way, you know."

"I don't like it," she mouthed silently. Gusti hesitated, then lowered his voice.

Many of those who knew both Mancika and Anikó, my mother, drew comparisons unfavourable to my father's first wife. Anikó was as different from Mancika as two women could be. Compared to my beautiful, temperamental mother, Mancika seemed flat and insipid. Anikó of the jet hair and flashing eyes – and a temper to match – added colour to Gusti's life that it never had before. It was the difference between a movie in Technicolor and one in black and white.

Yet Mancika was a hard act for the competitive, effervescent Anikó to follow, for to compete with Mancika, she had to wrestle with the dead. And the spectre of Gusti's decent, well-bred first wife haunted my parents' marriage from the beginning: from the walls of the Budapest apartment where she looked down on us in white brocade and wedding veil; from the repetitions of the saga of Gusti's wooing which Anikó endured through gritted teeth; and, hardest of all, from my own quaint interest and childish revenge in invoking Mancika's name when my mother slapped me for misbehaving.

With time, too, my father clung more and more to his dead family. In Montreal while he endured the dreariness of his bookkeeping job in the needle trade, his inner and imaginative life revolved once again around the people of the Rákóczi Estate. In his outward existence he lived in North American suburbia, devoted husband and father to his second family. But beneath that alias, he remained the master of the Rákóczi Estate for all time, a son of Ilona and Kálmán Weinberger, married to Mancika Mandula – not for a brief seven years, but for eternity.

I see my father in the hospital after his second stroke that paralysed him and destroyed much of his remarkable mind, that mind that had conjured up for all of us his first world. I see the Florida-tanned neurologist testily measuring by some arbitrary yardstick the extent of my father's brain damage. Irritably asking him: the day of the week, the month, the year, questions that leave my father vacant-eyed, nonplussed, and increasingly distressed. I see my mother, grey-haired, ashen, and disbelieving by his side. The neurologist, about to give up, glances at Anikó for inspiration, then asks a last irritated question.

"What's your wife's name?"

And without a second's hesitation, Gustav Kalman, né Gusti Weinberger, answers in Hungarian, "My wife is Mancika Mandula."

In 1984, Mancika had been dead forty years, thirty-eight of which my father had shared with my mother.

In the Budapest of the early Fifties, remnants of a once-huge family and surviving pre-war friends regrouped around Gusti and Anikó in their east-end apartment. Not because they were the oldest survivors, not because their home was the largest or the most centrally located: quite simply, Gusti was temperamentally best-suited to assume the role of mentor and protector that had always fallen on the master of the Rákóczi Estate.

The post-war Seders uniting friends and family were held in our apartment on tablecloths bearing Mary Ratzesdorfer's monogram and set with the remains of Ilona's silver. Siggie Morvay's wedding reception was hosted and prepared by my parents in our dining room. Aggie Békés and her fiancé boarded with us for a winter until they found an apartment. Ilona's impoverished, emotionally afflicted youngest sisters frequently required both financial and physical support in return for which they heaped abuse on the heads of their benefactors.

The mantle of the Rákóczi Estate did not always rest comfortably on the shoulders of Gusti's second wife. Thirteen years his junior, Anikó had grown up in a small town quite different from the rural setting of Szabolcs farmsteads. Love of her husband, genuine curiosity about his past, and a strong sense of duty helped to fill the emotional void left by her own terrible losses. In Anikó, members of Gusti's family found a ready listener and a fresh audience, and she became the recipient of confidences her husband preferred not to hear.

Blanche, the former cook on the Rákóczi Estate, survivor of Auschwitz and other camps, slowly wound her way back to the Nyírség and, like most of those who did so, finally moved to the capital. Communism had wiped away archaic forms of address and some social inequalities. When Gusti introduced Blanche to Anikó, the two women immediately used the familiar *te* reciprocally, something the old order would not have allowed. They liked each other as well, although Blanche, who clung uncompromisingly to orthodoxy, was saddened by my father's abandonment of religious observance and by my mother's seeming lack of religious feeling.

It was during one of Gusti's absences from the capital that Blanche, in a singularly agitated and mysterious manner, asked Anikó to tell him that she had a matter of import to discuss with him. What was it about? my mother inquired with considerable curiosity. It was about Gusti's father's great attachment to her, Blanche answered proudly.

My mother relayed the message to my father on his return from the state farm he had been inspecting. My father, uncharacteristically curt, replied, "Let her keep this belated news to herself."

It thus fell to Anikó to hear the insubstantial details of Kálmán Weinberger's lapse from morality with the plain-featured Blanche, the cook young enough to be his daughter, whom his sons had once mocked for her excessive religious zeal and peasant-like stolidity. Yet to Kálmán in the Thirties and Forties, soured by his sons' unsatisfactory romances, beleaguered by the increasingly threatening political climate, shut out by the walls of Ilona's silence, Blanche with her frizzy blonde hair and thick ankles was a source of much solace. The bare-headed, clean-shaven young Kálmán with the open countenance and dreamer's eyes in the old engagement photograph had aged into a dapper little man sporting a white goatee and black fedora. The young Kálmán who had been too shy and polite to admit that no, he did not eat giblets, in his old age commanded enormous respect for his acts of charity, his good sense, his polished manners, and wide-ranging knowledge. His wife, once a smooth-cheeked, merry girl, was now a well-padded matron in a white wimple. Alternately plunged into silence or manic activity, she surfaced from illness only sporadically until the birth of her granddaughters literally gave her a new lease on life.

Blanche confided in my mother in our Budapest apartment that Kálmán had called her his golden girl, that she had brightened his old age with her love and devotion. Was their love ever physically consummated? Blanche did not explicitly say, although she hinted that it had been. Whether this affair – surely no more possible to cover up in that hermetic farm life than any of the many other affairs conducted there – was the cause or effect of Ilona's melancholy seems now impossible to say. When I met Blanche in Budapest half a century after the first stirrings of that unlikeliest of illicit romances, she made no allusion to it. Instead, she spoke of her filial affection for both Ilona and Kálmán, of the love they mutually all bore each other, and of her privileged position as a quasi-family member during her employment.

Only once did her plain, honest face with its lashless eyes and flat nose cloud over and assume, for an instant, an expression of hurt. She knew, she said, that they had hidden away valuables for their children to find on their return home. They had not, however, revealed these hiding places to her so that she might have led my father to them when the time came. For a moment she was catapulted back into that old order in which – no matter how devoted and loving the connection between her and the master and the mistress – in the final analysis, they showed her no more trust than any other *servant*.

Journey to Vaja

Working as an executive at the Hungarian Cattlebreeding Trust in the 1950s, my father spent a good deal of time inspecting the national network of collective farms. On rare and very special occasions, he would take me along with him to the country for a day.

We would waken very early, in the dark, when it was still chilly although it was summer. By sunrise a grey taxi with red-and-white chequered standard was waiting for us at the curb. We drove through the empty streets of Budapest to a cavernous train station where steam locomotives blew and hissed like great draught horses impatient for departure. A real horse and cart met us when we got off the train, the coachman invariably sporting a handlebar moustache and wearing a loose white shirt and high leather boots caked with mud.

I believe that the Vaja of my fantasies must have been based on these childhood trips: on drives along deeply rutted country roads which bisected emerald fields touched by early morning sunshine, on the smiling welcome at the collective farm of peasant women who rustled in many-layered skirts. We would begin to tour the white-washed cow pens, my father inhaling the ripe odour of the animals with apparent relish, while I held my nose. Men with pitchforks hauled out excrement and brought in fresh straw. The animals flicked their tails, their udders straining with milk, as one by one they were led to the scales. Numbers were called out by one cowhand, noted on a pad by another, and then posted on a board near the animal's head. My father stood by the scales, eyeing the tallies sharply and frequently questioning the workers. The peasants' attitude towards him seemed both friendly and respectful. Some called him Comrade Kálmán (by this time he had Hungarianized his surname by adopting his father's first name), but most of them used the affectionate and informal "Uncle Gusti."

On different assignments and working with other national trusts, my father regularly criss-crossed the country on business. It would have been easy for him to check on what was happening in his native village in the postwar years. Had he wished, he might even have taken me with him, and we could have journeyed to Vaja together. In fact, he never returned to Vaja after the war, not while we still lived in Hungary, nor on visits after we had emigrated to Canada. His old college chums wrote to us in Montreal to say that the house where he had been born was now the headquarters of the local circuit doctor. Later they noted that it had been converted into a small school. László and Siggie, independently of each other, sent newspaper clippings when the ancient Vay Castle in the village was restored to a measure of its former splendour and turned into a museum. Then came a report that an award-winning collective farm in the region was named, like the old estate itself, after Prince Ferenc Rákóczi. Could it be on the site of the old Vay estate? Shrugging an indifferent shoulder as each tidbit of interest arrived in the mail, my father refused to be drawn into such speculations. Though he spent much of his second, postwar life looking back and reviewing the first, in a literal sense he never looked back, and he never went back.

In the spring of 1983 I told my father that I was planning a visit to Vaja. A year earlier he had suffered a series of little strokes that had affected his memory and his ability to speak, read, and write. Though he was then still mobile and living at home, the changes in him were devastating. After the onset of the illness, he would sit in silence, shoulders crumpled and face slack, an unfolded newspaper on his knees as he gazed into nothingness. Or he'd try to tackle the mounting pile of correspondence at his desk and, after an hour of concerted effort, produce three or four words in a bizarrely crabbed version of his once-beautiful rounded hand.

Yet he could still be a force to be reckoned with when something galvanized him out of apathy – as I found out when I announced that I was going to Vaja. The newspaper fell off his lap as he jerked himself straight on the couch. My father, who had never struck anyone in his life, swung his hand wildly through the air in my direction. I was sitting across from him at a safe distance, a coffee table between us, but I instinctively pulled back in my armchair. A menacing finger shook in my face. "I forbid you to go!"

I was thirty-five years old and had not dreamed of needing his permission for anything for decades. Since my adolescence, he had not forbidden me anything and, even as a teenager, there had not been much that I had not been allowed.

"They will kill you if you set foot there."

He would not say who "they" were. He was an old, crotchety, and irrational man in whose mind by then the Hitlerian cataclysm was often fresher than the present. But as he became more and more agitated, it became clear that he wasn't talking about Nazis.

"They'll call you a member of the land-owning classes ... They'll tear the clothes off your back. You'll be thrown in prison ... Mark my words, you'll never see your family again."

There seemed to be no limit to this sudden burst of absurdity. Although in 1983 *glasnost* was not yet in the offing in the Soviet Union, Hungary enjoyed the most liberalized form of communism in the entire Eastern bloc. My father had experienced that himself first hand, having visited his old homeland many times as a Canadian with complete ease.

"*Ilushka*" – his eyes behind their square tortoise shell frames glinted with a demented spark as he called me by my Hungarian nickname – "you have two small children. You have no right to endanger your life. I forbid you to go to Vaja."

I was completely shaken by the sight of him in this role of crazed oracle. And I felt furious because I could feel myself being sucked into the vortex of his paranoia. Uncannily, he had pushed all the right buttons. At the time, I was unsteady after a six-month illness that had shaken my commitment to the project and my confidence in my ability to write this book. I felt guilty in advance about leaving my small family on what might be an expensive wild-goose chase. I knew that my husband – who had lent his support by paying for the trip and shouldering much of the extra child care it would necessitate – deeply distrusted my passion for the Hungarian past. When my father had given me the family correspondence two years earlier, my husband had been appalled by the way I had let it take hold of me and rule my emotional life until I cracked under the strain.

Of all people, I had expected my father to be the one most encouraging about my Hungarian trip. I had even believed he would feel proud because I wanted to undertake it. But for weeks until I left, he would phone me every day and bark out a fresh version of the scenario of hostile peasants tearing me to pieces on my arrival to Vaja. By the time of my departure I was thoroughly rattled, displacing all my own anxiety on my equipment: would I be able to get into Hungary with my tape recorders and camera, would I be able to get my cassettes and film out safely afterwards?

On the eve of my flight I went to say goodbye to my parents. We chatted desultorily in their kitchen, surrounded by the pottery vases, decorative spoons, and woven hangings that were mementoes of their own trips to Hungary. When I hugged my father goodbye, I was not so much surprised by his tears – I was crying, too – as by his words.

"Go in good health. I admit I'm sorry I'm not going too." He held me at arm's length and then added, "I let you go with full confidence that you'll come home safe."

Despite this unaccountable about-face and even though no one looked at me crosswise even once during my three weeks in Hungary, I felt uneasy throughout my stay. At the National Library, the words "Canadian researcher" opened doors that did not always open for Hungarians. Family members were kind beyond kindness. My father's friends László and Siggie showered me with all the affection and attention they would have shown my father had he come instead. But my whole trip was coloured by unsettling first impressions. From the window of the descending plane, my first sight of Ferihegy Airport had been of fully armed soldiers standing at attention on the tarmac. My first outing in Budapest was an obligatory visit to a police station. On subsequent days, even while engaged in activities that gave me enormous pleasure, an undercurrent of anxiety nagged at me that I wouldn't be able to get out of the country when my visit was up.

The Hungarian economy was booming, there were tourists everywhere, fledgling private-enterprise restaurants and shops were the fashionable places to be seen, and even in state-run stores there were decent consumer goods available. But the stylish shop windows and people sipping espresso at sidewalk cafés seemed less real to me than the gory history evoked by Budapest place names.

Vérmező. Vérhalom Tér. Törökvész.

Field of Blood. Pile of Blood Square. Destruction of the Turks.

For a long time I had believed that, although I had never set foot in Vaja, that tiny spot on the map of Hungary was where I came from. Somehow its soil would be sacred to me. But I no longer believed it when I finally arrived in Vaja on a hot day in May 1983.

The five of us wedged into the red Lada ranged in age from early twenties to mid-eighties and represented three generations. In front with the driver was the senior member of the party, Uncle Samuel, a namesake and grandson of my great-great-grandfather Samuel Schwarcz who more than a century earlier kissed an aristocrat's baby and became a landed proprietor. A frail little man lost in the depths of a suit that had once fit him snugly, Uncle Samuel had a diametrically different way from my father of memorializing his Holocaust losses. Uncle Samuel pilgrimaged at least twice a year to the ancestral villages of his own past – Derzs and Gyulaj – to make sure that old family graves were kept in good repair and to remind villagers of his family's erstwhile presence in these parts.

For both Uncle Samuel and Aggie Békés, who sat in the back with me, the trip meant stirring up memories at once deeply painful and pleasurable. Aggie more than anyone had urged me to come to Hungary, promising that if I did so, she would travel to Vaja with me and help me find the old sights. Grey-haired and stooping slightly, she was now, at sixty-odd, the same age as the Uncle Kálmán and Aunt Ilona of her memories. She had not set foot on the Rákóczi Estate for forty years. In the interim she had become a distinguished educator, lexicographer, and translator, and possessed a memory that was second to none – not even my father's at its most acute – in her recall of the old house's every cranny. Although the estate had never been her home, she knew it intimately. She had written to me from Budapest, "You have no idea what that old place means to me. I spent every holiday of an idyllically happy childhood there ... The older I get, the more often I dream about the Rákóczi Estate.

But not just dreams. Sometimes these days I'll be rummaging through the apartment here and find myself suddenly thinking, 'Whatever was the colour of that particular doorknob?' Or 'In what order did we use to sit around the big table?'"

Squeezed between me and Aggie in the back of the car was her daughter, Zsuzsika, like me, weaned on stories of Vaja; she had come along out of curiosity and a sense of solidarity with her mother. The owner and driver of the car was Shanyi, a twenty-three-year-old friend of Uncle Samuel from Budapest who had volunteered the car and his services as chauffeur for the day and who, in retrospect, provided its small measure of comic relief. While I had travelled thousands of miles to get to Vaja and wanted to savour my impressions once there, Shanyi kept us moving briskly so we could return to Budapest (a four-hour drive) in time for him to give his infant daughter her bath before nightfall.

On the way down Aggie and Samuel reminisced about old times and played guessing games about what kind of changes we would find. Aggie maintained that, of all the estate's buildings, the distillery had been the sturdiest, a bulky, square edifice with a chimney like a giant exclamation point that was the tallest landmark of the region. "We'll see the chimney from far away," she said with absolute confidence, "and we'll be able to orient ourselves in relation to it."

The distillery had been erected by Count Adam Vay in the 1870s and renovated by Yakab at the turn of the century. It had stood about halfway between the two ancient bailiffs' houses, one of which had evolved into the manor house in which my father had been born, and the other which eventually became Zoltán's home.

"What do you think will be worse, Sammy?" Aggie spoke up again, an ironic edge to her voice this time. "To find everything still in place? Or to find a complete ruin?"

"It's impossible that everything should be the same," Samuel threw over his shoulder dismissively. "After forty years."

"But if the collective farm is exactly on the site of the old place," Aggie persisted, "they'll be using the old buildings."

"*Anyuci*, we'll soon be there and we'll know for sure," Zsuzsika put in.

"I don't know what will be worse," repeated Aggie, "to find everything the same, or completely changed."

We almost didn't find the place at all. Neither Aggie nor Samuel had ever travelled to the Rákóczi Estate by car – Aggie had always come by train from Debrecen, Samuel by carriage or on horseback from Gyulaj. Once off the main highway, the changes were startling. As late as the 1940s all the roads in this part of the countryside had been unpaved, and thatched roofs were common. Once one of the most backward parts of Hungary, Szabolcs County had belatedly entered the twentieth century. Vaja looked to be one of the Nyírség's more prosperous communities, with neat, pastel-hued houses dotting its paved roads and mature apple trees in the many orchards. Apples had apparently thrived in the sand since the postwar collectivization of agriculture. The sturdy stucco village homes were painted yellow, blue, and pink and wore steeply pitched hats of grey or red slate. The newer sections of the cemetery even boasted some stone monuments festooned with plastic flower arrangements.

But once off historic Main Street, the outlying streets were still unpaved and, in the haze of an unseasonably hot day, a car on these dirt roads was a rarity. Cyclists and pedestrians craned their necks at the Lada raising clouds of dust; chickens pecking in the road squawked and flapped out of our path. We kept on trying to approach the estate along the routes that Aggie and Samuel recalled, which all petered out in sandy trails. While Aggie vainly scanned the horizon for a glimpse of the distillery chimney, Shanyi began to steer the car gingerly alongside the railway tracks, hoping to find a familiar landmark before we ran aground in mud.

And that's how we came upon the neat rectangular building in perfect repair that bore the sign *Rákóczi Tanya*. Like some gingerbread cottage straight out of Grimm, the Rákóczi Estate station house built for great-grandfather Yakab stood in impeccable condition, squared off by a tall hedge and apparently still in use.

Had everything else been as of old, there would have been a vineyard and a kitchen garden sloping upwards beyond the station, and beyond them the house on the hillock, with the distillery looming behind it. Instead, a slightly undulating field of scrub lay fallow, patches of green sprouting in its clumpy, yellowish sand. Towards the crest of a mound we could just make out the outlines of a red roof dwarfed by a massive configuration of trees. In the 1920s Ilona had planted a grove of pine saplings next to the manor house and they had obviously taken. It was they, not the distillery, that led us to the Rákóczi Estate.

Abandoning the car, we began walking towards the house. Aggie had her bearings now. "This was where the walnut trees were," she pointed to a field at either end of which stood a soccer goalpost. "And here were the rose beds, I think."

But she couldn't be certain, because the house itself was unrecognizable. All of Yakab's additions and improvements had somehow been sloughed off over the intervening decades, and we were looking at the ruins of a primitive dwelling. It retained the yellowish stucco of Aggie's memories, but all its charming details – the verandah, the "tent," the famous bathroom – were gone. More than anything else, it probably resembled the bailiff's house that Yakab had renovated a century earlier.

Above one door hung the state emblem of the Hungarian school system in mute testimony to the rumour we had heard about the house once being a school. On the other side, tattered lace curtains of unknown vintage dangled over a couple of cracked and dirty windows. All the doors were bolted from the inside so we could not gain entry.

While I snapped pictures and made notes by reflex action, Aggie and Samuel wandered off morosely. Then Aggie reappeared wearing a tattered smile. "I *knew* the distillery couldn't disappear without a trace," she murmured with an undertone of triumph in her voice, and led me through ankle-high weeds past what she said had once been the carriage-drive where coachmen used to bustle the horses and carriages of family members and visitors.

Four two-storey new houses stood side by side near the site of Zoltán's old home, beneath a signpost that said "Distillery Street." A little further distant, where the estate's old smithies and barns had once been, a row of tiny cottages lined up in rainbow-coloured stucco. In front of them, a few short, sunburnt men and girls with aprons over their jeans were lounging in the shade. They greeted Shanyi politely when he approached them. The large homes, they told him, belonged to the management of the award-winning collective farm two kilometres away. They themselves worked at the collective and lived here. No, they didn't know why the street was called "Distillery Street." There had never been a distillery here.

"Let's go," I mumbled to Aggie. I was suddenly nervous lest someone ask me what I was doing here.

But no one asked us anything at all. We said good day, and they answered politely, "Good day to you, too."

We headed back to the village because Aggie asked to visit the old castle that had been turned into a museum. I wanted to say "No, let's get back to Budapest, there's nothing here for any of us." Normally outgoing and sociable, I felt choked by shyness and a desire for total anonymity. Until I'd seen the cottagers, I had felt nothing but a researcher's curiosity. But the sight of the farmers by their little gardens had unsettled me. Their lack of interest in us – welcome as it was – underscored the fact that we were interlopers.

It was not just my father's paranoia newly reborn in my cells in the days before the fall of communism when the descendant of erstwhile masters might meet a rude welcome. It was not just the sense of not belonging. More than anything, it was a feeling of not wanting to belong, of simply not wanting to be known here at all.

No one had uttered a protesting cry when my family was driven away from here. My father's refusal to set foot here not only seemed understandable to me now, but the only self-respecting course.

But an extraordinary change seemed to have come over Aggie as we drove through the iron gates of the castle and unfolded ourselves from the Lada. Her shoulders were squared, no longer slumped as they had been at the ruins of the farmhouse, and she addressed the swarthy museum custodian at the entrance to the castle with an almost girlish animation. She had been dreading visiting the old estate, and that visit was behind us now. The castle held only pleasant associations.

Aggie had last been here as a girl with my father and his brothers on a summer outing when the count had been away and when, as his tenants, they had been allowed to wander through the park and the grand chambers of the interior. As then, the late-Renaissance castle with its square guard-tower still held the place of honour in the village centre. Now, its interior was handsomely restored and housed artifacts of Rákóczi and his era, but the yellowing lawn and neglected grounds – once the counts' proud park – was a jarring setting for the imposing staircase, polished parquet, and period furniture inside.

The custodian who showed us through the building introduced herself as Zsuzsa Gebelyes, and could not get over the fact that we had come all the way from Budapest just to see the village. She was a striking-looking woman of perhaps fifty-five, with a broad, sun-baked face marked by deep white creases. Stout, with crinkly salt and pepper hair drawn back, her most arresting features were violet blue eyes that shone with good will. When she heard that I was my father's daughter, that I had come all the way from Canada, her hands sprang to her face in surprise.

Obviously eager to establish some common ground, she told us that her dead sister had worked "on the domain" in the old days. She herself, who became the village postmistress after the war, had often contracted to glean on the estate during the summers of her youth. She spoke of the hum and smoke of the threshing machines, recalling that she often met my father and his uncle Zoltán by its side. She remembered the ready song of the harvester girls, the spare, muscular form of the foreman who, as first scytheman, set the pace for the rest of the team. Behind him, and following his rhythm, mowers swished their scythes in staggered formation. Sickles in hand, it was the job of the gleaner girls to scrape together the mowers' leavings which would be bound with thick twine into sheaves the next day.

"There was the harvest festival," Mrs Gebelyes said with unmistakable fondness, "when we would tie up your father for a forfeit." That had been a time-honoured ritual; for untying him, the peasants would be ceremonially rewarded with bottles of sour Szabolcs wine. They in turn presented the master with a wreath braided of ears of wheat interwoven with bright paper streamers, which he kept in the office building until the following harvest.

Warmed by her reminiscences, Mrs Gebelyes walked to the iron

213

gates of the castle to send for her great-niece, a granddaughter of the dead sister who once lived and worked on the estate. A few minutes later a plump girl of nineteen arrived out of breath, her bright apron and blue jeans straining over a pregnant belly. She eyed us with obvious perplexity. For a moment, Mrs Gebelyes also seemed at a loss as she gestured towards me. Her violet eyes blinked as she searched for a title for me that would somehow describe the reality of yesteryear and yet remain ideologically correct, given the communist context.

All at once inspired, she motioned towards me and said with the exquisite tact of a seasoned diplomat, "This lady's father was once the *supervisor* of the old domain." I resisted a violent urge to giggle and yet was grateful. *Bourgeois exploiter*, after all, would have been the classic textbook term.

On parting, Mrs Gebelyes pressed on us a gift of small golden local apples, sweet but mushy from the previous year's harvest. As a final farewell, she dredged up one more positive memory: "Your father always had a good word for us. And a ready joke ... Always. Tell Mister Gusti that I wish him good health and a long life."

Back in Budapest that evening in good time for Shanyi to bathe his baby, Zsuzsika and I repaired to a neighbourhood restaurant and proceeded to drink too much. I remember little else of that evening besides asking her, "What did you feel when you saw the old house?"

"Nothing," she said, downing the last of a pilsner. "I wanted to feel something really badly. I knew how important this place was to my mother and to my grandmother. But I felt nothing at all ... And how about you?"

"Nothing. I could have been anywhere in the world and felt more."

I returned to the Rákóczi Estate once more in 1986. A forest of wild lilacs had engulfed much of what we had seen of the house three years earlier. By now the lilacs must have swallowed it altogether.

The Liberation of a Magyar Jew

I believe that if we spent five hundred, a thousand years simply ploughing
through the documents of the Holocaust, there still wouldn't be enough
time to learn in every detail what happened.
Cynthia Ozick, in an interview with Eleanor Wachtel,
Writers and Company.

I asked my father many times over the years, "But why didn't you
leave Hungary when you still could?" It seemed so obvious – with
hindsight – that the solution had been emigration: to Palestine? to
America? Anywhere, as long as it was out of Europe.

And no matter how insistent I was about the course – so obvious
– he should have taken, his answer remained the same: "You don't
understand ... We would never have left our parents behind. And
our parents would never have left Hungary behind." He said it heavily, with a fatalistic shrug.

It was not that my grandparents were unaware of the crush of
world events that was gradually eroding their safety. But my grandfather Kálmán, who set the tone for the whole family, would always
view Hungary through the liberal-tinted glasses he had donned in
turn-of-the-century Nagyvárad. He was a product of Hungarian Jewry's Golden Age; his personal heroes remained the great Hungarian
liberals of 1848 and, even against mounting evidence to the contrary,
his homeland that of the Emancipation Act of 1867.

The idiosyncratic evolution of Hungarian-Jewish life after the 1848
Revolution accounted for a strident, flag-waving brand of patriotism
among many Magyar Jews. The gift of Hungarian Emancipation
which followed Austrian repression bred in them a gratitude that
made them outdo even their gentile countrymen in displays of Magyar
nationalism. Theodor Herzl called Hungarian Jews "the withered
branch on the tree of world Jewry." Indeed, despite his profound
religious sense of solidarity with the Jewish people as a whole,
Kálmán was deeply suspicious of the Zionist movement, fearing that
supranational manifestations of Jewish unity would endanger the position of Jews in their native lands.

The powerful hold on Kálmán of his own native land was both emotional and practical. The Weinbergers viewed the soil where their ancestors had struck root as a latter-day land flowing with milk and honey. It not only gave them their livelihood, but its rhythms and demands defined their lives and exacted their loyalty. And though my father and his brothers came of age in a viciously anti-Semitic climate in stark contrast to that which Kálmán knew, they nevertheless heeded him when he declared, "This country has been very good to us for a long time. And will prove so again." Their own initially bitter experiences at the academy seemed, in fact, to prove that hatred could be surmounted by patience and diligence. Echoes of the boundless optimism inspired by the old legend of the rabbi's blessing reverberated in my grandfather's last conversation with my father in February 1944. Summarizing the belief system of a lifetime, Kálmán pronounced, "I am a Magyar and a Jew in absolutely equal measures."

Barely three months after that meeting and two months after the German occupation of Hungary, on May 23, 1944, my father's luck appeared to have run out.

"Luck" is a textured word meaning many things during a war. "Luck" could mean privilege, even though you had been stripped of wedding ring and watch, because there was still some money sewn into your trousers, and opportunities could still be found for turning it into the rashers of bacon that made the difference between subsistence and want. "Luck" could mean that the occasional censored postcard still managed to arrive from, if not home, then those who knew of those who once lived at home. It could mean that there was at least one soul in a company of motley, miserable, and uncouth Jews with whom Gusti had forged a meaningful bond. Now that he and his brother Feri had been separated, he would have felt a lost man without Dr András Rosenfeld, the company physician.

But to have fallen under the command of the dreaded Pioneer Corps of Engineers did not constitute luck. Not only did Jewish labour servicemen working under the Pioneers bear a heavy physical burden – building fortifications, bridges, and roads – but their masters were university-educated men, products of the very hotbeds of Hungarian anti-Semitism in the 1920s and 1930s that had bred a militant ideological viciousness. And Ensign Garamszegi who was in charge of Gusti's platoon was not just a doctrinaire anti-Semite but a sadist. At the sight of him, men turned to jelly.

The previous day, it had happened to Gusti's strapping young work partner. The two formed part of a chaingang digging a trench in the mountains of Transylvania. Snow still covered the highest peaks, in weather as wet and frosty as late fall, although the calendar indicated spring. Muscular and thickset, Gusti's comrade wielded a pickaxe slightly in front of him, breaking the rocky ground. Gusti behind him had the easier job, shovelling out the earth piling up in the trench.

Down the double row of labouring men, a mutter made itself suddenly heard: "Here comes Ensign Garamszegi!"

At the very mention of the officer's name, Gusti's partner reared back in fright with a sudden wild swing of his axe. Gusti's right hand shot up in self-protection, the axe striking it mid-palm and ripping out muscle and tendon. The resulting gash would leave a jagged scar to the end of his days.

Summoned to bandage the wound, Dr András sent Gusti back to camp. The following day, May 23, András once more pronounced him unfit for duty. When the work detail left early in the morning, Gusti, palm throbbing, gratefully stayed behind by a small fire.

Outside, there was a sudden small buzz at mid-morning as Ensign Garamszegi materialized for an unscheduled examination of the sick. Gusti jumped to attention to face an enraged officer. "Malingerer!" the ensign shouted, ordering Gusti out to work and András to leave the sick and follow suit. With a lance-sergeant for company, Garamszegi drove the two men from their camp to that of the Pioneers, a distance of some three kilometres. The officers rained blows upon them from behind as punishment for their crimes: Gusti's for "malingering," András for abetting him.

At the Pioneer camp, where building materials for the fortifications were stored, Garamszegi barked commands at the two labour servicemen to each hoist thick bales of wire on to their necks and to keep marching. András was younger and stronger than Gusti and managed to wrestle his load for the kilometre-long march reasonably well. But seeing Gusti's woeful attempts at shouldering the load, the lance-sergeant found additional sport in repeatedly kicking his legs out from under him. Over and over Gusti tripped and fell in the mud where the bale of wire rolled onto his head. Over and over he had to grovel for his load, struggle it back up and clamber to his feet. By then, the cold weather had become a blessing because the exercise was exacting an astonishing output of sweat. At noon when they reached their destination, my father's clothes were sudsing. Even his soldier's greatcoat foamed on the outside.

For the afternoon, Ensign Garamszegi had planned a roster of punishment for Gusti's and András's crimes for the whole company. The 200 men must run down the mountain, load up with a double-pack of lumber and, without resting, run back up. A normal load consisted of a stack of five planks slung between the shoulders of two men marching at regular speed. Doubled, it weighed some 90 kilos, to be lugged uphill and at a run.

The men paired off to the bawling of orders. Their feet slid tractionless in a mush of mud, rain, and snow. No defined road marked the mountainside, only serpentine snowy trails wending upwards. Sections of the path seemed steep enough to lead straight skyward. Gusti was lucky now to be partnered by a healthy young baker from Nagykálló, but András, as a physician, saw that his frail partner had a heart condition. Gusti's baker would effectively drag not only the planks of wood up the hill but his exhausted comrade with them. Out of compassion, not physical strength, András was obliged to do the same for his workmate.

At one point Gusti and András found themselves face to face. András was a handsome man, well-built and robust, a half dozen years younger than Gusti, but his complexion now had a ghastly, yellowish pallor from complete exhaustion. His eyes bulged. The physician who usually bolstered the spirits of others rasped at my father, "We won't survive this ... This is not to be survived."

Now Gusti assumed the role of bolsterer and found the resources to feign a small laugh. "Don't talk such nonsense, of course we'll lick this. Of course we will."

Somewhere during the course of that ascent, the memory of his

father's words returned to him. "I am a Magyar and a Jew in absolutely equal measure."

Gusti memorized the date: May 23, 1944. And made a vow: *If
I am to have a life, it will be as a Jew before anything else.*

No one but fellow Magyars had taught him this lesson.

Less than six months later and with six months of the war yet to
be waged, Gusti and András liberated themselves and their company
of 200 men near András's Subcarpathian home town, Beregszász.
This act, a combination of intuition, cunning, and blind luck, marked
the parting of their ways. András remained in Beregszász, which
eventually fell to the Soviet Union. Gusti, with another friend from
the Nyírség, headed for home. They covered the eighty-kilometre
journey in four days on foot. On Friday, November 10, 1944, they
reached the outskirts of the Rákóczi Estate. A gentle autumnal driz-
zle fell from the grey sky. Petrified silence hung over the countryside
like a blight. The chorus of barking dogs so familiar in the ears
of the country traveller had been silenced; traumatized first by the
retreat of German troops, then by the occupying Russians, the animals cowered noiselessly in the fields, tails limp between their legs.

At the limits of the estate, Gusti encountered his first familiar
face, an ancient herdsman by the name of Huszti, lounging by a
straggling herd of pigs. His garb made an arresting sight; the man's
smock had been cut from the gold silk curtains that, at my father's
last visit home and for as long as he could remember, had draped
the holy Ark in the family synagogue.

Somehow this vision left my father reeling at the margins of his
own identity. *Who was he*? Who was Gusti Weinberger? Was he the
same man who had been here in February, in his own home, the
place where he had been born thirty-eight years earlier?

"Do you know who I am?" he asked the old man, feeling a genuine
curiosity about whether he would be recognized.

"Of course I know you, honourable master," the pigsherd replied,
removing his greasy cap. "How could I not know you?"

"Can you tell me what's going on here now?"

"Well," the old man hesitated, picking his words carefully, "when

... when it pleased all of you to go away from these parts, the count sent a manager from one of his other estates to look after things here for us. You can find him in the office building."

"*When it pleased all of us to go away*," my father repeated out loud in bitter irony to his friend. They began walking in the direction of the house, filled with trepidation. The stables they passed on either side of the trail were empty, the horses requisitioned long ago by the Hungarian army. Yet considering the time of year, considering all that had transpired in the last eight months since he had been here, except for the unearthly silence, things seemed eerily normal. The granaries were stocked with the summer harvest. Smoke wafted from the distillery chimney. The house stood intact.

Outside the office building, Gusti told his friend to wait for him and entered alone. An ancient ragamuffin sat behind Feri's desk, quaffing alcohol from a canteen. My father introduced himself. It took a while for the manager, who was in an advanced state of inebriation, to understand him.

"A Weinberger? ... One of the Weinbergers who used to live here? Well, Mr Weinberger, by all means you can come here ... We will provide for you, it goes without saying."

"I have a friend with me as well."

"Well, then, we will provide for your friend as well."

The two men went through to the bedroom next door and collapsed into bed. Throughout the next day old servants kept on coming by, shaking their heads as they clasped my father's hands. Always plump, he was now painfully thin but, except for his aching legs with their newly acquired network of varicose veins and for the body lice to which he had become unwilling host, he felt fit.

No, none of the other Jews of Vaja had yet returned, the farm hands informed him, but in Nyírmada, they did not know why Mr Ervin Friedmann and his old mother had never been taken away. András Vég, one of the estate's coachmen, was the one to break the news about his house in Nyíregyháza, the little suburban bungalow opposite the train station that he and Mancika had leased from his uncle Ferenc.

"They bombed the station, honourable master. There's only a hole in the ground where your house used to be."

Weeks later, Gusti travelled to Nyíregyháza for the first time since he had returned. By then he had the use of a couple of horses and a carriage, for proper rail service would not resume for years. With typical efficiency and economy, the Germans had broken every rail (not the pair, just one) all the way to Budapest.

In the absence of hard news, Gusti still retained vestiges of hope about the return of his loved ones. But the sight of the open crater where his former house had been, shook him with a terrible force. A thought ran through his mind like a tune one can't shake: *This is the most fitting ending.*

Aloud he said, as if talking to someone who could hear him rather than to all those who could not, "If a happy life can be destroyed, it's better that everything connected with it should go, too." He bent down and scooped randomly in the rubble for the papers that lay there half buried. Mancika had been a neat housekeeper with the true instincts of the collector. She had kept all her letters from her girlhood.

Gusti's fingers scrabbled in the wreckage. He wanted only a small memento. He would take away only that which came readily to hand. Dirt-encrusted but otherwise intact were cards and letters to Mancika written in German in unformed girlish hands from classmates in Frankfurt and Montreux, cards and letters from Mancika's siblings and parents immediately after her marriage, a few cards from himself in earlier labour service.

These souvenirs of his brief married life would supplement the rest of his legacy of letters. Since the day he left in February, a few weeks before the German occupation, he had kept every item of mail that reached him: from Ilona and Kálmán, from Paul and Feri, from Mancika. The notes laboriously printed in block capitals by his little daughter. Cards and letters from his father-in-law and Mancika's brothers and sisters, from the Békéses and Ullmanns in Debrecen, from perfect strangers who had been enlisted into the news network after his family were no longer allowed to write, and whose missives continued to arrive until July 1944. Life-supporting, life-sustaining, life-affirming words stamped "CENSORED" that had fed his hopes even as his own life hung on thin threads.

After July 1944, the cards had stopped. Of his former correspondents, after July 1944 only Paul and Feri and the Békéses were still alive.

From these letters and postcards, from the wartime diary of Charlie Békés, from transcripts of interviews recorded years after the events themselves, it is possible to piece together the history of the last years, in their drama and banality. For the most striking element revealed by these records is how daily life evolved to adapt itself around the extraordinary, the menacing, and the terrifying. And, in the fact that the Weinbergers of sixty years ago did not possess our hindsight, but continued single-mindedly to pursue their personal lives while discounting premonitions of evil, how different were they from most of us today?

Normality in the Tightening Noose

To Paul Weinberger, deeply in love with Mary in Vienna, 1935 was far more significant as the year in which he attempted to win his parents' blessing for his marriage than the year in which the Nuremberg Laws deprived German Jews of their civil rights. And as Gusti sat in his damp suit on a bus in the Bükk mountains beside Mancika Mandula on a late August day in 1936, wanting yet fearing to propose, why should he have spared a thought for Admiral Horthy, regent of Hungary, speeding from a hunting trip in Austria to pay his respects to Hitler in Bavaria?

In the autumn of 1936, as Mancika and Gusti selected furniture for their tidy little house in Nyíregyháza from the same fashionable cabinetmaker who had fashioned Paul's and Mary's walnut buffet, as Mancika's trousseau was being stitched according to Ilona Weinberger's specifications at Elizabeth Békés's lingerie salon, a military unit of Hungarian volunteers left for Spain, the Rome-Berlin Axis came into existence, and Edward VIII gave up the British throne.

The following year Gusti and Mancika married and took the almost obligatory Italian honeymoon of well-bred, middle-class Hungarians. A square stub from the Grand Hotel Bristol in Merano documents the stay of "Gustavo" Weinberger on March 10 and 11, 1937. By March 22 the honeymooners had returned and Mancika's mother wrote that she was counting the days until their visit to Miskolc. Mancika's backward and painfully shy sister, Ilonka, added a postscript: "Today, Sunday, I cleaned out the cupboards in the girls' room. Afterwards, I listened to the 'White Raven' [a soap opera] on the radio. You probably listened to it, too."

A month later, their Nyíregyháza home not yet ready to receive them, the newlyweds were still at the Rákóczi Estate. Sarolta Mandula, Mancika's mother, in a cramped, exquisitely even, purple-ink script, wrote them two pages before the Sabbath. The wedding photographs were still not ready, the medicine Mancika had requested had proved difficult to obtain but had at last been procured from an out-of-town pharmacy. The old woman chided Mancika gently for not supplying her with enough details of her new life: "I acknowledge that in this respect I'm a bit insatiable but, my dear, you write as briefly as if you had been away from home for years. Yet it cannot be possible that you've forgotten how very interested I am in even the slightest morsel of news relating to my dear children."

While Gusti and Mancika were settling into their two-bedroom home in Nyíregyháza, hiring a part-time gardener and full-time maid, Ferenc Szálasi, leader of the fascist Party of National Will, was jailed for three months on the charge of attempting to overturn the constitutional order. The Nyíregyháza suburban water supply proved stagnant, requiring Ferenc Székács to have an artesian well dug in the garden for his nephew-tenant. Gusti commuted every second day to Vaja to confer with his partners and keep abreast of business; on alternating days, he bought and sold on the Nyíregyháza market and kept the firm's accounts.

In the summer of 1937, the minister of the Interior instructed the police to keep Hungarians backing the Republican side in Spain under constant surveillance; General Badoglio, the Italian chief of staff, arrived on an official visit to Budapest, as did General Blomberg, the German minister of war, who promised German aid in equipping the Hungarian army.

By the end of the year, half of the Jews of Germany were unemployed. Signs on butcher shops, dairies, groceries, and pharmacies in that country carried the slogan NO JEWS ALLOWED.

In August 1937, Mancika conceived, though the newlyweds didn't breathe a word to anyone. Gusti arrived by noon at the farm three times a week and left by the six o'clock train. One afternoon, deep in conversation at the dining-room table with Kálmán, he was caught unawares by the whistle of the departing train at the foot of the garden. Looking at his watch, already on his feet, he grabbed his briefcase and wailed, "I've been left behind!" Tripping and scrambling, he somehow reached the little station in time, while Ilona remained seated in the three-legged armchair in the corner of the room.

"That tone of despair, as if he'd been left behind in *jail* instead of his own home," she wept. "I've never heard him use such a tragic voice before."

By the time the four parties of the extreme right fused as the Hungarian National Socialist Party under the future Arrow Cross Prime Minister Szálasi in late October, the whole family rejoiced at the news of Mancika's pregnancy. A month later Szálasi was jailed for ten months for attempting to overturn the constitutional order. And now Mary was pregnant, too, in Vienna.

On New Year's Eve 1938, 100,000 pamphlets littered the streets of Budapest. They bore a brief message in block capitals: "1938 SZÁLASI!"

On March 5, 1938, in an address to a public gathering in the industrial city of Győr, Hungary's prime minister, Kálmán Darányi, gave the first official indication that the government intended to pass legislation to restrict the role of Jews in the economy and the professions. Darányi said, "There was a Jewish question in Hungary ... The kernel of the problem ... consisted in the fact that Jews living in Hungary, partly by reason of a special predisposition for commerce and also because of the indifference shown by Hungarian Christians, played a quite disproportionate role in certain branches of ... economic life. Moreover, the large concentration of Jews in the Hungarian capital had naturally influenced the cultural and economic life of Budapest and that influence was not always congruent with the vital requirements of the Hungarian people."[6]

Jews at this time formed five per cent of Hungary's population but, in the fields of law, medicine, banking, culture, and the arts, their numbers approximated fifty per cent. Their share of the population in the national capital, impossible to pin down exactly, was estimated at between twenty, twenty-five, and thirty-three per cent. The anti-Jewish legislation that would be introduced in the following month aimed both at defusing the constitutional threat of the extremist parties of the right and of currying favour with the German state, which by the Anschluss of March 12 had been brought to the very gates of Hungary. Darányi claimed that reducing Jewish influence in both cultural and economic spheres would not only "grant to the Christian section of the community a just share in the industry, commerce, and finance of the country," but would also "be in the interests of the Jews themselves, for anti-Semitism and the propagation of extremist and intolerant movements would thus be greatly lessened."

In the prevailing domestic and international climate, Hungarian Jews were willing to acquiesce to the prospect of what they perceived to be largely token legislation. They were reassured by the government's repeated promises that it would act equitably and withstand pressure from the extreme right. Enacted and immediately put into effect on May 29, 1938, the law limited Jews to twenty per cent of the total composition of the professions, business, and industry. The term "Jew" was defined according to religion. Harsh and discriminatory as it was, the law of 1938 compared favourably with restrictions imposed upon Jews elsewhere in central Europe.

In early March 1938, while the prime minister cogitated over the "Jewish question," Gusti, ever cautious and protective, prepared for the imminent birth of the baby by moving Mancika to Debrecen where the great event was scheduled for the middle of the month. Mancika, installed at her sister's, Gusti back at the Rákóczi Estate, heard the news of the German occupation of Austria separately.

Suddenly the whole family was trembling for Paul, Mary, and Mary's son, who were then wintering in Vienna and who, in the meantime, were queued up at a train station, among the panicked hordes attempting to flee the city. Lined up at the ticket counter, Paul reached for his wallet and realized that in his rush to catch what he believed to be the last train for Budapest, he had forgotten it at home. With overwhelming relief, he caught sight of a couple of second cousins up ahead in line. Breathlessly explaining his predicament, he requested a quick loan – and was curtly refused.

"These are extraordinary times," his wealthy cousin told Paul without apology. "Have you any idea what we'll find when we get to

226

Budapest? I may need my every *fillér* for myself." Leaving Mary and her son at the platform to keep their place, Paul threw himself into a cab, rushed back to the apartment, picked up his wallet, and somehow managed to catch the train.

The next day, March 15, the Hungarian ambassador extended the good wishes of his country to Hitler in Berlin on the reunification of Austria and Germany, and the Hungarian government hurried to show its sympathy for the new order by preparing the (anti-)Jewish Law.

The end of March arrived without the birth of Mancika's baby. Evidently there was some error in the calculations, for as the days dragged by, there was still no change. Gusti and Mancika visited the Békéses several times a week, Mancika by now covering her face in real rather than mock embarrassment as she crossed the threshold: the baby had been due in mid-March! On one of these visits, Gusti teased his aunt with a completely serious mien, "What do you think, Elizabeth? Can an unborn child be *absorbed*?"

In the Austria abandoned by Paul and Mary, a veritable explosion of sadism and terror, surpassing atrocities even in Germany, was taking place. Thousands of Jews were thrown into concentration camps, cornered on streets, beaten and kicked by black-booted SS men. Rabbis were sent to clean latrines, Jewish men and women forced on their knees to scrub gutters, often with acid added to the scrub water.

On April 8, the Jewish Law was tabled in Hungary, turning the clock of emancipation back some seventy years.

Eleven days later, my father bolted out of Dr Zempléni's fashionable sanatorium in the Alföldi Palace in Debrecen, unable to bear the wails of his labouring wife. He fled along the Korzo, fled from the approaching birth as he had fled so many times on the farm when cows dropped their calves or mares foaled, as he would flee my mother at my birth nine years on. While Évike Weinberger made her delayed debut into the world on April 19, 1938, Gusti stood quaking in the churchyard of the twin-spired Great Church, holding the trunk of an enormous oak for support.

The infancy of Évike and of her cousin Marika, Mary and Paul's daughter born three months later, saw the Munich agreement, the dismemberment of Czechoslovakia (with Hungary receiving back all of Carpatho-Ruthenia and passing further anti-Jewish legislation in appreciation of the prize), the organized pogrom in Germany and Austria known as Kristallnacht, a terrorist attack on Budapest's famous Dohány Street synagogue, the German occupation of Czechoslovakia and, in September 1939, Hitler's attack on Poland.

The outbreak of war briefly brought Mancika's parents and her sister Ilonka for refuge to the Rákóczi Estate, but it was soon evident that, despite terrifying events elsewhere, in Hungary normal daily life would continue. After a brief holiday in Vaja, the Mandulas returned to Miskolc, while the Hungarian government kept up its delicate courtship of Germany, a fatal flirtation bent on reversing the injustices of the old Treaty of Trianon and simultaneously eluding Germany's fearsome embrace. Despite successive waves of discriminatory legislation, Hungary actually became a haven to which Jews from Poland and Slovakia could sometimes escape. By 1944, the annexation of new territories and the trickle of refugees had increased Hungary's Jewish population from half a million to about 800,000.

Only in relationship to the situation of Jews in occupied Europe, however, could that of Hungarian Jews be viewed as favourable. The Second Jewish Law of May 1939 reduced the proportion of Jews in economic, financial, and cultural occupations to six per cent. It limited Jewish service in the armed forces, and laid down that "Jews were to be used only in the line of fire." Unlike the previous law, which had defined Jews by religion, the law of 1939 defined them by race. It restricted the franchise to those Jews whose ancestors had lived continuously in Hungary since 1867 or who had themselves done so. Since, in 1939, the great majority of Hungarian Jews had been born after 1867, and since precise records were almost nonexistent, this restriction effectively disenfranchised most Jewish voters. Besides the social stigma caused by loss of the vote, the economic impact of the law was immediate and far-reaching. About 40,000 Jewish families lost their means of livelihood.

Military co-operation with Germany began in 1940 and, along with it, the establishment of special battalions of Jewish men in auxiliary labour units. Hundreds of thousands of men of military age classified as "unreliable" – and hence unfit to bear arms – were organized into military formations under the command of Hungarian Army officers. They were supplied with tools and employed in construction, road, and fortifications building for the military, both within Hungary and in Hungarian- and German-occupied parts of Ukraine and Yugoslavia. Originally intended for all "unreliables" – Romanians, Serbs, Slovaks, and communists as well as Jews – in short order the system was used as an anti-Jewish measure.

From the vantage point of the military leadership, the peculiar problem was how to induct Jews into the forces without actually arming them. In the spring of 1940, as Germany won notable victories in Denmark and Norway, the Hungarian chief of staff wrote to the minister of defence that "the Jews must be made liable for service and for special engineering duties in sectors where casualties were heaviest." Feverish preparations were under way for a campaign against Romania to recover areas of Transylvania formerly belonging to Hungary. In the general mobilization ordered at the end of May, Jews not summoned into the army were to be put into special labour-service units of which there were seventy formed by July.

On November 20, 1940, Hungary announced its adherence to the Rome-Berlin-Tokyo Axis, the first of the smaller nations to join the pact. The Jewish policy of the Hungarian government by now had the objective of placating the extreme right.

The Finger of God

Nine kilometres away
houses and haystacks are burning,
and at the edge of the meadow
mute and petrified peasants
puff at their pipes.
But here the tiny shepherdess
stirs the lake as she wades in,
and, bending to drink,
her curly sheep swallow a cloud.

Miklós Radnóti,
"Picture Postcards"
Cservenka, October 6, 1944

In my hand I hold the *Zsoldkönyv*, my father's labour service record book. Its cover bears the old Hungarian national arms, topped by a crown with the Hungarian tipped cross and borne by two apparently female angels in flowing gowns. Inside it lists my father's vital statistics, the names of his parents and of his wife, his physical description. Body build: average. Hair: brown. Eyes: brown. Face: Round. Height: 170 centimetres. According to particulars in the booklet, my father served his first term in Kisvárda from September 2 to December 15, 1940.

The most notable feature of this unremarkable stint of duty spent clearing a forest emerged only with hindsight. Three years later, Gusti's squadron commander, a likable forestry engineer by the name of Marton Weinberger – no relation – by one of those eerie coincidences that prove fact stranger than fiction, married one Anikó Schwartz.

Gusti's future second wife. My mother.

In the early days of Marton Weinberger's engagement, in a scene that might have sprung out of a Hollywood movie, two men – one rotund and slightly balding, the other young and dashing, blond and blue-eyed – literally collided on the platform of a railway station teeming with soldiers and labour servicemen like themselves, wearing

yellow armbands. Shaking hands heartily, they exchanged pleasant-
ries, good wishes, and news.

"Just look at this," Marton said, reaching into his wallet to extract
a snapshot lovingly. "My fiancée."

And there, on the dusty platform of an anonymous railway station,
my father first looked into the eyes of my mother. "Very pretty,"
he murmured, returning the photo, his mind on his own wife and
daughter waiting for him at the end of his journey.

The two men who had had such genuine regard for each other
in the days of their service in Kisvárda would meet only one more
time. Years later, they would shake hands again in a small dark room
in Budapest, after a divorce court had terminated the marriage of
Anikó and Marton, the sole union in their respective families that
had not been sundered in a death camp.

While Gusti was clearing forests in the fall of 1940, the rhythm of
family life adjusted to accommodate the forced absences of its sons.

Lawyer Charlie Békés of Debrecen kept an intermittent wartime
diary, minutely recording family events in a soft-covered black note-
book. The entries for 1940-41 include annual pilgrimages to the family cemetery in Lövő, Elizabeth's fiftieth birthday ("Aggie and I
bought a black wool dress for her for 28 *Pengő*. Aggie contributed
a quarter of the amount, I the balance"), family visits to Debrecen,
conversation topics at dinner parties.

Charlie's entry for the evening of February 26, 1941, arrests my
eyes with its pencilled scrawl. "I have just arrived from a business
trip to Nyíregyháza where, by coincidence, I happened to meet my
brother-in-law, Kálmán, and his son, Feri. They took me to see their
purchase yesterday: the house at No. 5 Vörösmarty Square, for 26,000
Pengő. Because of the early hour, 7 a.m., they couldn't show me
the interior, which consists of 5 rooms."

I know the history of this house. I have even visited it.

After my father completed his first stint of service in December 1940,
he resumed commuting between Nyíregyháza and the family estate.
At home, things were almost entirely normal but for the absence

of Paul who was in service. On February 25, the day before he bumped into Charlie, Feri travelled up to Nyíregyháza on the early morning train for a house-hunting expedition with my father. Labour service and war notwithstanding, the brothers still looked towards a future that held unlimited possibilities. Aged thirty-four and thirty-five respectively, Feri and Gusti were planning their retirement years.

In reality, what they were after was some property for investment. But the house they found on Vörösmarty Square held additional inducements: edged by mature fruit trees, it stood on a landscaped lot that could easily accommodate two extra city houses and gardens. Over lunch at the ornately appointed Crown Hotel, the brothers discussed the future with excitement. There would never be enough room for all three of them and their families in the existing two houses on the Rákóczi Estate. Certainly they could build on to the main house as great-grandfather Yakab had done, but they would only be making improvements that would benefit the count's family. The land on which they built would never be their own. On the other hand, with the acquisition of this property in Nyíregyháza, all three brothers could one day retire and live together, side by side. Gusti, already renting in Nyíregyháza, could start immediately to build a new house next to the existing one in Vörösmarty Square and move in as soon as it was ready. Eventually they'd build a third house as well. They concluded the sale the same day.

The house that Gusti planned to build next to the one already standing on the property was no idle dream. Much of the correspondence between him and Mancika in 1943 and 1944 dealt with the details of its completion: disputes with the contractor, difficulties with the delivery of the parquet floor, the necessity of settling for an off-white instead of pure white linen blind for the kitchen. As Hitler planned Operation Margarethe, as the Russians edged towards Hungary, as Gusti clerked in a Transylvanian station house in March 1944, Mancika struggled over details of the new house in which she would never live.

Immediately after the war, my father found himself briefly the sole owner of two houses in Nyíregyháza. He installed one of his surviving aunts into the house where Mancika had supervised construction. It was in this house that he and Anikó trysted on stolen occasions in the last days of 1946 and early in 1947, in this house that my mother believes I was conceived.

Today, with a population of 100,000, Nyíregyháza is double the size it was half a century ago. Still the county capital, a flat provincial rail and industrial centre barely rising out of the sand, it houses its citizens in sterile highrises that have supplanted many of the traditional stucco bungalows that used to characterize the town's architecture.

Forty-five years after Gusti and Feri bought the house on Vörösmarty Square, I combed the acacia and linden-scented small-town streets for the houses that family members had once inhabited. Purple wild roses clung to country fences on side streets that resembled village roads, the odd chicken pecking in the dirt. An apartment building occupied the site of the bungalow where Yakab had spent his retirement. The other family residences I had been trying to unearth yielded similar results.

Weary and depressed, I trekked back to my hotel and unfolded my map. The words Vörösmarty Square leapt from the page without warning, located astonishingly – if I was reading the map right – directly in back of my hotel.

The light was rapidly fading when I snapped a photograph of the only house my father ever built. Its gracious grounds had been lopped off; the house that once stood near it – the original purchase – was gone. Three shuttered windows framed by grey stucco and dark shingles stared back at me. Only the address was familiar. I did not yet know that my own life probably began behind one of those cane shutters.

Back home in Montreal, my mother would rifle through my many Hungarian snapshots but ask for a copy only of this one.

On April 23, 1941, Gusti began his second bout of labour service. Called up with Feri to the foothills of the Carpathians recently reannexed by Hungary, he felt in considerably greater danger now than in the previous service. Three weeks earlier, Hungarian Prime Minister Count Teleki had killed himself over Germany's demand that Hungarian forces join in the invasion of Yugoslavia, a country to which Teleki had pledged "eternal friendship" a year before. On May 19, Jews in labour-service units were ordered to wear yellow armbands. Rumours abounded that the units would shortly begin to serve outside the country.

Indeed, on June 27, 1941, five days after the beginning of the German onslaught on Russia, Hungary also declared war on the Soviet Union over the pretext of a Russian air attack (actually staged by Germany) on the Hungarian city of Kassa (Kosice). Within days Company 108/32 received orders to cross the mountain pass at Toronya and follow the Hungarian Army into Ukraine as an auxiliary road-maintenance company.

A photograph taken of the two Weinberger brothers at that time captures them in identical khaki uniforms, peaked caps on their heads, leather side packs and boots. Gusti frowns mistrustfully over his round spectacles at the camera, but Feri, ever more optimistic, flashes a suave smile. As they performed their monotonous tasks, two things mitigated the uncertainty and dreariness of their duties: they had had the good fortune to be assigned a benign officer, and letters and parcels from home continued to boost their morale.

But even in the correspondence, there were hints of the larger, grim picture. Interspersed in the chatty news of daily life on the farm – of women putting up red currants and sour cherries, of Évike learning to recite nursery rhymes – Mancika let drop a sudden illuminating glimpse of the outside world: the youngest Ullmann cousin had managed to escape from occupied Belgium to Cuba.

In the meantime, the Hungarian Parliament passed the Race Protection Law that defined the term "Jew" according to racial principles in the spirit of the Nuremberg Laws of Germany. It prohibited marriages between Jews and non-Jews and defined as Jewish anyone who belonged to the "Israel faith," or one of whose parents, or two of whose grandparents had been or were members of that faith.

And while Charlie and Elizabeth Békés were celebrating their twenty-second wedding anniversary in Vaja on August 17 and, three days later, twenty-two family members sat down for tea in honour of the sons now unexpectedly home on leave, steps were being taken by the Hungarian government that were a direct consequence of the political climate which had given rise to the Race Protection Law.

During the month of August, some 18,500 stateless Jews in Hungary, most of them Polish nationals, were being rounded up for expulsion to Galicia or Ukraine. At the end of August, German SS units and Hungarian army engineer units massacred most of them in Kamenetz-Podolsk.

"The idea of deportation was conceived and implemented at the time when the Lower House was debating the Race Protection Law, when the public was subjected to incessant tirades advocating the segregation of Jews from Magyars," writes historian Nathaniel Katzburg.[7] The first instance of such segregation and deportation was targeted at those of allegedly non-Hungarian nationality. While these events, shadowy and unpublicized, were being planned, on August 1 Charlie Békés had confided to his diary, "*May God grant that we remain on Hungarian soil throughout.*"

In Germany, meanwhile, preparatory regulations were being drawn up for the liquidation of the Jews. Eichmann was visiting the killing centres in the East and organizing his first mass deportations from Germany and the Protectorate. January 1942 saw the Proclamation of the Final Solution at the Wannsee Conference. The machinery of destruction that was now set up would be refined and perfected by March 1944, when it would be applied to Hungary.

Hannah Arendt has written, "In country after country, the Jews had to register, were forced to wear the yellow armband for easy identification, were assembled and deported, the various shipments being directed to one or another of the extermination centres in the East, depending on their relative capacity at the moment; when a trainload of Jews arrived at a centre, the strong among them were selected for work, often operating the extermination machinery, all others were immediately killed."[8]

By the time Hungary's turn arrived, all the kinks had been ironed out of the system.

But it did look as if Hungary's turn would not arrive. In January 1942, for instance, Kálmán Weinberger travelled with ease to his old home in Kajdanó, now once again belonging to Hungary and no longer in Czech territory. Kálmán's reason for going was to arrange for the manufacture of ox-bows for the new teams of oxen his sons planned to purchase to replace the horses they were selling off from the Rákóczi Estate before they could be requisitioned by the army. A month later, Kálmán's brother Béla, thoroughly experienced at working with oxen, wrote from Kajdanó with advice about the projected purchase, concluding his letter with the words, "The days pass in the greatest monotony – until outside events jolt us out of our complacency."

Those "outside events" included the mobilization of all of Hungary's available manpower to the Russian front in January 1942 at Germany's behest. In response, Britain and the United States declared war on Hungary. In March the new Hungarian prime minister, Miklós Kállay, began to pursue the duplicitous policy of trying to make peace with the West while aiding the German war effort and publicly speaking friendship for Germany. This "see-saw" policy permitted relative internal freedom for Hungary's Jews – although on March 12 legislation was introduced to expropriate their lands, and on March 17, with the mobilization of the Second Hungarian Army to the East, Army Command issued an order for "the utilization of the Jews for war purposes."

Verbal instructions to officers in charge of labour units from High Command made explicit what this "utilization" implied. "I see a good officer as one who brings back few Jews," witnesses quoted the words of one officer at his subsequent trial as a war criminal.[9] Kállay's war minister, a singularly decent man, wrote in his memoirs, "the men of the Labour Service sent to the Ukraine carried in their knapsacks their death sentences."[10] In this malevolent atmosphere Paul began a new service in June, and his brothers waited for their next call-up.

In the summer of 1942, while the Warsaw Ghetto was being "evacuated" and some 300,000 Jews "resettled" in Treblinka at the rate of 5,000 a day, Charlie Békés wrote of his summer holidays: "Wonderful swimming in the Bodrog. The heat is very great." On August 19, he noted poignantly, "At Vaja, Ilona, Elizabeth ... and I congratulated Mary on her 6th wedding anniversary today; Paul is in labour camp."

The occasional "outside event" also found its way into Charlie's diary. A fervent Hungarian patriot, he recorded on August 12: "12 o'clock. At Vaja, we are shocked to hear on the radio that Vitéz István Horthy de Nagybánya, the regent's son and deputy, died the death of a hero on the Soviet battlefield." And on Yom Kippur in Debrecen, the sight of a squadron of labour servicemen elicited a rare critical comment from Charlie; a much-decorated first lieutenant in World War I, he was stung by the spectacle of Jewish soldiers not accorded their proper rank. "They serve in their own clothes, yellow armbands on their left arms, on their heads soldiers' caps; among them are two in full uniform, without being ranked. One used to be a lieutenant, the other a sergeant. This is what I find painful."

"Every Jew who survived in occupied Europe is a kind of itinerant miracle, the result of incredible endeavours and struggles," declared the Israeli diplomat Aryeh Leon Kubowy, shortly after the conclusion of the war.[11] My father didn't know Kubowy, but he shared with him the idea of miraculous deliverance. In recounting his experiences – those many near misses and alternate routes that might well have led him where all, or nearly all, the other members of his family ended up – Gusti frequently spoke of the "finger of God" that had guided him out of disaster, that had pointed him in the right direction.

This is strange when I think of my father's belief system. Although his parents and grandparents had believed in the most personal of gods, one who paid attention – in the words of the Christian hymn – to even a falling sparrow, Gusti had abandoned that kind of faith under Zolka Rochlitz's tutelage in Varsány. There, he became a rationalist who believed in the laws of nature. To him God was a guiding principle, the force that had created life, set it in motion, and then stood watch as it unfolded beneath His gaze.

But that was the grand and distant God who could be relegated to omnipotent impersonality when all was well with the world. In wartime, the God of miracles had to be invoked. And, indeed, my father would invoke Him, bless His name and His miraculous finger whenever he spoke of his own many escapes. Unlike Elie Wiesel who, in works such as *Night*, railed against the God who had abandoned the Jews, my father could accept the mystery of his own survival as a divine gift. But he too railed – increasingly, as he got older.

He railed at Hitler and his henchmen as the incarnation of Satan in our day. God had not so much abandoned the Jews as proved weaker than His adversary.

The "finger of God" appeared almost in the flesh in October 1942 when Gusti was called up with his company to the town of Sárospatak, in nearby Zemplén county. For a number of reasons the posting seemed particularly fortuitous. His youngest aunt, Augusta, and her husband, Nándor, lived in Sárospatak in a comfortable, centrally located house already requisitioned as a billet. Gusti's commanding officer, a first lieutenant called Kassai, had himself been assigned quarters there.

Kassai belonged to a rare breed of Hungarian soldier: he was so well-disposed towards his Jews that it was said to be a pleasure to serve under him. In no time Augusta had persuaded him to allow Gusti to live under her roof as well, instead of in the barracks. "On one condition," Kassai joked, "that on pay day he'll report to duty like every other man."

In fact, there was no real work for the other men either. They had been called to Sárospatak to await the formation of several other companies, each consisting of 207 men, each presumably destined for the Russian front. Gusti knew many in this throng, including two of his own cousins and a nephew of his uncle Nándor, one Andor Klein. Since it looked as if the companies would not be moving for a while, Augusta invited Mancika and Évike to the house as well. It was an enviable situation in which to find oneself, so enviable that Gusti tried not to show his face too much about town, making sorties only to visit his cousins in barracks and pick up his pay.

Uncle Nándor, on the other hand, was a popular gadabout who fed off the choice morsels of gossip circulating in town concerning the influx of Jewish soldiers. The juiciest tidbit – deliberately gotten up, as it later turned out, by military brass prospecting for bribes – was the rumour that Company No. 32, to which both Gusti and Andor Klein had been assigned, was a so-called "home company." It was said with the greatest assurance that the 32nd Company was not intended for the front but for certain undefined duties that would keep it indefinitely in Hungary. Regardless of what happened to Companies 33 through 37 which were all being drawn up as well, only the 32nd would have domestic duties.

Early each morning Nándor made his ritual trip to the barber on Main Street to find out who had switched out of which company in order to be admitted to the 32nd, as monied servicemen greased palms to obtain the necessary permits and transfers. In the meantime, Gusti and Andor reflected on their good fortune in having been assigned to this favoured company.

Every tenth day Lieutenant Kassai would remind Gusti to turn up for his pay. When he did so, he invariably found himself in a transformed platoon. The 32nd Company kept on expanding; at roll call he always had new neighbours.

Suddenly the pleasant monotony of these days was broken by the news that all six companies must prepare to be made road-ready. But even now the odd man found a way to worm himself into the 32nd. The alert, however, had signalled a genuine problem: the 32nd Company, it was announced, had over-enlisted. It numbered 277 men instead of the requisite 207. Seventy men would have to be cut from the roster.

That evening Gusti bumped into Andor Klein, and told him he was heading over to the company office "to check things out." The younger man fell into step with him and they headed for the administration building together. In the dingy, dimly lit office assigned to the 32nd, men jostled irritably in a haze of cigarette smoke. Disgruntled servicemen formed straggling lines by the desk of the company clerk. The poorer members of the company complained loudly about rich Jews inflating the roster. Why should poor men have to be cut and transferred to the front when they had been originally assigned to a favoured home company?

Gusti drifted about the room listening before taking up a position behind the desk of the beleaguered clerk where he could hear the man's answers to his questioners. It appeared that, instead of being evenly distributed among the six existing companies, the seventy men who would be cut were to be transferred to a newly forming company in Sárospatak. They would then be joined by another newly recruited group until their numbers were large enough to form a brand new outfit. Its commander was said to be a member of the dread Pioneer Corps of Engineers.

Gusti listened intently for a while, then beckoned his friend to a corner. "I'm thinking, Andor," he said, "of stepping out of the 32nd."

"Are you *crazy*?" The young man's eyebrows were working in alarm.

"Just listen for a moment. This new company they're planning to form with seventy men ... it can't just be taken from here from one day to the next. It's got to wait for the other group they're talking about, which hasn't even arrived. It'll be a while before they're road-ready. Whereas the 32nd Company –"

"– Is a *home company*!" Andor wailed. "Even if we've got to go today, with a man like Kassai at the helm, it'll be a pleasure!"

"Suit yourself," Gusti said. "As for me, I'm getting out."

The other man looked at him, then shrugged. "The blind leading the blind ... I must be crazy, too."

My father made his way back to the hapless clerk still warding off belligerents. "Please sign me out of the 32nd," Gusti said, passing him a folded bill. The clerk gave him a searching glance, scanned his roster, then scratched his name. Why protest? Everyone else wanted in.

The 32nd Company, like the other five formed in Sárospatak in the fall of 1942, left town a few days later, destined, for the Russian front. At the Hungarian border the military gendarmerie relieved First Lieutenant Kassai of his command. The 32nd was assigned to the care of the infamous Pioneers and put into immediate action. After liberation Gusti would meet a Dr Moskovits, who had once been a member of his first platoon in the 32nd. Moskovits was one of seven of the original 207 to have returned home alive.

In the winter of 1943, the Second Hungarian Army disintegrated completely. Out of 200,000 soldiers, 140,000 were killed. Of 50,000 Jews, between 40,000 and 43,000 perished, victims of German soldiers, Hungarian militiamen, or Russian bullets. The sixty-eight who had been struck out of the 32nd (and the two who had voluntarily withdrawn) were sent home for a winter holiday until the other section of the company arrived. They were recalled to Sárospatak in February 1943 and immediately discharged.

Two months later Gusti began his final labour service, in which eventually his own life was daily on the line when he too fell into the hands of the dreaded Pioneers. But his miraculous journey of survival had begun long before his deliverance from Ensign Garamszegi, amidst the rumours and smoke swirling in the company office in Sárospatak, when "God's finger," as he would always maintain, pointed his way in the direction of life.

In the spring of 1943 Prime Minister Kállay's "see-saw" policy reached its zenith. Three months after the rout of Hungary's forces at Veronezh, in a tactical concession to the Germans, Kállay dispatched twenty-two fresh labour-service battalions to the doomed Russian front. And yet he repeatedly refused German requests that the country's Jews be "transferred to areas of the East" (for this, read "murdered"), on the grounds that this would destroy Hungary's economy. Simultaneously he launched several initiatives to parlay with the West. As Germany continued to lose in the East, and Anglo-American troops landed in Sicily in the summer of 1943, liberal voices were being heard in Hungary on behalf of the country's labour servicemen. A famous romantic patriot, editor, and politician, Endre Bajcsy-Zsilinszky, called for the abrogation of the anti-Jewish laws.

In this period of hope mitigated by departures to the front, of a thaw in public opinion counterbalanced by the expropriation of Jewish lands, Charlie Békés continued to record the everyday events of the family's life in Debrecen. In the wake of the expropriation of Jewish lands, eighteen-year-old Zsuzsi Rochlitz, who had dreamed of studying early childhood education in Budapest, had been apprenticed to Elizabeth's lingerie salon. On March 7, 1943, Charlie wrote: "22 o'clock. Zolka and Yanchika have come from Mándok where they have been living since their enormous estate and home were taken away by the Jewish laws of December last year to visit their daughter Zsuzsi who is staying with us. Tomorrow, Laskod, too, where Gisela and Béla live, will have its critical day. It, too, is being taken over by the National Organizing Tribunal for Landed Property, so that, for the time being, it will be leased to Dr Jozsef

Okolicsán." In a further disruption of normal life, the Békéses had begun to take in Jewish boarders in an attempt to prevent their spacious flat from being used as a billet.

Meanwhile, Mancika, Évike, and Gusti had decided on spending Gusti's last days of leave at the old family home in Vaja. Mancika's cards to her parents anxiously detail the steps of the little girl's recovery from chicken pox in May: "Yesterday, Saturday, I let her get up from bed ... Tomorrow, God willing, I'll give her a bath." The Mandula family had reached such a state of poverty that Mancika's sister asked for her cast-off clothes, and poultry was sent weekly to Miskolc from the Rákóczi Estate.

After Gusti departed for his new posting in Kassa on March 7, Mancika could not keep a note of bitterness from her upbeat missives to her parents: "Unfortunately it appears that for our family the good Lord has so decreed that all three boys should stay in service. As long as it ends well and His will be done. Others have had better luck."

From Kassa, reported Mancika, Gusti had written "that they are well accommodated and are well." Had she known the true nature of those accommodations, she might have sounded even more bitter and anxious. Later, my father called the trooping together in Kassa of thousands of Jewish men "the greatest human slave market I ever saw." Put up in huts and tents at a makeshift encampment, they slept virtually out of doors, although the balmy May weather was no great hardship. In the morning they faced the humiliating command to strip and parade naked until they were sorted out into their companies: a rag-tag crew of oddly shaped figures, many still with waist-long beards and curly sidelocks.

And yet the rules of humanity had not yet been altogether suspended. A month later when Mancika's mother died suddenly, Gusti obtained immediate compassionate leave to return to Miskolc for the funeral. The days of easy service had come to an end, however. On June 30, Germany, Austria, and the German Protectorate were declared *Judenrein*. And from Kassa, Gusti's company was transported in the new mode being perfected for Jews across Europe: forty men packed literally like sardines, head to foot, foot to head for a three-day journey to Transylvania. Their job would be to lay tracks and build stations for the new line reconnecting Transylvania to Hungary.

Meanwhile Feri received his final posting as well. Wrote Charlie Békés on the evening of July 14, 1943: "My dear nephew Feri Weinberger is travelling back to his garrison in Bükkszállás, near Zombor, as deputy platoon commander of auxiliary labor regiment 108/81." Feri's destination, unknown to him as yet, was the copper mines of Bor, in Serbia.

"I escorted him to the station," continued Charlie. "Pouring rain. Dark station house. Long, crowded train. He got two days' leave to equip himself with winter clothes. Ilona also accompanied him."

My grandmother had come as far as Debrecen with Feri, but she refused to go to the station. Aggie witnessed the final leave-taking between mother and son in the foyer of the Békés apartment, as Charlie stood by the door hat in hand, ready for departure. External crises always galvanized Ilona out of her melancholy periods. She tried to shield the family as much as she could from fully realizing the extent of her dark moods. Her letters to her sons in service, for instance, were unfailingly cheerful, belying tear-drenched pillows that the chambermaid changed each morning when she came to make the bed. Exercising supreme self-command, Ilona now bade Feri a steadfast good-bye. But when he and Charlie left the apartment, her unshed tears burst forth in hysterical sobs. She tore into the next room, plucking and rending her clothes, before collapsing unconscious on the floor. None of them ever saw Feri again.

About 200 kilometres southeast of Belgrade, the Bor mines supplied about half of the copper requirements of the German war industry. In 1943 the German corporate authorities in charge arranged for the transfer of 6,000 Hungarian-Jewish servicemen to meet the labour shortage there. The majority of them worked in gruelling conditions with inadequate diet for over a year before facing the forced evacuation of the mines in the fall of 1944 under pressure of the Red Army and Yugoslav partisans. Feri was among the more fortunate in being assigned to a road-construction unit rather than the mine itself or its access tunnel where conditions were the worst.

In response to an advertisement I placed in the North American

Hungarian-language weekly *Menora* for information about my uncle's fate, a New York psychiatrist wrote me in 1982: "I was with
him in Bor. He bore the life of the *lager* well. He always maintained
that 'soup's not eaten at the temperature at which it's cooked.'" That
homely Hungarian proverb roughly signifying "things are not as bad
as they seem" is of a piece with everything I have ever heard of
my uncle. Sophisticated, easy-going, an optimist, he had a survivor's
spirit, but no survivor's luck. The "finger of God" failed him.

He survived the inhuman conditions and the massacres of the
month-long forced march out of Bor. At Cservenka, on the night
of October 7, between 700 to 1,000 men were slaughtered. He was
there, but he did not even know of the massacre at the time. On
October 15, his column reached the southern Hungarian town of
Baja. His friend, the physician who answered my ad, along with
many other Bor survivors, managed to escape there. Those who
stayed with their regiments were deported to concentration camps
in Germany.

Among the Jewish labour servicemen being evacuated from Bor was
the brilliant, thirty-five-year-old poet Miklós Radnóti. He continued
to write almost until the day he was felled by an SS bullet in November 1944. He was buried in a mass grave. Upon exhumation after
the war, his last poems were found on his body.

According to the International Tracing Service of the Red Cross,
my uncle Feri Weinberger, Prisoner No. 34971, was committed to
Concentration Camp Flossenburg on November 9, 1944, one day
before my father arrived back home with his friend on the Rákóczi
Estate. He was "transferred to Concentration Camp Flossenburg/
Commando Hersbruck on December 3, 1944, where he died on December 26, 1944. Cause of death not indicated. Category: *Jude*."

In the desultory entries Charlie Békés penned in his diary during
the summer and fall of 1943 is evidence that wartime exigencies were
finally undercutting the pursuit of normality. When Aggie left for
a holiday in Sárospatak at Augusta's as she usually did every summer,
because of the increased scarcity of food she took bread and flour

with her for an eight-day stay. Still, all was not completely bleak, even in the menu department. On November 7 Elizabeth made a little party to celebrate Aggie's acceptance as a substitute teacher at the Jewish *gimnázium* (Aggie was still pursuing her doctoral studies at the University of Debrecen). Eight people attended the soirée of conversation and radio listening, leaving at two in the morning. "My Elizabeth," wrote the diarist with fond pride, "served sandwiches filled with goose liver, *real* coffee, quince leather, walnuts and sweet cakes. There was excellent wine and finely aged brandy. Lesko [one of the guests] read out loud the poem I composed for Aggie with modest success."

Counterbalancing this image of well-fed hospitality is the following entry of November 23: "My Elizabeth says that, since the financial clouds are truly blackening over the heads of Zsuzsi [Rochlitz]'s parents – ever since the expropriation of their estate and home a year ago, the cost of keeping Péter in Budapest and Zsuzsi here is barely covered – today she told Zsuzsi that until things become more affordable and the estate is given back to them, she doesn't have to pay us anything. Zsuzsi kissed her. I approved." Formerly the wealthiest branch of the extended family, the Rochlitzes had been reduced to such penury that covering their daughter's room and board in Debrecen had become unaffordable.

"The Greatest
and Most Horrible Crime"

At the end of February 1944 Gusti travelled home to Vaja from Transylvania on what turned out to be his final leave. (By this time, Mancika and Évike had moved to the Rákóczi Estate from Nyiregyháza for reasons of safety and economy.) Only in retrospect does his sense of hope on this leave take on a dreadful irony. He would later maintain that he had never said his farewells as lightheartedly as he did on February 27, 1944. The Red Army had reached Tarnopol in Ukraine and seemed unstoppable on its path towards the Carpathians and the Hungarian border. The Hungarian government was attempting desperately to reach a separate armistice with the West as Italy had done the previous year. For 800,000 Jews and 150,000 Christianized Jews, Hungary remained an "island of safety in an ocean of destruction."[12]

To every member of his family – his parents, his wife, his brother Paul (home on sick leave after a hernia operation) – Gusti spoke with hearty confidence and almost uncharacteristic optimism. A great change was at hand, he told them, as he cautioned all to look out for their own safety when the liberating Russians arrived. He predicted a time of chaos and upheaval in which everyone would have to fend for themselves. Only to Mancika did he put a different spin on the instructions: "Whatever happens, whatever you do, don't ever let go of the child's hand."

Once upon a time I was a rapt little girl hanging onto my *Apu*'s hand as he told me stories about Vaja and the people who used to live there. Many years later, I listened as an adult to his voice on tape, and later still to the voices of others. They helped me to piece together parts of the jigsaw world I didn't know, couldn't fully know. I tried hard to be true to all that I had learned about the role of a historian. I tried to be objective. I wanted to recreate a family and a world destroyed during the Holocaust, all their warts and virtues intact.

How does the pain of others become one's own particular pain? When does objectivity fly out of the window?

Once upon a time, I had translated into English the letters that my father had hoarded over the years, and transcribed them onto index cards in exemplary historical mode. But I found that, after all, I could not be professional about some of them. Even now, years later, I keep the little notes that Évike sent my father in a separate little box, lest I stumble upon them by accident, unwary, unprepared. They have no place amongst the neat piles of index cards arranged chronologically on my desk, month by month, year by year.

She used charming little-girl stationery decorated with flowers, like my own daughters when they were small. The notes were neatly folded into miniature matching envelopes. Unfold the yellowing paper and inside a child's painstaking words run together in immense block capitals. She had never been taught to write formally, never had a chance to go to school, but had taught herself to read out of story-books and daily newspapers.

I never memorized her letters, yet I know many of them by heart. "DEAR APU, one of them begins, YOULLNEVERGUESS. GRAND-MOTHERMADESCRAMBLEDEGGSANDIBITONSOMETHINGHARD. ITWAS MYTOOTH. ILOSTMYFIRSTTOOTH.

Her favourite toys were a doll and a teddy bear, both named after her absent father. Being a boy, the teddy was Gusti; the doll had a girl's name, Augusta. In Évike's letters to *Apu*, both toys invariably sent their love.

I cannot find it in me to be detached or objective about the two little girls, one my sister, the other my cousin, who appear together, often dressed in identical white rabbit coats, muffs, and hoods, in the last pages of the old family album. Marika was a picture-book baby with fair curls and rosy cheeks, so beautiful that a photographer from the local paper tried (vainly) to persuade her parents to let him submit her photo for the New Year's film clip of 1939, so that movie-goers could ring in the new year with Marika before their eyes. Five years later she was a lovely child with golden ringlets to her shoulders and a lively, open nature that captivated all who met her. Évike, plainer, was shy and introspective but precociously intelligent.

In April 1944 Count László Vay of Berkesz was charged by the new law of the land to repossess the lease of the Rákóczi Estate on behalf of his wards, the three mad Counts Vay in Budapest. After the grim legal transaction had taken place, the count left the house and noticed the two little cousins playing together in the sun on the verandah. Évike as usual hung back when she saw a stranger. But Marika, sunny-faced and flirtatious, charmed the visitor instantly. Impulsively, he turned to her father. "Let me have her, let me keep her for you ... Who can know what will happen in these times?"

Paul could only gaze back in silence.

"No one will know who she is, what she is! I'll send her directly to my place in Mohara, on the train, instantly! With a footman ... She'll be waiting for you when you come back. Say you'll let me have her."

Paul refused. Marika would enter the gas chamber in Auschwitz, like Évike, like all the other little children, holding their mothers' hands. The count would be clubbed to death months later as he tried vainly to defend the honour of his wife and daughters from the Russian soldiers who raped them.

After the war, Gusti frequently had business to conduct at Mohara, at the count's former castle. Unfailingly he thought of his one-time landlord's offer with a heavy heart. He knew he too, in his brother's place, would have made the same decision, yet, had Paul been willing to part with his child, Marika would almost certainly have survived.

Though Gusti returned to his regiment in February 1944 buoyed with confidence over the expected liberation, he left behind a dispirited family. They might write of the ordinary round of farm events – the birth of some 300 piglets, the sale of forty foals, the scarcity of straw – but their description of the approaching Purim holiday revealed the true bleakness of their spirits. For the first time, Gusti and Feri would not be home for this most joyous and carefree date on the Jewish calendar. Their absence cast a pall over the entire family. On March 7 Kálmán wrote, "Purim this time is the holiday of inward-looking and penitence. We hope that the debt left by Purim will be paid by Passover."

On the afternoon of the holiday two days later, Mancika wrote, "It's significantly quieter than usual. The children's joy is great, they received presents. I bought Évike *Uncle Posa's Book of Verses* ... from which she already knows a few ... I bought a book for Marika, too ... and our customary Purim gift for your parents, the fish."

Instead of the usual night of revelry, the evening passed "in a mood of pained depression," according to Kálmán. The Gypsies knew better than to come unbidden, and the only guests were Schoolmaster Sas and Ilona's brother Sándor from Nyírmada. Instead of celebrating until the early hours, the family retired at 9:30.

Passover preparations follow hard upon the heels of Purim, and three days later Mancika was already toying with the idea of visiting her widowed father for the holiday, taking Évike along. She decided against it, "though you can imagine, my dear," she wrote Gusti, "how my heart aches that I can't be together with them." Instead, she decided to make a quick trip home alone before the holiday.

While Mancika was spinning these plans, on March 12, unbeknownst to Hungarians, Adolf Eichmann brought his Sondereinsatzkommando to Mauthausen to prepare his activities in Hungary.

Mancika travelled by train to Miskolc on March 16 but was already too late to see her youngest brother, who had suddenly been called up for active duty. She found her father ailing but cheerful and her sister recovering from a nervous breakdown.

Back in Vaja, Ilona too had succumbed to melancholy but now roused herself for Évike's sake. She wrote to Gusti, "Our sweet Évike stayed home without fuss. She is playing nicely, there's no problem with her at all."

Mancika's Miskolc visit passed uneventfully. On March 19 she wrote to Gusti twice, once from Miskolc in the morning before departure, and then upon her arrival in Vaja. These were the last missives before the family learned of the German occupation. In a postscript, an unsuspecting Kálmán noted an unusual event: "Yesterday evening there was a circus performance at the farm with an *artiste* from Nyíregyháza."

Later that day, Charlie Békés made a terse entry in his diary in Debrecen: "18 o'clock. In the Golden Bull Coffee House I hear that the Germans have occupied Budapest by surprise. Our Lord Regent and Kállay were at the German general headquarters."

What do you do when your world caves in? Rend your garments and rail at the sky? Succumb to madness? On the Rákóczi Estate, numbed with horror, the family did what they would always do at this time of year: they prepared for Passover. But descriptions of the weather reflected their inner turmoil: on April 1, it snowed, and the next day Mancika wrote, "a gale of great strength is raging, constantly raising the roofs of the buildings."

On April 10 Kálmán sent Gusti a poignant summary of the last Seder at the Rákóczi Estate: "The first 2 days of the holiday were spent in the tightest family circle and, on account of your absences, in downcast spirits and amidst painful remembrances. We made an effort to conjure up all the memories of the beautiful and uplifting old Passovers we spent together and to draw strength from the past for the future."

Just how much strength would be required became evident a few days later. On April 16 the family learned of impending plans to ghettoize the Jews of the Nyírség. In the wake of the German occupation, Hungary's Jewish policy changed from one of discrimination and exclusion to one of annihilation.

Jews were to be segregated and concentrated in ghettos as the last step before their deportation. Because of the approach of the Red Army from the east, Eichmann's orders stipulated that the country would be "combed from East to West," to rule out the liberation of Jews in the direct path of the Russians. The process began in Subcarpathia, then shifted to Szabolcs and Szatmár Counties, and progressed westwards towards the capital, where in July the pressure of world opinion finally forced a halt to the nightmarish deportations.

(The majority of Hungarian Jews to survive were those who lived in the capital.)

Nowhere else but in Hungary were so many people deported and murdered as rapidly and efficiently. In less than two months, 147 trains carrying 434,351 people in freight cars left the country, causing a near glut in the gas chambers of Auschwitz. In a minute of July 11, Winston Churchill alluded to the barbarity and speed of the Nazis who, knowing full well that they had lost the war, were yet hell-bent on destroying the only Jewish community left in their thrall: Churchill referred to the annihilation of Hungarian Jewry as "probably the greatest and most horrible crime ever committed in the whole history of the world."[3]

An undisguised note of terror crept into Mancika's letter of April 16. Too frightened to write of approaching events except in veiled terms, she dared not name Kisvárda, the nearby small town where a hastily erected ghetto had begun a week earlier to receive its first Jews from the surrounding countryside. Instead, she referred to an aunt who lived in the town, and alluded to deportation only by using the name of a friend who earlier met this fate:

"Up to now we have always been able to reassure you, my darling, about our situation, in the present case, regrettably we can't. Our situation is completely uncertain. It has been held out as a likely prospect that quite shortly we'll probably go to Aunt Seréna's and will share Lisike's fate. I ask the good Lord to give me strength to bear the future, I will try as much as possible to take care of our darling child and of myself and I beseech the good Lord to protect all of us, so that we may meet each other in a happier, better future. My heart is filled with gratitude towards the good Creator for those days which we spent together, so that I had the opportunity to enjoy your goodness and noble nature. Sadly, time was short, but I trust in the good Lord that we will find each other again."

In the following days Mancika fleshed out the bare bones of the dreadful chronicle and in uncharacteristically disjointed passages made little attempt to spare Gusti her mounting anguish. On April

17 she wrote, "One moment I dare hope, the next I'm in despair over the total uncertainty the future holds – what will become of us, what will become of our beloved children who up to now we have protected from every evil? ... One is allowed a 50-kilo package per person which has to include food for 14 days. Everything else is taken over by the state. They allow 30 Pengő in cash per person ... I must say it hurts, it hurts very much to leave behind everything to which one is so attached – why, I even looked after the child's toys so carefully! – and now all is over."

Thought tumbled after haphazard, horrifying thought in Mancika's slanting, green-inked words. Évike, watching the grown-ups packing, had made a parcel of her Gusti teddy bear and a few books. "They are going to every household to take inventory, they itemize everything on lists and they say how much one is allowed to take of each thing. As we hear, in the larger cities they are establishing a ghetto system."

On April 19, Évike's sixth birthday, Mancika had news of the family living in Kisvárda and of the housing situation in the ghetto. "The [Jewish] people of Vaja left yesterday, transported in what used to be our farm wagons. They will be housed in the synagogue and its vicinity." She catalogued the heart-rending details of the encroaching horror: "Even wedding rings have to be given in. You will buy me another one day, if, God willing, we meet again once more. Today is the darling child's birthday, we congratulated her in tears and I wish that she will attain all her future birthdays under happier circumstances."

In the remaining time at home – the family expected to leave the estate on April 24, but in the end were reprieved by an extra day – Mancika's hold on herself strengthened. Now, at the age of thirty-four, her parcels packed for the journey, she was taking stock of her life. She drew courage from the past and from the kindnesses of old friends, a veterinarian and a doctor who had offered to help Gusti, should he require assistance. "I am grateful to the good Lord," she wrote on April 21, "for that which He has given me in my life: blessed good Parents and such a life-partner as you, my Gusti, with whom I could have lived so happily if they had let us ... The only thing that keeps the spirit in me is my hope that we will see each other again, and my responsibility for the child."

This steadfastness of spirit seemed to rule the rest of the family as well. Ilona had regained mastery of herself after the latest bout of depression and was now displaying the iron control she had manifested in bidding Feri good-bye. On April 23, in a long farewell letter, she wrote, "If you could see me, you would say I am a veritable hero and I owe this to the fact that, thank God, I am perfectly healthy and also to my unshakable faith to which I cling convulsively. We all have to fortify ourselves greatly so we can bear it all. Don't worry, I will do everything for the two sweet children, after all they have always been the light of my life along with all of you."

My grandfather's last formal message to my father was both prayer and blessing, a benediction bestowed even upon future children. He would never have dreamed that these unborn grandchildren would have a mother other than Mancika. Yet this indirect blessing is my only direct legacy from him:

"From my heart I wish that the good Lord will bless you with your beloved Family and that He will guard you, them, and us. Let the mercy and love of the Almighty not leave us for even a moment in these critical and difficult times. Let Him help us that we may all be together again and, happy with one another and striving for each other, begin again to rebuild the ruins.

"Thank you my beloved good son for the great joy which you have given us and let your precious Évike and your yet-to-be-born Children also give you great joy ...

"Heads up! Luck belongs to the courageous and the strong!"

On April 25, 1944, three generations of Weinbergers piled into two carriages headed for Kisvárda, the nearest town designated as a collection ghetto. It had been receiving transports of Jews from the surrounding countryside since April 8. Kálmán and Ilona, Mancika and Évike, Paul, Mary, and Marika were among the last Jews of Szabolcs County to arrive. From Debrecen Elizabeth Békés alerted the remaining family of the sad journey, taking personal solace from the fact that the Weinbergers had been permitted to make the trip by carriage rather than peasant cart.

Kálmán himself managed to smuggle a pencilled scrawl to my father that same day, "Don't be anxious if you don't hear from us for a long time because for now it's impossible to write."

Under normal conditions, the Weinberger family had pleasant associations with Kisvárda, where Yakab and Karolina had lived for five years in the 1890s and where two of Ilona's siblings had been born. A country town of mixed commercial and agricultural interests with a sizable Jewish population, it was a place where the Weinbergers shopped and visited regularly. Now nearly 7,000 Jews found themselves crammed into four streets, two lumberyards, and the courtyard of the beautiful baroque synagogue, all cordoned off from the rest of the town. During the month-long stay in the ghetto, the Weinbergers were assigned accommodation in a corner of an attic of one of the lumberyards. They cooked for themselves there while their supplies from home lasted, although within two weeks their food ran out.

Even now they kept Gusti informed by means of smuggled notes and verbal messages passed to labour servicemen on the march. Blanche, their former cook, who lived in the town proper until being herself forced into the ghetto, was instrumental in smuggling the messages in and out. Falling into her mistress's arms on her visits to the attic, Blanche would weep more from the knowledge of Ilona's reduced circumstances than from her own privations.

Thus the odd pencilled epistle from Paul or Mancika reached my father with brief bulletins of ghetto life. Ever trying to emphasize the normal and to reassure a desperately worried Gusti, both Mancika and Paul noted that Évike and Marika had made a good adjustment to the new routines. Having grown up with no other playmates on the farm, the little girls seemed to enjoy the sudden company of other children. The two were now browned by the May sun and even Évike's thin hair was growing profusely after the radical cropping it had received on arrival.

In the meantime Elizabeth Békés, who had not as yet been incarcerated in Debrecen, managed with typical resourcefulness and generosity to send care packages to the rest of the family: to Gusti in Transylvania, Feri in Bor, to the Weinbergers and Rochlitzes in Kisvárda. She wrote to Gusti that on May 13 Aggie had mounted the podium at the University of Debrecen to receive her doctorate. Despite the bright yellow star of David on his daughter's breast, this proud moment gave Charlie his last true moment of happiness. Two days later the Békéses themselves entered Debrecen's ghetto.

Of the misery in the squalid, overcrowded quarters in Kisvárda, of the endless humiliations and beatings meted out by the gendarmerie who tried to elicit information from the wealthy about hidden valuables, of the howling in the night and bloodied, battered men slinking back to their quarters in the morning – of these things the Weinbergers did not choose or did not dare to write in their letters to Gusti. But rumours had travelled swiftly as far away as the capital that the Jews in the countryside were receiving inhumane treatment.

To dispel these rumours, the new state secretary for Jewish Affairs, László Endre, embarked on a tour of the ghettos of the northeast. Endre was a rabid anti-Semite, whose cruelty and fanaticism Regent Horthy – no friend of the Jews himself – described as "insane." Endre, Eichmann's Hungarian henchman, the embodiment of evil and terror for every Jew in the country, chose to inspect in detail the attic that housed my family. Endre mounted the ladder to the attic at a moment when Blanche happened to be visiting Ilona. But for this peculiar coincidence, there would have been no surviving eyewitness to the exchange between László Endre – who would be executed by judgment of the People's Court of Hungary in 1946 – and my grandmother.

Ilona – who from the time of the German occupation had written the most sanguine bulletins to her labour-servicemen sons; who believed that God would yet reunite them all in this life; whose ostensible optimism bolstered the faith of everyone around her – had nonetheless packed in her baggage allowance of life's necessities the white clothing she wore every year on Yom Kippur. It was the outfit that she had destined for her shroud.

And now László Endre was rummaging through the Weinbergers' remaining possessions. Flanked by gendarmes on each side, he pointed to this and that item, demanding explanation and justification. Rifling through Ilona's burlap sack, he yanked out first the white kimono, then the fringed white shawl that she always wore on the Day of Days.

He gestured contemptuously towards her. "And what are *those* things?"

The dumpy little old woman drew back her shoulders. "Those are clothes to die in."

Once the Jews of the neighbourhood had been gathered in, the ghetto of Kisvárda opened its gates only twice. On May 29, the second day of the Jewish holiday of Shavuoth, it disgorged 3,475 Jews, including Blanche and Helen B., the two former cooks. Two days later, thirty-four members of the Weinberger, Székács, and Rochlitz families managed to organize themselves into a unit occupying one wagon, thirty-four out of 3,421 bound that day from Kisvárda to the border town of Kassa. Here, a day later, the sealed cattle cars were briefly opened and those inside – dead and alive – were counted by Hungarian gendarmes. The gendarmes then gave up their charges to the Gestapo, while Hungarian railway engineers switched with their Slovakian counterparts. Two days later the second Kisvárda transport arrived in Auschwitz. Zsuzsi Rochlitz was the only one of the thirty-four family members who would return a year later.

Memory is a selective, individual process. Someone else would have retained entirely other impressions of this three-day journey than did Zsuzsi. But our last glimpse of the family all together has been filtered through her memory and consciousness. Decades later she recalled not her own parents, not her brother Péter, not her beloved bossy Aunt Gisela. She did not speak of stench, thirst, or airless heat. Zsuzsi's life's work has been with small children, but she did not speak of the children in the wagon either.

Emil Bihari was Zsuzsi's favourite uncle, tall and sparely elegant. A lawyer in his seventies, he had been my grandfather's counsel, representing the Weinbergers in their endless business dealings with the Vays. Urbane Uncle Emil had always been extraordinarily popular with Count László Vay, who said he actually enjoyed litigating with the Weinbergers because he liked to spar with Emil Bihari. "Now you make sure you bring Bihari with you," he would joke with Kálmán on the eve of a hearing at the Agricultural Tribunal. "I'm excessively fond of him, you know." What Zsuzsi Rochlitz remembered were the excruciatingly embarrassing trips to the waste bucket at one end of the wagon, trips the nineteen-year-old girl could only negotiate by holding on to Uncle Emil, grasping his hand convulsively in order to be able to urinate.

And she remembered my grandmother and Mancika. Like an oasis in a desert of despair, the sight of Ilona sitting on her bundles in stoical calm, her aged moon face entirely smooth, her manner un-ruffled as she dispensed peppermint candies to anyone who would take them, had a soothing, almost hypnotic effect on Zsuzsi. And Mancika's low voice somehow reassured Zsuzsi more than it did quer-ulous little Évike, in answer to whom Mancika repeated over and over and over, with endless patience, "It's a place where we'll work until we'll be together with *Apu* ... Perhaps he's already waiting for us there ... We're going somewhere where you'll see *Apu.*"

Epilogue: Circle of Stories

My father died in 1990 in his eighty-fifth year. His prolonged illness took its toll on our whole family. The last few years he sank ever deeper into apathy, yet almost until the end, he would surface for brief respites into himself.

He lived his final years in the hospital wing of a chronic-care facility. Painstakingly he would wheel himself to the wide picture window in his room, taking up his post. He stared at the blue and silver buses below, counted the airplanes on the flight path to Dorval airport, cocked his ear to the shrieking of seagulls swooping in the gardens below. Periodically his attention lit on the teenagers who poured out of the suburban high school across the street. My older daughter, his oldest grandchild, attended this high school then. When I first began taping my father's stories, she had been a baby. It had been her birth that had prompted our recordings, so that one day she could appreciate where she came from, in his words, as I then thought, not mine.

I felt no need in those days to be particularly efficient in my work habits. In fact it wasn't work at all, simply a tapping into an unnamed nostalgia. Years later I would use index cards and translate directly into English, but when I started, the first stories unwound from the tape in Hungarian. I filled four brown spiral notebooks before putting them aside for years. When I began to research the book properly, I berated myself for my earlier inefficiency. Laboriously, I translated the Hungarian transcripts into English to fit the format of the rest of my sources.

During my father's illness, I learned, however, that nothing over which we labour with love is ever really wasted. After his strokes, *Apu* gradually lost all his English, all his interests. Every day it became more difficult to find a bridge from my world to whatever remained of his. The brown notebooks became that bridge. On days that he was cranky, when he waved away my news of the world outside, I began to read to him from the transcripts of our early conversations. In my childish Hungarian, I stumbled over the sentences in which he had once summed up his life, starting with his first stilted words for posterity about the beginning of his beginnings.

"I really don't know if my life is worthwhile that its story should be put on record. I didn't become an Einstein or a Sigmund Freud or a Moshe Dayan. But perhaps one can learn something from the life of anyone, so perhaps you can learn something from my life."

My father in his eighties, his face vacant and his eyes often wild, bore an uncanny resemblance to the portrait of my great-grandfather, Reb Hersh K'danever Weinberger. His brows bristled, his face was set in angry lines. But on hearing these words – his own – he righted himself in the wheelchair. His eyes sharpened with attention.

Outwardly *Apu* may have resembled old Herman Weinberger, but the emotion he displayed next was the pure, uninhibited legacy of another great-grandfather, my father's grandfather Yakab. Tears ran down his face. He sniffled as I read on:

"My history begins on February 5, 1906 when, after three days of labour, my late mother brought me into the world. And, as later on family members told of it, I was lemon-yellow in colour, and when my late grandmother, my mother's mother showed me off to her oldest son, my uncle Andor, saying, 'Look, what a beautiful little boy Ilona has given birth to,' Andor replied, '*This* is beautiful?' and spat all over me."

I paused a second for effect. "Go on," my father said, crotchetiness forgotten, tears of remembrance and pleasure flowing in runnels down his face. "Go on. *Don't change a word.*"

And so I would go on in the waning light of day, the seagulls below screeching, the drone of airplanes forgotten, as once again *Apu* and I travelled back to Vaja.

Together.

Glossary

Anyuci	(Hungarian) diminutive of "Mummy," literally "little Mummy"
Apu	(Hungarian) "Daddy"
Apuka	(Hungarian) diminutive of "Daddy," literally "little Daddy"
barkes	(Yiddish) festive loaf
bajtársok	(Hungarian) literally "comrades," used here for members of the Society of Awakening Magyars
Chevra Kadisha	(Hebrew) literally "Holy Brotherhood," made up of a community's most respected men responsible for all aspects of burial of the dead
chupah	(Hebrew) wedding canopy
chosed	Yiddish form of "Hasid"
chumash	(Hebrew) the Torah, the five books of Moses
daven	(Yiddish) to pray
gabeh	(Hebrew) synagogue official
gimnázium	(Hungarian) academic secondary school
Haggadah	(Hebrew) a collection of historical and biblical texts, psalms, and songs, recited at the Seder
hold	(Hungarian) Hungarian land measure equalling .57 hectares or 1.42 English acres
jeles	(Hungarian) academic grading: excellent
kaddish	(Hebrew) the prayer for the dead recited daily for a year by a close relative, usually the son, and then on each anniversary (*yahrzeit*)
kichel	(Yiddish) a kind of cookie
kittel	(Hebrew) white robe worn by men on Day of Atonement in the synagogue; also traditionally worn as a wedding garment and used for a shroud

knaidlach	(Yiddish) dumpling made out of matzoh-meal, eggs, and oil and served in soup
konflis	(Hungarian) one-horse hansom cab
kvitli	Hungarian form of *kvitle* (Yiddish), letter of request to a holy man
matzoh	(Hebrew) unleavened bread eaten during Passover
mechetonem	(Hebrew) in-laws
mezuzah	(Hebrew) small tube containing blessing attached to doorpost
mikvah	(Hebrew) ritual bath of purification
minyan	(Hebrew) ten men required for a public religious service
mitzvah	(Hebrew) good deed
nyírfa	(Hungarian) birch tree
polgári	(Hungarian) middle school
putz	(Yiddish) scatological, "prick"
rebbe	(Yiddish) teacher or scholar, Hasidic rabbi
Seder	(Hebrew) literally "order." A ritually prescribed meal held in the home on the first two nights of Passover at which the *Haggadah* is recited
Shavuoth	(Hebrew) springtime two-day "Festival of Weeks" commemorating the season when the Torah was given to the Jews
shiva	(Hebrew) the traditional seven-day period of deep mourning observed in Jewish homes after the death of a close relative
shul	(Yiddish) synagogue
Simchat Torah	(Hebrew) holiday celebrating the completion of the year's reading of the Torah
sukkah	(Hebrew) festival booth where a family partakes its meals during the seven-day Feast of Tabernacles
talles	Yiddish form of the Hebrew "tallith" or prayer shawl
tate	(Yiddish) father
traif	(Hebrew) unkosher, ritually unclean
tzaddik	(Hebrew) holy man, wise man

yahrzeit	(Yiddish) anniversary of the death of a loved one commemorated by the lighting of a twenty-four-hour candle and the recitation of the mourner's prayer
yarmulke	(Hebrew) skull-cap
yeshiva	(Hebrew) Jewish academy devoted to religious study
yevorechecho	(Hebrew) "may you be blessed"

Notes

1 In 1735 the Jewish population of Hungary numbered some 12,000. By 1880 it had risen to 625,000, slightly more than 4 per cent of the population.

2 Iván Ballasa, "*Adatok a zsidók szerepéhez Tokaj-Hegyalja vidékének szőlőművelésében és borkereskedéseben* (1791–1841)" ("Data on the Role of Jews in the Viticulture of the Tokay and its Foothills,") 1981–1982 *Évkönyv* (*Yearbook*) of the Agency of Hungarian Jews, Sándôr Scheiber, editor, 8.

In the twentieth century, the stigma against Polish immigrants to Hungary took on a life-and-death connotation. During the implementation of anti-Jewish legislation in World War II, Jews had to prove that their ancestors had been born on Hungarian soil for several generations. Recently arrived Jewish refugees fleeing from destruction in Poland were the first to be deported from Hungary in 1941 when 18,500 of them were slaughtered in Novi Sad (Yugoslavia) and Kamenets Podolsk (Ukraine).

3 Quoted by Ruth Ellen Gruber in *Upon the Doorposts of Thy House: Jewish Life in East-Central Europe, Yesterday and Today* (New York: John Wiley & Sons, 1994), 151.

4 Arrow Cross party program, quoted by Nathaniel Katzburg, *Hungary and the Jews: Policy and Legislation 1920–1943* (Ramat Gan: Bar Ilan University Press, 1981), 86.

5 The peasants all spoke generically of the family as "Székács," both because the Hungarianized name came more easily to them than did the Germanic "Weinberger," and because both Zoltán and Andor were flashier and more visible in public than my grandfather.

6 *Hungary and the Jews*, 96.

7 Ibid., 183.

8 *Eichmann in Jerusalem: A Report on the Banality of Evil* (New York: Penguin, 1977), 114.

9 "Development of Anti-Semitism and Persecution of the Jews in Hungary, 1920–1945," introductory essay by Livia Rothkirchen to Moshe Sandberg's *My Longest Year in the Hungarian Labour Service and in the Nazi Camps* (Jerusalem: The Jerusalem Post Press, 1972), xix.

10 Ibid.

11 Kubowy [aka Kubowitzki] was cited by Jenő Levai in the epigraph to *Black Book on the Martyrdom of Hungarian Jewry* (Zurich: Central European Times Publishing, 1948), Lawrence P. Davis, editor.

12 *Eichmann in Jerusalem*, 195.

13 Minute to Anthony Eden, quoted by Martin Gilbert, *Winston S. Churchill, Volume VII: Road to Victory, 1941–1945* (London: Heinemann, 1986), 847.

Selected Bibliography

PRIMARY SOURCES

I am indebted to my late cousin Sámuel Derzsi for giving me full rights to use material from his unpublished 1966 manuscript *A Kidőlt Sírkő Helyett* (*In Place of the Fallen Gravestone*), from which I drew many of the family legends and the description of the *yahrzeit* observances in Gyulaj.

I have also made free use of information found in *Kastély a Faluban: Vajai Beszélgetések* (*Castle in the Village: Conversations in Vaja*), an oral-history project of Class IId (1981) of Budapest's Kálmán Könyves High School.

SECONDARY SOURCES

Out of the scores of books consulted, I particularly drew on Péter Ujvári's *Magyar Zsidó Lexikon* (*Hungarian Jewish Lexicon*) (Budapest: Pallas, 1929), for general biographical and geographical information; Yad Vashem's *Pinkas Hakehilloth* (*Encyclopaedia of Jewish Communities*): *Hungary* (Jerusalem: Yad Vashem, 1976), for statistical and historical data on Jewish life in Hungary; and Dr Samu Borovszky's *Magyarország Vármegyei és Városai: Szabolcs Vármegye* (*Hungary's Counties and Cities: Szabolcs County*) (published circa 1900 and colloquially referred to as the *Monográfia*) for the historical lore of the various villages of the Nyírség.

The most helpful works on Nagykálló and its famous Tzaddik were László Szilágyi-Windt's *A Kállói Cádik: A Nagykállói Zsidóság Története* (*The Tzaddik of Kálló: A History of the Jews of Nagykálló*), (Tel Aviv: Neographika, 1959), and Andrew Handler's *Rabbi Eizik: Hasidic Stories about the Zaddik of Kálló* (Cranberry, N.J.: Associated University Presses, 1978).

As a general survey of Hungarian history, Paul Ignotus's *Hungary* (New York: Praeger Publishers, 1972) was helpful, and for specifics *Magyarország Történeti Kronológiája* (*Hungary's Historical Chronology*), volumes 2–4 (Budapest: Akadémia Kiadó, 1982), general editor Kálmán Benda, was excellent.

For background on the town of Nagyvárad at turn of the century, Géza Hegedüs's *Előjátékok Egy Önéletrajzhoz* (*Overture to an Autobiography*) (Budapest: Szépirodalmi Könyvkiadó, 1982) was fascinating. For the history of Debrecen and its Jews, I consulted Moshe Elijahu Gonda's *A Debreceni Zsidóság Száz Éve* (*One Hundred Years of Jewry in Debrecen*) (Tel Aviv: Linotur, n.d.). A similar work on Kisvárda is *Emlékkönyv: Kisvárda és Környéke* (*Memorial Book of Kisvárda and its Environs*) (Tel Aviv: Lahav, 1980), edited by Dr Károly Jolesz.

The classic work on the Holocaust in Hungary is Randolph Braham's *The Politics of Genocide: The Holocaust in Hungary*, 2 volumes (New York: Columbia University Press, 1981), an indispensable source. Also helpful on the subject were Livia Rothkirchen's introduction to Moshe Sandburg's wartime memoir, *My Longest Year* (Jerusalem: The Jerusalem Post Press, 1972), and Andrew Handler's *The Holocaust in Hungary: An Anthology of Jewish Response* (Alabama: University of Alabama Press, 1982).

For an analysis of anti-Jewish policy and legislation during the war years, Nathaniel Katzburg's *Hungary and the Jews: Policy and Legislation 1920–1943* (Ramat Gan: Bar Ilan University Press, 1981) was illuminating. And Hannah Arendt's *Eichmann in Jerusalem: A Report on the Banality of Evil* (Penguin: New York, 1977) remains essential reading more than thirty years after it was first published.

Two monographs, Joseph Held's *The Modernization of Agriculture: Rural Transformation in Hungary, 1848–1875* (New York: Columbia University Press, 1980) and William O. McCagg's *Jewish Nobles and Geniuses in Modern Hungary* (Boulder, Colorado: East European Quarterly, 1972), helped shed light on social and economic conditions in nineteenth-century Hungary. Imre Heller and Zsigmond Vajda's *The Synagogues of Hungary: An Album* (New York: Diplomatic Press, 1968) was evocative and yielded a photograph of the old synagogue of Vaja.

The poem "Picture Postcards" on page 230 is my translation, in collaboration with Susan Rochlitz Szőke, of Miklós Radnóti's "Rezglenicák" and is taken from his *Összes Versei és Műforditásai* (*Complete Poems and Translations*) (Budapest: Szépirodalmi Könyvkiadó, 1959), 271.

DATE DUE

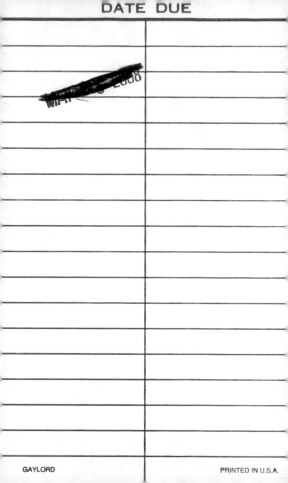